AFRICAN HISTORICAL DICTIONARIES
Edited by Jon Woronoff

Historical Dictionary

of

KENYA

by

Bethwell A. Ogot

African Historical Dictionaries, No. 29

THE SCARECROW PRESS, INC.
METUCHEN, N.J., & LONDON
1981

Library of Congress Cataloging in Publication Data

Ogot, Bethwell A.
  Historical dictionary of Kenya.

  (African historical dictionaries ; no. 29)
  Bibliography: p.
  1. Kenya--History--Dictionaries. I. Title.
II. Series.
DT433.515.O36   967.6'2'00321   81-1815
ISBN 0-8108-1419-6   AACR2

DEDICATED

To the Memory of all those Kenyans whose ideas, toil, and blood
have contributed to the creation
of a more just and humane nation.

CONTENTS

v

EDITOR'S FOREWORD

Although not significantly different from other African territories prior to decolonization, independent Kenya has been considerably more successful than many of them. Despite the broad range of ethnic groups, some with a heritage of distrust toward their neighbors, they have managed to get along quite well together. More surprisingly, despite the bitterness that preceded statehood, an exceptional number of Arabs, Asians and Europeans have remained and made their contribution to the country. The economy was radically changed at certain levels, with a substantial redistribution of land and property. But it built on the past rather than launching into novel or unproven schemes and managed to attain relatively rapid growth. With none of the fanfare that characterized some countries, Kenya has gained a respected place in world councils.

Perhaps what has impressed outsiders most is that Kenya has been able to negotiate the succession from its first generation of indigenous leaders to another generation so successfully. Many thought that it would be far from easy for Jomo Kenyatta, whose ascendancy over the state had been so great, to be replaced by a younger man, despite the careful preparations. Yet, the government of Daniel arap Moi did take over smoothly and has begun moving in new, if not strikingly different, directions with considerable ability.

The key to Kenya's success doubtlessly lies with the people who ruled it in both pre- and post-independence days. They include not just a handful of chiefs, governors and politicians but a broad array of leaders in many circles: administrative, business, educational, religious and others. It is also rooted in the customs and traditions of its many ethnic groups. An amazing number of these leaders are presented in this volume along with many other elements that should be known by friends of Kenya and by Kenyans in general.

The entries were written with such insight because their author, Bethwell A. Ogot, was a witness to much of the recent past and a student of earlier days. One of Kenya's leading historians, he has served as professor and head of the history department at Nairobi University, Director of the Institute of African Studies, and Director of the International Louis Leakey Memorial Institute for African Prehistory. He has also been active in UNESCO's Committee on History of Africa, the International African Institute in London, and the Pan-African Association for Prehistory and Related Studies. He has written and edited over a dozen books including Kenya Before 1900, A Place to Feel at Home, A History of the Southern Luo, and East Africa, Past and Present. This volume in the African Historical Dictionaries series is just the latest of his endeavors in making Africa better known to the world.

Jon Woronoff
Series Editor

SELECTED CHRONOLOGY

1498 Vasco da Gama reached Mombasa and Malindi on his way to India.

1592 Mombasa captured by the Portuguese; beginning of Portuguese rule.

1593 Fort Jesus in Mombasa built by the Portuguese.

1698 The Omani captured Mombasa and effectively ended Portuguese rule in East Africa.

1746 Mazrui rule established in Mombasa.

1824 Captain W. F. W. Owen set up Protectorate over Mombasa which ended in 1826.

1837 End of Mazrui rule and beginning of the rule of the Busaidi dynasty led by Seyyid Said in East Africa.

1840 Seyyid Said moved his headquarters from Muscat to Zanzibar and created the Zanzibar Sultanate, whose overlordship extended to the coastal region of Kenya.

1844 Dr. Johann Krapf founded the Rabai CMS station.

1883-4 Joseph Thomson traveled through Masailand to Lake Victoria.

1884-5 Berlin Conference laid down rules for the partition of Africa.

1886 The Anglo-German Agreement--partitioned East Africa between the two powers and placed Kenya in the British sphere.

1887 The Imperial British East Africa Company formed by William Mackinnon to exploit the British sphere.

1890	The Second Anglo-German Agreement--tidied up the East African partition.
1895	1st July: British Protectorate declared over future Kenya. Start of the building of Uganda Railway at Mombasa.
1901	Uganda Railway reached Kisumu.
1902	East Uganda Province transferred to East Africa Protectorate.
1904	Sir Charles Eliot, the Commissioner, enunciated his "Whiteman's Country" policy.
	First Masai Agreement. The Masai were moved to Laikipia district to make room for white settlers.
1905	East Africa Protectorate transferred from the Foreign Office to the Colonial Office. The Colonialist Association formed.
1906	Title of "Commissioner" changed to "Governor." The establishment of the Legislative and Executive Councils was accepted.
1907	The Legislative Council was established.
1911	The Second Masai Agreement. Moved them from Laikipia to make room for European settlers.
1914	The East African Indian National Congress formed.
1915	Crown Lands Ordinance was passed.
	Native Registration Ordinance introducing the "pass" system was passed.
1917	A system of electing Europeans to the Legislative Council recommended. Asians continued to be nominated and Arabs and Africans were represented by Government officials.
1919	The Kikuyu Association was formed.
1920	East African Association and Young Kavirondo Association (Piny Owacho) were formed. East

x

Africa "Protectorate" becomes the "Colony" of Kenya. The Protectorate is restricted to the ten-mile coastal strip.

1922   Harry Thuku was arrested and deported to Kismayu. Africans organized a protest march in Nairobi; as a result, 25 people, including women, were killed.

1923   The Young Kavirondo Association became the Kavirondo Taxpayers Welfare Association.

The Devonshire Declaration enunciated the paramountcy principle.

1924   Dr. J. W. Arthur was appointed to the Legislative Council to represent African interests--without their mandate.

1925   Kikuyu Central Association formed.

1929   Kenyatta's first visit to England.

1930   Kenyatta returned to Kenya.

1931   Kenyatta's second visit to England.

Harry Thuku was released from detention.

1934   North Kavirondo Central Association was formed.

The Report of the Kenya Land Commission was published.

1935   Harry Thuku resigned from Kikuyu Central Association to form Kikuyu Provincial Association.

1938   Ukamba Members Association was formed.

Kenya African Teachers' Training College was established at Githunguri by Mbiyu Koinange.

1940   Kikuyu Central Association, the Ukamba Members Association, and the Taita Hills Association were proscribed and their leaders arrested and detained.

1943   The Rev. L. J. Beecher was appointed to the Legislative Council to represent African interests.

1944   Mr. Eliud W. Mathu became the first African to
         be nominated to the Legislative Council.

         Kenya African Study Union was formed.

1945   The Membership System by which some unofficial
         European members of the Executive Council were
         given portfolios was introduced.

         The Fifth Pan-African Congress, in which Kenyatta
         participated, held in Manchester.

1946   Kenya African Study Union became Kenya African
         Union.

         Jomo Kenyatta returned to Kenya.

1947   Kenyatta became President of the Kenya African
         Union.

         Kipande system abolished and replaced by an iden-
         tity card system.

1948   East African High Commission formed.

1949   East African Trade Union Congress formed by
         Makhan Singh and Fred Kubai.

1950   Nairobi became a city.

         Mau Mau was declared an illegal society.

1952   19 October: A State of Emergency declared.

         Kenyatta, Paul Ngei, Achieng' Oneko, Bildad Kag-
         gia, Fred Kubai and Kungu Karumba were arrested.

1954   Lyttleton Plan introduced the principle of a multi-
         racial government.

1956   Dedan Kimathi was captured and executed.

1957   First Election of African Members of the Legisla-
         tive Council.

1958   Lennox-Boyd Constitution introduced.

1960   March: Kenya African National Union formed.

        August: Kenya African Democratic Union formed.

        State of Emergency ended.

        Kenya Freedom Party formed by some Asians.

        First Lancaster House Constitutional Conference
        held in London.

1961   February: General elections won by KANU.

        August: Kenyatta was released from detention.

        28 October: Kenyatta became President of KANU.

        East African Common Services Organization was
        formed.

1962   Second Lancaster House Conference was held in
        London.

        April: Coalition Government was formed.

1963   May: General Elections won by KANU.

        June: Internal Self-Government (Madaraka) intro-
        duced, with Kenyatta as Prime Minister.

        September: Third Lancaster House Conference.

        12 December: Kenya became independent.

1964   24 January: Attempted mutiny by Eleventh Battalion
        Kenya Rifles at Lanet, Nakuru.

        5 February: Kenya Airforce was formed.

        26 February: Emergency declared in North Eastern
        Province because of the Shifta war.

        10 November: KADU was voluntarily dissolved.

        12 December: Kenya became a Republic.

        16 December: Kenya Navy was formed in Mombasa.

1965	24 February: Mr. Pio Gama Pinto, a freedom fighter and Member of Parliament, was assassinated.

1965   24 February: Mr. Pio Gama Pinto, a freedom fighter and Member of Parliament, was assassinated.

5 March: The Seven Forks Hydro-Electric Development Scheme at Kindaruma was launched.

27 April: Sessional Paper No. 10 on African Socialism, the cornerstone of Kenya's economic policy, announced.

1 June: Central Bank of Kenya inaugurated.

1 September: Government dissolved the rival trade union groups: Kenya Federation of Labour and Kenya African Workers Congress and decided to set up Central Organisation of Trade Unions (COTU).

1966   14 March: KANU Reorganisation Conference in Limuru abolished the post of Vice-President and consequently ousted Oginga Odinga as Vice-President.

14 April: Vice-President Odinga resigned. He subsequently formed the Kenya People's Union.

28 April: Parliament passed a new Act requiring members of the Opposition to vacate their seats in Parliament. Thirty MPs lost their seats under the Act.

2 May: Parliament was prorogued for the "Little General Election."

4 May: Mr. Joseph Murumbi, Minister for Foreign Affairs, appointed Vice-President.

14 September: Kenya's first national currency was issued.

21 September: Mr. Joseph Murumbi resigned as Vice-President.

1967   5 January: Minister for Home Affairs, Mr. Daniel arap Moi, appointed Vice-President.

1968   25 June: Constitution of Kenya (Amendment) Bill dealing with the election of a President was passed by Parliament.

3 July: Mr. Kitili Mwendwa appointed the First African Chief Justice.

1969   5 July: Minister for Economic Planning and Development, Mr. Tom Mboya was assassinated.

26 October: During the opening of the Russian-built Nyanza Hospital in Kisumu, by Jomo Kenyatta, there was an incident, and at least nine people were killed.   On the following day, all KPU MPs, including Mr. Oginga Odinga, were detained and the Party proscribed.

6 December: First Parliamentary Election after independence.

1970   10 December: University of Nairobi inaugurated.

1971   28 March: Odinga released from detention and rejoined KANU on 9 September.

1973   2 October: United Nations Environment Programme (UNEP).   Secretariat opened in Nairobi.

1974   14 October: Second Parliamentary elections unseated 88 MPs.

1975   2 March: Mutilated body of Member of Parliament for Nyandarua North, Mr. Josiah Mwangi Kariuki, was found in the Ngong Hills.

10 October: Achieng' Oneko was released after six years of detention.

1977   2 February: The formation of Kenya Airways announced.

26 October: The Kenya Court of Appeal established.

1978   22 August: President Jomo Kenyatta died at State House, Mombasa.

Vice-President Daniel arap Moi became the new President of Kenya.

6 October: President Moi was elected President of Kenya's ruling Party, KANU.

11 October: Minister of Finance, Mr. Mwai Kibaki, was appointed Vice-President.

12 December: President Moi released all political detainees.

1979   31 January: A ten-year Kenya-Ethiopia treaty of amity and co-operation signed in Addis-Ababa.

8 November: Third Parliamentary elections unseated 76 MPs.

12 December: President Moi sworn in as President for a five-year term of office.

ABBREVIATIONS AND ACRONYMS

AIM	African Inland Mission
CDC	Commonwealth Development Corporation
CMS	Church Missionary Society
COTU	Central Organisation of Trade Unions
CSM	Church of Scottish Mission
DC	District Commissioner
EAA	East African Association
EAC	East African Community
ECA	Economic Commission for Africa
EGH	Elder of the Golden Heart
GEMA	Gikuyu, Embu and Meru Association
ICDC	Industrial and Commercial Development Corporation
KA	Kikuyu Association
KADU	Kenya African Democratic Union
KANU	Kenya African National Union
KAR	Kenya African Rifles
KAU	Kenya African Union
KCA	Kikuyu Central Association
KLFA	Kenya Land Freedom Army
KNA	Kenya News Agency
KPU	Kenya People's Union
KTDA	Kenya Tourist Development Corporation
KTWA	Kavirondo Taxpayers Welfare Association
LEGCO	Legislative Council
LUM	Luo United Movement
OAU	Organisation of African Union
PAFMECA	Pan-African Freedom Movement of East and Central Africa
UMA	Ukama Members Association
VOK	Voice of Kenya
YKA	Young Kavirondo Association

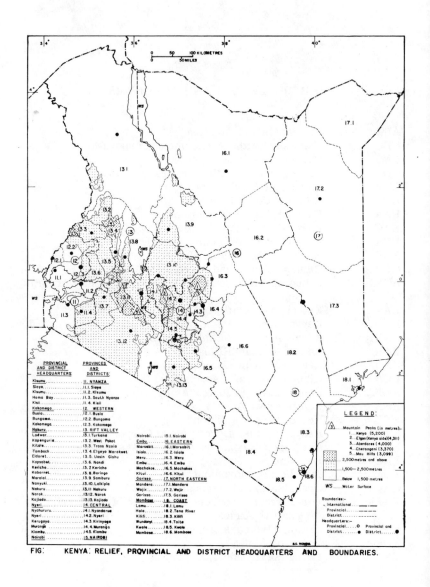

FIG. KENYA: RELIEF, PROVINCIAL AND DISTRICT HEADQUARTERS AND BOUNDARIES.

Kenya: Relief, Provincial and District
Headquarters, and Boundaries

INTRODUCTION

Kenya has been called a land of contrast. Her people waged one of the most violent anti-colonial wars against the British, and yet she has remained politically very stable since independence due largely to the policy of reconciliation which the Government has pursued. She has an honorable place in the world in the studies of early man, and yet her own nationals are least involved in such activities which continue to be the exclusive preserve of foreign scholars. She has rich and varied cultures of which her people are rightly proud while at the same time the cultural scene in the country continues to be dominated by foreign ideologies. The Government has done more than most African governments toward improving the quality of life of the people while continuing to accept a substantial measure of foreign control of the economy.

Location and Topography

The Republic of Kenya is almost bisected by the Equator and is located approximately between latitudes 4° 28' S and N, and between 34 and 40 degrees east meridians. Its size encompasses 582,646.4 sq. km. of which 13,396 sq. km. are water surface. Of the remaining land surface, about two thirds is semi-arid or desert. The surface area includes several lakes, the largest being Lake Victoria (the largest lake in Africa and the second largest in the world-- 62,937 sq. km.) although only 3,831 sq. km. of it form part of Kenya. Lake Turkana covers 2,473 sq. km. The smaller lakes include Naivasha (210 sq. km.), Baringo (129 sq. km.), Bogoria (34 sq. km.), Nakuru (52 sq. km.) and Elementeita (21 sq. km.). Lake Magadi, which lies in the Rift Valley near the Tanzania border, is an important source of soda ash and salt. The Indian Ocean coastline, stretching from the Somalia border in the north to Tanzania in the south, is 608 kilometers long.

1

Kenya is bordered by Tanzania in the south, Uganda to the west, the Republic of Somalia to the east, and the Sudan and Ethiopia to the north.

Internally, the country is divided into seven administrative provinces plus Nairobi, which ranks as an extra-provincial district. The provinces, in order of size, are the Rift Valley (173, 869. 3 sq. km.), Eastern (157, 026. 5 sq. km.), North-Eastern (126, 902. 2 sq. km.), Coast (86, 467. 2 sq. km.), Nyanza (16, 612. 3 sq. km.), Central (13, 175. 3 sq. km.), Western (7, 909. 9 sq. km.), and Nairobi (683. 8 sq. km.).

The topography varies from the hot, humid coastal belt to the savannah grasslands and the plateau foreland where the tops of the hills may rise to well over 2, 500 meters. Kenya is cut by the Great Rift Valley which runs from the north to the south between 610 meters and 914 meters below the country on both sides, and which varies in depth. A considerable area of the Rift Valley is ideal for mixed farming. On the western rim of the Rift Valley, the land slopes down towards Lake Victoria and the Uganda border. The vast expanse of the North-Eastern province varies from featureless desert in the east to the more rugged area west of Lake Turkana.

Population

The population of Kenya is of diverse origins. The vast majority of Kenyans, over 98 percent of the population, are persons of African origin. Of these, about 69 percent are Bantu-speakers, 27 percent are Nilotic-speakers, and 3 percent are Cushitic-speakers. The remaining elements of the population of Kenya originated in Europe and Southwest Asia.

This population is mainly rural, with only about 14. 6 percent, according to the August 1979 Census, living in urban centers. The estimated total population was 15, 322, 000 as compared to 10, 943, 000 at the previous census in 1969. The breakdown for the different provinces is as follows: Nairobi, 835, 000; Central Province, 2, 348, 000; Coast Province, 1, 339, 000; Eastern Province, 2, 717, 000; North-Eastern Province, 373, 000; Nyanza Province, 2, 634, 000; Rift Valley Province, 3, 240, 000; and Western Province, 1, 836, 000.

The 1979 Census also revealed that the number of
urban centers has increased significantly since 1969.   In
that year there were 48 urban centers of 2000 or more people and the total urban population was 1,082,437 (9.89 percent of the total population of Kenya).   By 1979, the number of centers had increased to 90 and the total urban population had risen to 2,238,000.   The figure for urban centers with populations over 10,000 as reported in the 1979
Census included Nairobi, 834,500; Mombasa, 341,500; Kisumu, 150,400; Nakuru, 92,600; Machakos, 84,300; Meru,
72,400; Eldoret, 50,200; Thika, 41,300; Nyeri, 35,800;
Kakamega, 31,800; Kisii, 30,700; Kericho, 29,600; Kitale,
28,400; Bungoma, 25,100; Busia, 25,000; Malindi, 23,300;
Nanyuki, 19,100; Webuye, 17,600; Embu, 16,200; Murang'a,
15,300; Garissa, 14,000; Narok, 13,000; Isiolo, 11,400;
Nyahururu, 11,200; Naivasha, 11,200; Maralal, 10,200; and
Athi River, 10,000.   These give a total of 2,048,700 urban
inhabitants.   There were twenty-two centers with populations
between 5,000 and 10,00, and with a total population of
156,300; forty-one centers had populations between 2,000
and 5,000, with a total population of 125,800.

Prehistory

Kenya has long been known to geologists, palaeontol-
ogists and archaeologists as a region notably rich in fossil
and artifactual remains.   Western Kenya, for instance, contains a fossil record of Miocene age (from about 20 million
to about 5.5 million years ago) unparalleled in Africa for
the richness and diversity of the material preserved at sites
on Rusinga Island, at Fort Ternan, Kanjera and Kanam,
which includes a variety of hominoids.   Archaeological sites
of Pleistocene age (from about 2.5 million until 10,000
years ago) are found in the Rift Valley and on the shores
of Pleistocene Lake Victoria.   Famous sites such as Olor-
gesailie (which belongs to the Middle Pleistocene and which
lies on the floor of the Gregory Rift Valley 65 kilometers
southwest of Nairobi), Chesowanja (which is located in the
north Kenya Rift Valley, to the East of Lake Baringo), Kil-
ombe (in the Rift Valley, northwest of Nakuru), the Kapthurin Formation (in the Baringo district), Koobi Fora (east of
Lake Turkana), Kariandusi (on the Nairobi-Nakuru road),
Ngira (near Karungu in South Nyanza), and Muguruk (near
Kisumu) are all known internationally.   The final period,
the Iron Age, is more widespread, and representative sites
are found scattered all over the country.

History

When we move to the historical period, during which
Kenya was peopled by the present inhabitants, it is conven-
ient to look at the history of each language group. As we
have already observed, the indigenous languages of Kenya
can be divided into three major categories: Bantu, Nilotic
and Cushitic. Each of these categories is further sub-divid-
ed. For example, the Bantu group comprises (1) Western
Bantu (Luyia, Gusii, Suba, Kuria); 2) Central Bantu (Kikuyu,
Embu, Meru, Kamba); and 3) Eastern Bantu (Taita, Taveta,
Mijikenda, Pokomo and Swahili). Similarly, the Nilotic languages of Kenya embrace 1) Western Nilotic represented by
the Luo; 2) Eastern Nilotic (Teso-Turkana and the Maa-
group: Masai, Njemps and Samburu); and 3) Southern Nilotic (Omotic and Kalenjin: Pokot, Marakwet, Elgeyo, Tugen, Kipsigis, Nandi and Terik). The Cushitic group has
two major sub-divisions: 1) Western Cushitic: Shangala,
Burji, Oromo, Somali, El Molo and Rendille; and 2) Southern Cushitic represented by Dahalo.

The Western Kenya societies have evolved as a result of a long and complex process of interaction between
the Cushitic, the Kalenjin, the Bantu Luyia, Gusii and Kuria,
and the Nilotic Luo, stretching back to the period before
1000 A.D.

In the Rift Valley, we find that the Southern Cushitic
who had expanded into the area from Southern Ethiopia were
assimilated by the Kalenjin and central Bantu-speakers. The
expansion of the Masai southwards along the Rift Valley,
which dates from about 1600 A.D., drove the Kalenjin from
the eastern grazing lands in the Nakuru and Tugen areas
towards the present Elgeyo, Elgon, Nandi and Kipsigis. It
was during this period that the different Kalenjin groups
emerged.

By the first half of the nineteenth century, the Masai
society began to disintegrate as a result of internecine wars.
The Kalenjin, especially the Nandi, having consolidated their
position, began to expand again into the Western Highlands
at the expense of the Masai. Some Bantu communities, especially the Kikuyu and Kamba, also exploited the situation
to extend their territories into former Masai lands.

When we move to Central Kenya, we find that the
precolonial history is dominated by the stories of the Kikuyu,

Meru and Kamba. The ancestors of the Kikuyu appear to
have emigrated from Meru and Tharaka via Mbere, Mwea
and Ndia in the seventeenth century. They regrouped in the
area between the rivers North Mathioya and Gura before
they expanded westwards towards the Aberderes Range, southwards towards Kiambu and northwards towards Nyeri, where
they arrived in the nineteenth century. The Meru claim to
have reached the present Tharaka in the 1730's from the
coast. They expanded into the lower portions of the Mt.
Kenya and Nyambeni forests where they encountered the
Oromo-speakers who had migrated southwards from Ethiopia.
Many Oromo-speakers were absorbed, especially into the
northern Meru society. By 1800, the Meru were already
evolving as a distinct society.

The Kamba affirm that they moved into their present
homes from the region of Mt. Kilimanjaro starting in the
seventeenth century. By 1700 they had reached Mbooni Hills,
and Kitui was settled in the eighteenth century. They expanded into the rest of Ukambani during the nineteenth century.

In the coastal region, the histories of the Mijikenda
and the Swahili predominate. The former comprise the
Rabai, Duruma, Kauma, Chonyi, Jibana, Kambe, Digo, Ribe
and Giriama. They adopted the name "Mijikenda" ("the nine
villages") in this century in place of the pejorative term
"Nyika" meaning "bush," which had earlier been applied to
the group. They claim to have migrated to their present
homes from a place called Shungwaya in southern Somalia,
where they lived together with the Taita, Pokomo, Segeju
and Oromo, in the seventeenth century. In the seventeenth
and eighteenth centuries, they settled in nine fortified hill-
top kaya, or villages, in the area between Kilifi Creek and
the Shimba Hills. They moved to their present homes in
the nineteenth century. By this time, their history was already intertwined with that of the coast, where a relationship of equality and interdependence was already established
between them and the Swahili.

In 1895 a British Protectorate was declared over the
territory between the coast and Uganda. The area was administered by career diplomats based at Zanzibar until 1902,
when, with the transfer of the Eastern Province of Uganda
to East Africa Protectorate, the Government headquarters
were moved to Mombasa, and then to Nairobi in 1907.

Soon a policy of turning Kenya into a "whiteman's

country" was evolved and from 1904 strenuous efforts were
made to attract European settlers to the country. In 1907,
a Legislative Council was established to provide the white
settlers with a political forum.

The establishment of British rule in Kenya marked
the formal incorporation of the region into the worldwide
capitalist system. Capitalist production in the forms of
corporate plantations and settler farming was introduced.
This did not, however, kill the indigenous household commodity production which continued to compete for dominance
with the capitalist production. The result was that the various Kenya societies were subjected to social contradictions.
The period from 1895 to 1905 was characterized by punitive
expeditions which resulted in the appropriation of African
resources. Large numbers of livestock looted were partly
given to collaborators, partly sold to the white settlers and
the majority kept for government purposes. The African
labor was appropriated by coercion and through a Hut Tax.
By 1910 the Africans were paying at least 40 percent of
total revenue in tax and import duties as opposed to 20 percent by the settlers. Household production continued to expand. By 1913 productions of African origin provided three
quarters of export earnings, and it was these that paid for
the Railways operating deficit. The amendment of the Crown
Lands Ordinance in 1915 established a free market in land
and thereby introduced concessionaire development. The
leases of land for the white settlers were extended from 99
to 999 years. After the First World War, a further 12,000
sq. km. of land were made available for white settlement.
The country, now renamed Kenya, was formally annexed
and declared a Crown Colony.

The contradiction between the two forms of production, capitalist and household, was to reach a crisis point
in the 1920's. Before the First World War, many Africans
earned more by domestic sales than through wage-employ-
ment. Hence, African peasant agriculture provided a real
threat to capitalist production. It was the First World War
that intensified the social contraditions within the colony.
There had been 190,000 military carriers recruited for the
war, out of which between 15 percent and 20 percent died.
Also, the 1917 drought, influenza, and dysentery killed many
people, especially in Nyanza and Central Provinces. The
peasants became restless. The Giriama and the Masai re-
resisted recruitment and the anti-European Mumbo Cult started in Nyanza. Several resistance groups emerged in the

1920's. In Nyanza the opposing factions compromised by
later forming the moderate Kavirondo Taxpayers Welfare
Association while in Central Kenya two parallel organizations emerged: the Kikuyu Association dominated by the
Chiefs who were protecting their pre-war economic gains,
and the Kikuyu Central Association, a radical organization
which championed the rights of the peasants. In an attempt
to control the radical leaders, the Local Native Councils
were established in 1925 to divert them from national issues.

African labor continued to be exploited through the
use of the Registration Ordinance. However, African peasant production continued to expand, exploiting the growing
domestic market. At the same time, the capitalist production expanded both in terms of acreage as well as in terms
of number of settlers. They were assisted by statutory systems of organized marketing that came into existence in the
1930's.

With the outbreak of the Second World War a ban
was placed on African political activity and several political
leaders were detained. The Europeans, on the other hand,
were again quick to exploit a war situation to consolidate
their position, as they had done during the 1914-18 war.
Their influence on the Executive Council and on the statutory boards was enhanced, and labor was conscripted for
their farms. At the end of the war, a "Membership" system was introduced, which meant that European unofficial
members of the Executive Council could now be given portfolios. The first to be given to European settlers (Agriculture and Local Government) were those which affected
Africans most intimately.

The war also aggravated the contradictions between
the colonizers and the Kenyans. Produce from peasants
was bought at low prices through a tightly controlled marketing system. Even though prices of foodstuffs, and man-
ufactured goods quadrupled, African wages were kept at pre-
war level. The workers, whose numbers had risen from
377,000 in 1946 to 620,000 in 1960, increasingly resorted
to the strike weapon.

A new type of African leader emerged, being better
educated than the earlier leaders. In order to contain the
situation, the Government decided to offer opportunity for
so-called moderate African voices to be heard by nominat-
ing them to the Legislative Council. On October 5, 1944,

Mr. E. W. Mathu was nominated as the first African unofficial member of the Legislative Council.

As a result of this nomination, the Kenya African
Union (the first national political party) was founded in October 1944 to give him support.   Jomo Kenyatta, who had
returned from Britain in 1946 after a long sojourn, became
the President of KAU in June 1947.   The Africans' demand
for political independence became more and more radical,
eventually resulting in an armed conflict between the Africans and the colonialists, a conflict which is popularly known
as "Mau Mau."

Thousands of Africans were killed, while others were
detained or restricted.   As a counter-revolutionary move,
the colonial Government introduced a major program of land
reform which paved the way for increased agricultural production.   This was the beginning of the political bargain that
climaxed in the One-million Acre Scheme.

The ban on African political parties that had been in
force since 1952 was lifted in 1960.   Although there was
general agreement on political independence as the goal there
was a sharp difference of opinion among the African leaders
as to how political power in an independent Kenya should be
distributed.   This led to the formation of two political parties: the Kenya African National Union (KANU) led by Mr.
Jomo Kenyatta after his release from detention in August
1961, and the Kenya African Democratic Union (KADU) led
by Mr. Ronald Ngala.   On December 12, 1963, Kenya
achieved independence under a KANU government with a complex constitution (known as the Majimbo Constitution) which
conceded much autonomy to the regions.

On the first anniversary of independence, however,
Kenya became a Republic and the KADU-inspired regional
constitution was replaced with one that restored strong, central powers.

How those powers have been used, is in essence, the
story of the post-independence era in Kenya.

THE DICTIONARY

ABALUHYA. The name "Luhya" was selected by the North
Nyanza Branch of the Kavirondo Taxpayers Welfare Association in 1929 in preference to the "abalimi" (the cultivators). The origin of the name lay in "oluyia, " the
fireplace around which clan elders congregated. The
fireplace was thus the center of public life of the clan.
Most of the Bantu groups in Western Kenya, despite
linguistic variation among the different groups, share this
term and concept.

By 1935, the term had been accepted by most of
the groups, and the Abaluhya as a national group emerged
between 1935 and 1945. Like the Mijikenda and the
Kalenjin in Kenya, the Abaluhya came into existence
through a combination of reasonable cultural similarity
with colonial administrative convenience and the desire
of younger and more educated men and women for wider
levels of organization to enable them to exert more effective pressure on events. Previous attempts had included organizations such as the North Kavirondo Central
Association and Bantu Kavirondo Taxpayers and Welfare
Association. Their history in Western Kenya extends
back to the 14th century A. D. , although some of the
groups did not arrive in the area until the latter half of
the 19th century. They are the third largest ethnic
grouping in the country, numbering about two million,
and living largely in the three districts of Kakamega,
Bungoma, and Busia in the Western Province.

The Abaluhya are mixed farmers who grow maize,
millet, tea, sugar-cane, and cotton as well as keep cattle, goats and sheep.

ABALUYIA ASSOCIATION, THE. Founded in 1954 with Mr.
Musa Amalemba as its first President. Its aims are
similar to those of other welfare associations in Kenya,
and include the promotion of social, cultural, economic
and welfare activities. Its headquarters are in Nairobi.

ABERDARE MOUNTAINS. The range was named by J. J.
Thomson in 1884 after Lord Aberdare, then the President of the Royal Geographical Society. The Kikuyu
name for them is Nyandarua. They are of volcanic origin and lie north of Nairobi. For over 40 miles, the
range is over 9,000 ft.

ACHARIAR, SITARAM. Arrived in Kenya in the early twenties when the "Indian Question" loomed large on the political horizon. The white settlers, under the guise of
protecting African interests, wanted the "yellow menace"
removed. The East Africa Indian National Congress
fought hard against such racial discrimination. The
Congress was provided with a forum in 1923, when
Sitaram Achariar founded the Democrat. He voiced the
Indian viewpoint in pungently-worded editorials. Unfortunately, due to financial reasons, the Democrat had
to close down in 1931.

        Achariar was employed for a short time by Sir
Ali bin Salim. He then migrated to Bombay to edit the
Sun. He died there in 1939--an unsung and unhonored
hero of the Indian struggle for equal rights in Kenya.

ADAMSON, JOY. Author, artist and conservationist. Born
Frederike Gessner in January 1910 in Austria. Married
to Victor von Klarwill, who did not accompany her to
Kenya in 1937. Met her second husband, Peter Bally,
on shipboard. A painter of distinction, her most ambi-
tious project in this field was to produce a large series
of portraits of Kenya peoples. Today these are housed
in the National Museums of Kenya, Nairobi. She was
also a botanical painter. Her drawings of East African
plants and wild plants which were commissioned by Lady
Muriel Jex-Blake, the founder of the Horticultural Society
of Kenya, to illustrate Gardening in East Africa, are
classics. But it was the story of Elsa, the lion cub that
she and her game warden third husband reared as one
of the family and released as a full-grown lioness, that
won Joy Adamson an international reputation. The books
Born Free, Living Free, and Forever Free, and the
films based on them, did much to create a public aware-
ness of African wildlife. She was murdered in the Shaba
game reserve in Kenya in January 1980, where for two
years she had reared a leopardess named Penny.

        In addition to the previously mentioned books, she
published The Story of Elsa, Elsa and Her Cubs, The
Spotted Sphinx, Pippa's Challenge, Pippa--The Cheetah

and her Cubs, The People of Kenya, Joy Adamson's Africa, The Searching Spirit (which is the story of her life), and Penny: Queen of Shaba (posthumously).

AFRICAN CARRIER CORPS. One of the biggest problems facing the British during the First World War was how to move the equipment and supplies needed for military operations in Tanganyika. With the inadequate road system, motor transport was out of question; the prevalence of the tsetse fly made the use of ox-drawn carts difficult. The only solution lay in human porterage. Mass recruitment resulted in about 160,000 Africans from the East Africa Protectorate (the future Kenya) joining the Carrier Corps. This mobilization of Africans was far more extensive than any previous recruitment of Africans for public or private undertakings and the white settlers were to demand after the war that similar steps should be taken to recruit African labor for their farms. About 50,000 Africans died in Tanganyika, due largely to poor diet and health facilities. Nairobi Municipality built its first housing estate, called "Kariokor," in 1929 on the site of the old Carrier Corps Camp.

AFRICAN DEVELOPMENT BANK, THE. Established in 1964 as a joint venture by thirty independent African states with an authorized initial capital of £250 million. Kenya holds 2.8 percent of the total capital and its annual subscription to the Bank is approximately K.£160,000. The Bank is empowered to borrow money in the capital markets of the world, to buy and sell securities, to guarantee or underwrite securities or invest directly in enterprises and institutions, and to provide technical assistance. The African Development Bank made its first loan to Kenya in 1967 which was to help finance the improvement of roads between Kenya and Tanzania and Kenya and Uganda.

AFRICAN INLAND MISSION, THE. Founded as a result of the American revival movement that had been started by the evangelist Dwight L. Moody in the last part of the nineteenth century. It was a socially conservative, fundamentalist, evangelical, bible-centered movement that concentrated primarily on winning souls for Christ. Initially, Moody concentrated his efforts in the United States and Great Britain. Later, he was interested in extending his crusade to Asia and Africa. It was to meet this need that the Africa Inland Mission (later to change

its name to Africa Inland Church) was established
through the initiative of Peter Cameron Scott, a Scottish immigrant to the United States who had been a missionary in the Congo from 1890 to 1892.

Scott arrived in Kenya in 1895 with a small team,
and they established their first station at Nzaui in Ukambani. Unfortunately, Scott died in 1896 and the Mission
was only saved by the dedicated work of C. E. Hurlburt
who was in charge of it from 1898 to 1925. The mission
established its headquarters at Kijabe among the Kikuyu.
It also had stations among the Kamba and Masai. Between 1906 and 1907, it opened stations in Western Kenya. It also opened stations in Tanzania among the Ny-
amwezi in 1909 and in eastern Zaire in 1912. Compared to such other missions operating in Kenya as the
Church of Scotland Mission, the Church Missionary Society, and the Roman Catholic Missions, AIM paid little
attention to education, and many of its leaders were not
well educated. The mission's main aim was evangelism.

AFRICAN SOCIALISM. In November 1964, KADU dissolved
itself and joined the ruling party KANU. In December
1964, Regionalism was abolished and Kenya became a
de facto one-party Republic. Soon ideological differences developed within the party between the small group
of radicals led by Odinga and Kaggia and the majority
of party members led by Kenyatta and Mboya. It was
in this context that the Kenya government decided to
formulate its ideology. It was embodied in a policy
statement called African Socialism and its Application
to Planning in Kenya (Sessional Paper No. 10 of 1965)
which was published in April 1965. Kenyatta described
it as Kenya's economic "bible." According to the paper, Kenya's socialism had to be derived from Kenya's
cultural roots and not from Marxist analysis. Private
foreign investment was to be encouraged; private property was to be protected, and there would be no expropri-
ation without full compensation; nationalization would only be practiced under certain special circumstances; in-
equitable distribution of wealth was to be controlled to
avoid the use of economic power as a political base;
foreign firms had to be encouraged to Africanize their
management and to make their shares available to Africans who wished to buy them; and Africans were to
be established in private enterprise through loans and
by restricting certain trades and trading areas to citizen traders.

AFRIKANERS, THE.   First arrived in Kenya in 1903, and
   settled in Nakuru and the Uasin Gishu Plateau. Between
   1905 and 1908, small groups of Afrikaner trekkers, with
   their families, arrived from South Africa. In 1908,
   about 50 Afrikaner families with over 250 persons, led
   by Jan Van Rensburg, arrived from South Africa and
   went to settle on the Plateau. In 1911, another large
   trek, the Cloete Trek, which had 60 Orange Free State
   trekkers, settled on the Plateau, making it the largest
   enclave of Afrikaners in East Africa.
        During the inter-war period, a second Afrikaner
   community sprang up in the Thomson's Falls area. They
   believed in "Africa for the Afrikaners," and regarded
   the Kenyan Afrikaans-speaking community as the outpost
   of Afrikanerdom. They brought with them the Dutch Re-
   formed Church. They also demanded that Dutch be
   used in Afrikaner schools. They built a central school
   at Eldoret in 1915, where Afrikaans was taught until
   1956, when the school, which since 1944 had been renamed Highlands School, became an all girls' school.
   Most of the Afrikaners migrated back to South Africa
   between 1961 and 1964 in fear of Kenyan independence.

AGA KHAN III, H.R.H.   Contributed immensely to the
   cause of Islam in Africa. He assumed the Spiritual
   Leadership on August 17, 1885, and first visited East
   Africa in 1899. He was greatly alarmed about the conditions of Muslims in East Africa. His Highness visited East Africa again in 1905, 1914, and 1926 to study
   the plight of Muslims. In 1937, the year of his Golden
   Jubilee, he called a Round Table Conference of all prominent Muslims to discuss the uplift of Muslims in East
   Africa. At this Conference, the East African Muslim
   Welfare Society was founded with Sheth Abdullah Kar-
   imjee as its first President. Not much progress was
   made during the period of the Second World War, but
   in 1945, His Highness visited East Africa and urged
   Muslims to organize themselves for a greater era of
   progress in the post-war Africa. A Major conference
   chaired by His Highness was convened at Mombasa attended by all sects and races from all parts of Africa.
   The task of leading the society fell on Sheth Abdul Hus-
   sein Kaderbhoy of Jinja, Uganda. From that day, His
   Highness contributed large sums of money on "a pound
   to pound basis" for mosques, schools, clinics, technical centers etc. He died at Geneva on July 13, 1957.

AGA KHAN IV, H.H. PRINCE KARIM.   Spiritual leader

and Iman of Ismaili Muslims, many of whom live in
Kenya. He was born on December 13, 1936, son of
the late Prince Aly Salomon Khan and Princess Joan
Aly Khan. He was educated at Le Rosey, Switzerland
and Harvard University, U.S.A. He became the Aga
Khan on the death of his grandfather, Sir Sultan Mohamed Shah, Aga Khan III, in 1957. In 1969 he married Sarah Frances Critchton-Stuart with whom he has
two sons and one daughter. He has visited Kenya several times to promote the spiritual as well as material
well-being of his followers.

AGAR, ELIJA OMOLO BARNABA. Born in 1927 in Karachuonyo. Educated at Kamagambo School, King's College, Budo, Uganda and Bombay University, where he
obtained an honors degree in Economics in 1958. Agar
worked as a teacher before going to India. He joined
politics on his return from India and became organizing
Secretary of Mboya's Nairobi People's Convention Party
as well as editor of its organ, Uhuru, 1958-59. He
was convicted and sentenced by the colonial government
to fourteen months imprisonment on May 21, 1959, for
subversive activities. He was subsequently restricted
in Lamu at the Coast until 1961. In 1962, he became
Assistant Organizing Secretary of KANU and in the following year he was elected Member for Karachuonyo in
the House of Representatives. Agar became an Assistant Minister in 1967 and died following a road accident
in 1969.

AGRICULTURAL DEVELOPMENT CORPORATION, THE.
A parastatal body established by an Act of Parliament
in 1965 to promote and execute schemes of agricultural
development and reconstruction in Kenya. Its initial
task was to undertake the Land Transfer Programme,
1966-72. The British government had provided K. £3.71
million for the purchase of large-scale farms owned by
British nationals for transfer to African farmers. At
the close of the programme in 1972, 201 farms with an
acreage of 320,896 were either sold or leased to African farmers. A number of key large farms were, however, retained in the national interest, by the ADC,
which consequently embarked on direct farming. By
1979, the ADC still managed some 25 farms all over
the country with a total acreage of nearly 500,000 and
is the largest supplier of milk to the Kenya Co-operative Creameries. The ADC has also invested in devel-

opment projects and agro-industries such as sugar industries, ranching schemes, fruit processing, vegetable products, cattle feeds, poultry farming, irrigation projects and horticultural schemes.

AGRICULTURAL FINANCE CORPORATION. Established by the Land and Agricultural Bank (Amendment) Bill No. 27 of 1963 under chapter 323 of the Laws of Kenya, to administer agricultural credit in Kenya. The Corporation grants loans to farmers for up to a maximum of fifteen years. In 1968 the Corporation was combined with the Land and Agricultural Bank of Kenya. It has facilitated the transition from European to African control of the agricultural sector of the Kenyan economy.

AGRICULTURAL SOCIETY OF KENYA. The first agricultural society in East Africa was formed in 1901 and was largely due to the efforts of Mr. John Ainsworth, the Sub-Commissioner for Ukamba, which then included Nairobi. A farming enthusiast, Ainsworth convened a meeting of a number of Nairobi district residents to form a society which they called the East African Agricultural and Horticultural Society, of which he was Secretary until 1906. The Society's first show was held in Nairobi early in 1902, and the following year a show was held at Mombasa. Three more shows were held in Nairobi and in 1907 the management of the society was taken over by the Department of Agriculture.

In 1919 three societies, The Pastoralists' Association of Nakuru, The Uasin Gishu Agricultural Society, and the Old Agricultural and Horticultural Society, amalgamated to form the Kenya Agricultural and Horticultural Society. Its main object was to hold shows at Nakuru, Eldoret, and Nairobi. Ten shows were held in Nairobi between 1919 and 1939. The one held in 1928 was visited by the Prince of Wales, after which the society was given the title "Royal" by King George V. It was known as the Royal Agricultural Society of Kenya until independence when it shed its "royal" connection. It was in 1952 that the first Royal Show took place at Mitchell Park (now Jamhuri Park) in Nairobi. The Society continued to stage shows in other parts of Kenya-- Mombasa, Nanyuki, Eldoret, and Kitale. Since 1963, the Society has expanded so rapidly that today it is one of the largest organizations of its kind in Africa.

AGRICULTURE. Agricultural activities form the core of

rural development. Since independence the old distinc-
tions between modern and traditional agricultural sectors and between subsistence and commercial holdings
have gradually disappeared. Agricultural production oc-
curs primarily on commercialized small holder farms,
supplemented by an important plantation industry. While
land is Kenya's most abundant natural resource, only
17 percent of it is potentially arable. Moreover, the
population is growing at a faster rate (about 3.5 percent
per year) than that at which new land can be made productive through drainage, irrigation and improved inputs
such as high-yielding food varieties and chemical varieties.

Between 1970 and 1979, there was substantially
increased production of cash crops, especially tea, coffee, and sugar-cane. The average annual increases in
the volume of output of tea, coffee, and sugar-cane during that period were 9.5 percent, 2.8 percent and 10.3
percent respectively. There were falls in output of
wheat, sisal, and some non-cereal crops and also of
livestock products other than dairy products. The values of production of agricultural commodities in 1976
and 1978 were as follows: Food crops--maize, wheat,
paddy rice, sorghum (millet), pulses, potatoes, fruits,
bananas and vegetables--K.£197,792,000 and K.£213,-
225,000; Industrial crops--oil seeds and nuts, sugar-
cane, seed cotton, tobacco and barley--K.£16,582,000
in 1976 and K.£17,606,000 in 1978; Export crops--cof-
fee, tea, sisal, pineapples, pyrethrum, cashew-nuts,
wattle--were valued at K.£142,746,000 in 1976 and
K.£175,260,000 in 1978; and last Livestock Products--
milk and dairy products, beef, coffee, sheep, goats, pigs,
poultry meat and eggs--were worth K.£129,436,000 in
1976 and K.£137,319,000 in 1978.

AINSWORTH, JOHN DAWSON. Born June 16th, 1864, at
Urmston, just outside the city of Manchester. One of
the most prominent British pioneer administrators in
Kenya where he first arrived in 1889 to serve the Imperial British East Africa Company. He retired in 1920
as Chief Native Commissioner of the Colony and Protectorate of Kenya.

Before he came to Kenya, he had gone to Congo
(now Zaire) at the age of twenty, where he worked for
a trading company with Roger (later Sir Roger) Case-
ment for five years. It was while in the Congo, that
he sent to Europe news about the H. M. Stanley's Emin

Pasha Relief Expedition which had gone to the Congo in
March 1887 and about which nothing had been heard.
He also met Major-General Sir Francis de Winton, one
of the Directors of IBEA Company in the Belgian Congo,
and it was Sir Francis who partly persuaded Ainsworth
to join IBEA Company in 1889. From 1889 to 1892, he
was based in Mombasa, where his main duty was to assist with the organization of transport into the interior.
He also travelled extensively along the east coast. In
January 1892, he was posted to Machakos to take charge
of the Ukambani district. He turned the station into a
safe stronghold and a valuable provisioning center on
the caravan route to Uganda. He also established good
relations with the Wakamba. On July 1, 1895, the
British Government took over the territory from the
IBEA Company, and Ainsworth was appointed Sub-Commissioner in charge of a province that included Kikuyu
country, Ukambani, Taita and Taveta districts. In
1896, he was made a Vice-Consul. From 1899 to 1906
he was Sub-Commissioner at Nairobi and played an important role in founding the city. He founded the East
Africa Agricultural and Horticultural Society.

Ainsworth was posted to Naivasha in 1906 and
from there he moved to Kisumu as Provincial Commissioner from 1907 to 1914. The Province then included
the present Nyanza and Western Provinces, plus Kericho and Nandi districts. He launched successful campaigns against malaria, sleeping-sickness and plague,
especially in Mumias and Kisumu areas. He also
played a leading role in road construction and agriculture. During the second Masai move from the Laikipia
area to the Southern reserve in 1911, Ainsworth was
put in charge of both the Nyanza Province as well as
the Naivasha Province. In December 1914, he was appointed a Member of the Legislative Council to represent African interests. In 1917 he was appointed Military Commissioner for Labor with the ranks of a Colonel, to organize porters who were to supply the forces
operating south of the Rufiji river. He moved back to
Nairobi, consequently covering about 10,000 miles by road,
steamer, and rail by 1918. About 162,000 Africans were recruited into Ainsworth's Military Labour Corps.

He was awarded the D.S.O. and the C.B.E. for
his services to the Protectorate during the war. In
September 1917, Ainsworth had been appointed Adviser
on Native Affairs and a Member of the Executive Council. In June 1918, while still Military Commissioner

of Labour, he was appointed Chief Native Commissioner,
a post he held until his retirement in 1920. He went
to Somerset West, about 30 miles from Cape Town,
South Africa, where he settled. In 1927, he became
Mayor of the town. Ainsworth died on March 31, 1946,
at the age of eighty-two.

AIR TRANSPORT see COMMUNICATIONS AND TRANS-
PORT

AJUOGA, ABERNEGO MATTHEW. Born at Kambare, Gem,
Central Nyanza; educated at C.M.S. Maseno School
1942-44; St. Mary's Yala, 1945-46; Advanced Theological Studies, Union Theological Seminary, New York
City, 1964-65. Ajuoga worked as Clerk at the Railway
Training School in 1948. He trained at St. Paul's United Theological College, Limuru, 1950-54, and was ordained Priest in the Anglican Order. He later left the
Anglican Church in 1957 to found the Church of Christ
in Africa, of which he is the Archbishop and Leader.

AKANG'O, ODERA. A Luo enlightened despot who tried to
modernize Luoland, especially Gem, during the early
stages of British rule in Kenya. He was born about
1878, when the first Europeans were arriving in Western Kenya. He was the son of a Luo ruoth or chief,
Oloo Ramoya of the ruling Ojuodhi clan in Gem. His
father died when he was still young, and his uncle,
Odera Ulalo, succeeded as ruoth. When Odera Ulalo
died in 1901, another uncle, Odera Sande, assumed the
leadership of North Gem. The British appointed Odera
Akang'o a sub-chief. By 1910, his power and influence
was felt throughout Gem and even beyond. He promoted
agriculture by making it compulsory for all adults to
work on their farms and idlers were severely punished.
        Akang'o set an example by establishing several
large farms where he planted new crops such as sugar
cane, maize, rice. He became a full chief in 1915.
In that year, he was one of the three chiefs who were
sent to Uganda on official tour. The tour made a deep
impression on him, especially the cleanliness, road
building, and quality of education of that country. On
his return, he introduced compulsory primary education
for all children and many schools were built on a harambee basis. He also constructed roads in all parts of
his location and he introduced extensive afforestation
schemes.

In 1916, the British transferred him to Teso
area in Bungoma district and appointed him chief. The
British had failed to bring the Teso people under their
rule, and they needed the power and influence of Odera
Akang'o to do this. He became very unpopular with the
Ateso, who accused him of all manner of crimes. The
British deposed him and sent him to Kismayu, where
he was detained until the end of the First World War.
He was transferred to Nairobi prison, and a day before
his release, he was mysteriously killed. He lies buried
at Langata cemetery in Nairobi--a martyr of British
imperialism.

AKUMU, JAMES DENIS. A prominent trade unionist born
in 1934 in Central Nyanza. Educated at Onjiko Secondary School (1947-49), Aggrey Memorial High School,
Uganda (1950-2), Medical Training School, Nairobi (1952-
4). Akumu worked as a laboratory technician for the
East African Breweries (1955-7). He became district
organizer of Kenya Local Government Workers Union in
1957; and Chairman of the Kenya Federation of Labour,
Coast Province 1958. From 1958 to 1963, he was Secretary-General of Dockworkers' Union. Between 1964
and 1965, he was director of organization for the African Workers' Congress. In 1965, he was appointed
Deputy General-Secretary of the newly established Central Organization of Trade Unions (COTU) by the President, and in 1969, he became the General-Secretary of
COTU. He had been a founder member of Nairobi People's Convention Party in 1957. In 1969 he contested
the General Election and became member of Parliament
for Nyakach. When the Organization of the African
Trade Union Unity (OATUU) based in Ghana was established in 1973, he was elected its first Secretary-General, a post he has held with distinction.

AL-IDRISI. A famous Arab geographer from Cordova, who
was born in North Africa and educated at Cordova. He
travelled in Spain, Asia Minor and Africa. He wrote
an important book, The Book of Roger, which dealt with
the empires of the Western and Central Sudanic regions
and the East African city-states. The work was completed in 1154.

AL-MASUDI, ABDUL HASSAN ALI. An Arab geographer
born in Baghdad in the late 9th century. Travelled
widely in Asia, Europe, North and East Africa. His

Eastern Africa journey was in 915-916, and he visited
several East African towns en route to Madagascar.
He was responsible for the theory of a centralized "Zanj
Empire," which historians have never confirmed. He
died in 956.

ALLIANCE HIGH SCHOOL, THE. Established in 1926 following a conference of the Protestant denominations in
Kenya at which it was decided to form an alliance--
hence the name. Also in 1926 the La Zoute conference
was held at which the Protestant Missions decided to
co-operate with the British Government in a new education policy for Africa. It was the first African Secondary School in Kenya, followed by Kabaa-Mangu (1927),
Maseno Secondary School 1938 and St. Mary's School,
Yala, 1939. The last two had been primary schools
for over thirty years. They were all established by
the missions--the Alliance High School and Maseno by
the Protestant Mission; Kabaa-Mangu and Yala by the
Catholic Mission. The Alliance High School played a
decisive role in the development of secondary education
in Kenya and in the creation of an educated elite. It
is particularly associated with Edward Carey Francis,
an English mathematician who abandoned a promising
career at Cambridge University first to teach at Maseno School and later to run the Alliance High School
as a Headmaster.

ALLIANCE OF MISSIONARY SOCIETIES IN EAST AFRICA.
Formed between the Church Missionary Society, the
Church of Scotland Mission, the African Inland Mission,
and the United Methodist Church Mission. The objective was to coordinate the work of the Protestant Missions in Kenya, with a hope of forming a United Church
of Kenya. It was this Alliance that planned and established the Alliance High School at Kikuyu in 1926 with
twenty-six pupils.

AMBOSELI GAME RESERVE. One of the largest of Kenya's
Parks and Reserves. It covers an area of 1,259 square
miles in the Kajiado District. Besides other game such
as elephants, buffalo, lions, cheetahs, giraffes, baboons,
monkeys, etc., it is most famous for its large numbers
of rhinos.

ANGAINE, JACKSON HARVESTER. Farmer, businessman,
and politician, born in 1903 in Meru. Educated at Al-

liance High School, Kikuyu. Appointed Secretary of
Meru A.D.C. 1935-48. He then left Local Government
Service to do business, 1948-52. He was Manager,
Meru Traders Ltd., 1957-58. Member of Meru A.D.C.
1959-62. He was first elected to the Legislative Council in 1961, and again in 1963 as a KANU Member for
Meru. During the Coalition Government, he was appointed Parliamentary Secretary in the Ministry of Education. In 1963, he was appointed Minister for Land
and Settlement, a portfolio he held up to November 1979.
He has thus been a key figure in the evolution of the
post-independence land policy in Kenya. He himself is
a leading large-scale farmer in Meru.

ANOKA. According to Akamba traditions, the Anoka were
hunter-gatherers who lived on Chyulu hills before the
arrival of the Akamba and Chagga in the area. They
either died out or more likely, they were absorbed by
the incoming groups.

ARABS. Today the Arabs number about twenty-six thousand
in Kenya and have been connected with the history of
Kenya since the ninth century when they visited the
coastal region as traders. They introduced Islam in
the area and played a leading role in the Indian Ocean
trade and the caravan trades. They were also active
in the slave trade and the establishment of plantation
slavery which continued in Kenya until 1907. Various
Arab dynasties also established regimes in places such
as Mombasa, Witu, Lamu, Pate and Malindi.

ARGWINGS-KODHEK, CHIEDO MORE GEM. A brilliant
lawyer, teacher and politician, born in 1923 in Gem,
Nyanza Province. Educated at St. Mary's College,
Kisubi, Entebbe in Uganda (1936-37), Makerere College
Kampala, 1937-40, where he obtained a teaching diploma. Taught for seven years in various schools in
the Rift Valley and Nyanza before he won a government
bursary in 1947 to study social science at the University
of South Wales and Monmouthshire. His ambition was
to study law, but Africans from Kenya were not allowed
to study law in Britain or anywhere else in the Commonwealth. He applied to the Kenya Government for per-
mission to study law, but this was flatly refused. He
decided to do it secretly with active support from his
University. Between November 1948 and December
1949, Argwings-Kodhek surprised everybody by passing

all his law examinations. He also obtained his Bachelors degree in social science. He was called to the
Bar at Lincoln's Inn in 1951. Before his return to
Kenya in 1952, he married Miss Mavis Tate, the daughter of an Irish engineer. He declined a job in the Attorney-General's Department where he was offered a
third of the salary of a whiteman and decided to go into private practice.

Argwings-Kodhek was the only African practicing
lawyer at the beginning of the Emergency, and he fought
fearlessly against colonial injustices and oppression.
With Fitz de Souza and A. R. Kapila, he became one
of KAU's three legal draftsmen. He defended most of
the Mau Mau cases, and was therefore nicknamed "the
Mau Mau lawyer" by the white settlers.

This "highly literate African" as the Kenya Weekly News described him, formed the first African political
party since KAU, the Nairobi African District Congress
in 1956. He was a Member of the Legislative Council
from 1961-63, during which period he was made Parliamentary Secretary in the Ministry of Lands, Surveys
and Town Planning in 1962. He was elected KANU Member of the House of Representatives for Gem in 1962 and
appointed Parliamentary Secretary in the Ministry of
Natural Resources. In 1963, he was transferred to the
Ministry of Health and Housing. From 1964-66, he was
Assistant Minister for Internal Security and Defence.
In 1966, he joined the Cabinet when he was appointed
Minister of Natural Resources. In 1968, he was appointed Minister for Foreign Affairs. Very accessible
and a man of the people, Argwings-Kodhek was a witty
and sharp debater who made a great impact on Kenya
Parliament. He died on the morning of January 29,
1969, following a road accident.

ARTHUR, JOHN WILLIAM, 1881-1952. Educated at Glasgow Academy and Glasgow University. Came to Kenya
in 1906 as a missionary and doctor. He rose to be the
head of the Church of Scotland Mission in Kenya and
organized the Kikuyu Missions Volunteer Corps (1917-18).
He was appointed a Member of the Kenya Legislative
Council to represent African interests 1924-26, and was
a Member of the Executive Council 1928-29. As Head
of the Church of Scotland in Kenya, Arthur took a very
active part in the fight against female circumcision in
Central Kenya, a fight which led to a direct confronta-
tion with the Kikuyu Central Association. He retired
in 1937.

ASIANS.   In Kenya this ethnic group numbers about 140,000,
   of whom only about 70,000 are Kenya citizens. They
   comprise several communities: the Hindus, the Sikhs,
   the Goans, and the Muslims (who are further subdivided
   into the Ismaili Khoja and the Bohra). The Asians have
   been largely a commercial Community since the nineteenth century when they started to arrive in Kenya in
   significant numbers.

ATHLETICS.   Kenya is famous for athletics, especially in
   track and field events. The country has produced several world-acclaimed athletes, starting with Wilson Ki-
   prugut Chuma, who won for Kenya the first Olympic
   medal at the Tokyo Olympics in 1964. This was followed by Kipchoge Keino setting two world records in
   1965 (3000 meters at Helsinki: 7.39.6 and 5,000 meters in New Zealand: 13.40.6.) In June 1973, Ben
   Jipcho broke the 3,000 meters steeplechase world record at Helsinki in a time of 8.14.10; and in June 1977,
   Kimombwa set a new world record in 10,000 meters at
   Helsinki (27.30.47). This Kenya reputation climaxed in
   Henry Rono becoming the first man in history to hold
   four world athletics records in 1978: 5,000 meters in
   April (13.8.4), 3,000 meters steeplechase in May (8.05.4),
   10,000 meters on June 11, (27.22.47) and 3,000 meters
   in June 28, (7.32.1). Besides these world-record hold-
   ers, Kenya has produced many athletes of international
   fame such as Nyandika Maiyoro, Seraphino Antao, Arere
   Anentia, Naftali Temu, Amos Biwot, Charles Asati,
   Robert Ouko, Sang, Mike Boit, John Kiprugat, Paul
   Mose, Richard Juma, John Ng'eno, Dan Omwanze, Alice
   Adala, John Mwebi, and Wilson Waigwa.

ATTORNEY-GENERAL.   The chief legal officer of the Government. It is his responsibility to decide whether to
   institute criminal proceeding; also, he can require the
   Commissioner of Police to investigate any matter that
   he thinks relates to any offense or alleged offense or
   suspected offense. He has also got a political role: he
   acts as chief legal advisor to the Government. He is a
   Member of the Cabinet and of Parliament, where he sits
   without a vote. He is thus the only Civil Servant who is
   a Minister.

AUSTRALOPITHECUS.   Meaning "southern ape," this term
   was first applied by Prof. R. A. Dart in 1924 to the

kind of creature represented by the fossil skull he found
at Taung in the Cape Province, South Africa. It has
since been identified as a genus of extinct members of
the hominids (or family of man) whose fossilized remains have been found in South Africa, in Tanzania
(Garusi, Olduvai, and Peninj), in Ethiopia in the Omo
Valley, and in Kenya (Kanapoi, Chemeron, Lothagam
and East Turkana). These creatures who lived in open-
savanna, along the lake-shores and in semi-desert en-
vironments lived roughly from the Pliocene period to
the Middle Pleistocene.

AWORI, WYCLIFE WORK WASWA. A prominent politician
and journalist, born in Nambale, Western Kenya in
1925. He was educated at Kakamega High School before going to Mulago Hospital in Kampala, Uganda, to
train as a health inspector. Later he worked as health
inspector with the Municipal Council of Nairobi. In
1945, he resigned and devoted his full time to politics
and journalism. He edited Radio Posta, Habari Za
Dunia, Tribune and other publications in preindepend-
ence days. With Pio Gama Pinto and E. K. Shaldah,
Awori used the press effectively to fight colonialism.
When the Kenya African Study Union was started in
1946, Awori was elected Treasurer. He later became
the Vice-President of the organization when it was renamed Kenya African Union. From 1952 to 1956, he
represented North Nyanza in the Colonial Legislative
Council, where he was a forceful critic of the colonial
administration. For a short time after independence,
he worked as an assistant editor of the Kenya Hansard.
He died on May 5, 1978, at the Aga Khan Hospital in
Nairobi.

AYANY, SAMUEL GERSON. Born in 1922 at Got Nyapong',
North Sakwa location, Siaya District. Educated at La-
ba 1933-37; Maseno Secondary School 1938-42; Alliance
High School 1943-44; and Makerere University College
1945-48, where he studied sociology, history, geography,
and English, and obtained a Diploma in Education. He
went back to teach at his old school at Maseno where
he remained for twelve years. In 1960, he went to
Howard University, U.S.A. where he studied history,
political science and Latin, which earned him B.A. and
M.A. degrees. On his return to Kenya in 1963, he
was posted to Kisumu as Deputy Provincial Education

Officer.   In the following year, he was appointed Headmaster of Kangaru School, thereby becoming the first
African to head a secondary school with a Form VI.
During the same year he moved to the headquarters of
the Ministry of Education in Nairobi to head the secondary education section.

In 1965, he left the Ministry of Education to become the Executive Director of the Central Housing
Board, which had been established in 1953 to act as a
clearing house for funds or other resources allocated
by the Government to facilitate housing development by
local authorities.   In 1967, it was renamed the National
Housing Corporation.   Under the direction of Mr. Ayany,
the Corporation has developed from a clearing house
consisting of seven expatriate staff in 1965 to a national
corporation employing over two hundred staff and empowered to acquire funds, participate in direct housing
construction, and lend funds to individuals and local
authorities.   From 1964 to 1977, the Corporation constructed 23,531 housing units at a cost of over £24
million.

Mr. Ayany has also been a Member of Central
Nyanza African District Council, 1951-59; Founder and
First President of the Kenya National Union of Teachers,
1958-60; and Co-founder and First Chairman of Maseno
Hospital League of Friends, 1959.   He is the author of
A History of Zanzibar: A Study in Constitutional De-
velopment 1934-1964 (1970).

AYODO, SAMUEL ONYANGO.   Teacher and politician, born
in 1930 at Kabondo, South Nyanza, son of William and
Drusila Sawala Ayodo.   Educated at Maseno Secondary
School, Makerere University College, Uganda 1950-51;
and Lincoln University, U.S.C. (1953-55), where he obtained a B.S.C. (Education).   On his return to Kenya
he taught at Kisii High School, 1956-59; Elected Member for South Nyanza 1959-61 in the Legislative Council;
and in 1961-63.   In 1963 he was elected to the House
of Representatives for Kasipul/Kabondo, where he remained until 1969.   He was appointed Minister for Local Government 1963-64; Minister for Natural Resources,
Tourism and Wildlife 1964-66; and Minister for Tourism
and Wildlife 1966-69.   He lost in the General Elections
of 1969, but won the Kabondo/Kasipul seat again in
1974.   He is Elder of the Golden Heart of Kenya; Grand
Band of the Star of Africa (Liberia), Grand Cordon,
Order of Star of Honour (Ethiopia) and a director of

several companies including Kuja Crafts Ltd.   Ayodo
was re-elected to Parliament in 1979.

- B -

BADEN-POWELL, ROBERT STEPHENSON SMYTH.   Founder
of the Boy Scout movement in 1908.   He was born in
1857 and joined the Indian Army in 1876.   Later he
fought in South Africa against the Zulu in 1888 and in
West Africa against the Asante in 1895-96.   In both of
these cases he acquired notoriety as a harsh and in-
sensitive war leader, especially to African war captives.
In 1896, he was again in Southern Africa, trying to sup-
press the Ndebele rebellion.   During the South African
War, he held Mafeking against an Afrikaner siege which
lasted seven months (1899-1900).   He retired from the
Army in 1910 and devoted the rest of his life to scout-
ing.   He died in Kenya in 1941 and is buried at Nyeri.

BAJUN.   The Bajun number about 30,000 people and live on
the Lamu archipelago in the Coast Province.   Historians
are not in agreement regarding their origins, but it is
evident that they represent a hybrid population whose
elements are similar to those of the Swahili group.
They cultivate coconut, fish, export mangrove poles to
Arabia and organize maritime transport.   They are also excellent woodcarvers and sandal makers.

BAKER, RICHARD EDWARD ST. BARBE.   A British Silvi-
culturist, born on October 9, 1889, at Southampton.
Educated at Dean Close School, Cheltenham, Saskat-
chewan University, Gonville and Cains College, Cambridge and Imperial Forestry Institute, Oxford University.   Student, farmer and lumber camp employee, Canada 1909-13; served in the Army 1914-17.   He was then
appointed Assistant Conservator of Forests, Kenya 1920-
23; Nigeria 1924-1929.   He founded Men of the Trees
in Kenya in 1922, Britain in 1924, Palestine in 1929;
and as a World-Wide Society in 1932.   He also founded
Junior Men of the Trees in 1956.   In 1959, he settled
in New Zealand where he established the Commonwealth
and Overseas Headquarters of Men of the Trees.   He
was the Convenor of the World Forestry Charter Gath-
erings 1945-56; founded Friends of Sahara (U.S.A. &
U.K.) and prepared a report and launched Sahara Reclamation Programme 1963-64.   He was founder and

editor of Trees and Life (Journal of Men of the Trees)
1934-1959, as well as author of several books dealing
with trees.

BARAZA. The oldest Swahili weekly newspaper in Kenya
until it ceased publication in 1979. Founded in 1939
to provide the Colonial Government with a forum for
war propaganda directed to the African population, it
nevertheless retained its independence and played a
pioneering role in the promotion and development of
Kiswahili as a lingua franca. Baraza was owned by
the Standard Group.

BARING, SIR EVELYN (later Lord Howick of Glendale).
Born in 1903, Baring was Governor of Southern Rhodesia 1942-44. He served as High Commissioner for
the United Kingdom in South Africa and Administrator
of the High Commission Territories of Basutoland,
Swaziland, and Bechwanaland 1944-51. Was appointed
Governor and Commander-in-Chief of Kenya, 1952-59.
He was thus in charge of Kenya during the critical period of the Mau Mau war, and the immediate post-Emer-
gency period. From 1961 to June 30, 1972, he was
Chairman of the Colonial (later Commonwealth) Development Corporation. He died in March 1973. Baring
was awarded GCMG and KCVO.

BARINGO, LAKE. Situated in the northern Rift Valley.
The surrounding area has yielded Pleistocene fossils,
including hominid remains. To the west of the lake
are older sediments known as the Chemeron beds (named
after the Chemeron River), which are rich in vertebrate
fossils, and younger sediments called the Kapthurin beds,
after the Kapthurin River nearby. These younger depos-
its contain fossilized human skeletal remains and stone
implements.

BARTH COMMISSION REPORT, THE (or The 1912-13 Native
Labour Commission Report). A major historical document. As the demand for cheap African labor increased
among the European settlers, the position of the African
laborer deteriorated fast. Alarmed by this, the Kenya
Government appointed a Labour Commission in 1912,
with Judge J. W. (later Sir Jacob) Barth, the most able
of the country's judges, as Chairman. The other members were A. F. Church, the Chief Engineer of the Railway; F. G. Hamilton, a district Commissioner; B. G.

Allen, a Nairobi solicitor; G. Williams, a farmer and
Chairman of the Convention; and two missionaries, Father G. Brandsma and the Rev. Dr. John Arthur.

Over two hundred European and over sixty African witnesses gave evidence, all of which was eventually included in the published Report. This is what makes it a valuable historical source. The settlers wanted the administration to "exploit the native for Europeans," to quote Hollis, one of the administrators. The evidence revealed the appalling conditions under which the African laborer worked: poor, monotonous food; bad housing; employer ill-treatment; hardship on journeys; and starvation wages. Chiefs, assisted by retainers and headmen, supplied labor to professional recruiters, who paid them in cash. The Commission's Report rejected any form of direct government recruiting as amounting to compulsion. It recommended the creation of a Chief Native Commissioner; a system of identification to deal with desertion; the abolition of "Kaffir farming"; the abolition of professional recruiter; the establishment of government labor camps to which district officers would direct work seekers; the improvement of travel conditions; and the establishment of a system of labor inspection. Finally, the Commission recommended the expansion of technical and agricultural education.

BATTUTA, IBN (MUHAMMAD IBN ABDULLAH IBN BATTUTA). A famous Moroccan traveller and chronicler, born in 1304. Between 1325 and 1354 he visited most of the Muslim world, recording in detail what he saw. In 1331, he visited the East Coast down to Kilwa. His description of the region at that time is an invaluable eye-witness account. He died in 1377.

BEAUTTAH, JAMES. His original name was Mbutu wa Ruhara and he was born in 1888 at Lower Muhito in Mukuruwe-ini Division of Nyeri District. Lost both his parents while still a child. Escaped to Fort Hall town when he was twelve years old to work as a houseboy for a Mnyamwezi policeman, with whom he moved to Nairobi in 1903. Went to Mombasa and studied at Rabai mission school and Buxton High School. He joined the Post Office as a telegraphist trainee at Rabai. On completion of the course he was posted, in 1911, to Bombo, a military post in Buganda. From here he was transferred, every two years, to different stations, until 1932 when he resigned. He worked at Kikuyu, Nairobi, Mom-

basa, Eldoret, Naivasha, Kisumu, Maseno, etc. It
was during one of his spells in Mombasa in 1918 that
he decided to Anglicize his name. He had been christened James and he decided to change his Kikuyu name
Mbutu to Beauttah. By 1919 he was back in Nairobi,
and it was during this period that the East African Association (EAA) was formed by Harry Thuku, Norman
Mboya, Joseph Kangethe, Jesse Kariuki, Abdulla Taira-
ra and a Muganda called Ssentongo. He attended their
meetings as an onlooker. In 1921, he was posted to
Maseno, where he met the future leaders of Young Kavirondo Association (Piny Owacho) such as Rev. Reuben
Omulo, Matthew Otieno, Jonathan Okwiri and Joel Om-
ino. In 1924, he was posted back to Nairobi. With
Joseph Kang'ethe, George Kirongozi Ndegwa, James
Njoroge, Jesse Kariuki, Kumo Kahacho (all from Murang'a) he decided to form another political organization:
the Kikuyu Central Association in 1924 to replace the
EAA which had been banned in 1922 after the Thuku
riots. From 1926 to 1929, he worked in Eastern Uganda. He was then posted back to Mombasa, where he
founded a branch of the KCA, but which, for security
reasons, he called Kiama kia Kunyamara, the "Society
of the Destitute."

Beauttah resigned from the Post Office in November 1932 to devote more time to politics. In 1936,
he went to settle in Maragua, Murang'a. The next year
he was elected with Job Muchuchu, to the Murang'a Lo-
cal Native Council. In 1940, the government banned
KCA and arrested its leaders such as Joseph Kang'ethe,
George K. Ndegwa, Job Muchuchu, Jesse Kariuki. But
Beauttah was not arrested. He founded the Murang'a
Land Board Association to fight for lost lands, and the
Kenya African Traders Association to help Africans get
control of the marketing of wattle bark. In fact, the
KAFTA was a front for the KCA.

In 1945, after the resignation of Harry Thuku
as President of the Kenya African Study Union, Beauttah joined its Executive Committee. Later he became
a Vice-President of KAU representing Central Province.
In 1946, he joined the Labour Trades Union of East Africa which Makhan Singh had founded in 1935; and with
the return of the latter from India in August 1947, Beauttah tried to get the trade unions, with the help of Makhan Singh, to join KAU. On February 12, 1952, the
Court sentenced him to two years imprisonment for organizing anti-inoculation protests in Murang'a. This was

followed by six years of detention, for the Government
was convinced he played a leading role in organizing
Mau Mau.   He unsuccessfully contested the 1963 General
Election.   It is thus difficult to understand African, and
especially Kikuyu, politics during the colonial period,
without reference to Beauttah.

BEECHER, LEONARD JAMES, C. M. G.   Born in 1906 in
London and educated at St. Olaves School Southwerk and
Imperial College, London obtaining a Dip. Ed. (London)
and B. Sc. (London).   He later earned a D. D. (Lambeth).
He came to Kenya in 1927 with the Christian Missionary
Society to teach physics and mathematics at the newly-
founded Alliance High School, Kikuyu.   From there he
went to Kahuhia Teacher Training College to become
the headmaster there.
          In 1929, he married Gladys Leakey, the second
daughter of Canon Leakey, the first Anglican missionary
at Kabete, and the father of the famous anthropologist
Dr. L. S. B. Leakey.   In the 1940's, he was ordained
into priesthood and subsequently became a nominated
Member of the Legislative Council, representing African
interests prior to African nominations and elections.
Beecher was Chairman of the famous education commission which produced the Beecher Report.   Eventually he
became the Archbishop of the Church of the Province of
East Africa until his retirement in 1970.

BLIXEN OF RUNGSTEDLUND, BARONESS KAREN (pen name
ISAK DINESEN) 1885-1962.   Married to a cousin in 1914,
she came with him to Kenya, where they established
and successfully operated a coffee plantation.   Her book
Out of Africa vividly records many of her experiences
in Kenya.   In 1921, she was divorced from her husband,
but she continued to manage the plantation for another
ten years, until the collapse of the coffee market forced
her to return to Denmark.   In 1961, Shadows on the
Grass, containing four stories based on her memories
of life in Kenya, was published.   Karen suburb in Nairobi is named after her.

BLUNDELL, SIR MICHAEL, M. B. E., K. B. E.   Born in
1907 in London. The son of an English solicitor, he
was educated at Wellington College.   In 1925 he came
to farm in Kenya.   His public career began in 1938 when
he was elected to the Coffee Board of Kenya.   During
the Second World War, he served in the Royal Engin-

eers, 1940-47, becoming a Colonel.   As Chairman of
the European Settlement Board, 1946-47, he initiated
the post-war European Settlement Schemes.   In 1948-
57, Blundell was the European Elected Member for Rift
Valley and in 1952 he became Leader of European Elected Members Organization.   In 1954 he was appointed
Minister without Portfolio to the Emergency War Council where he played a key role in the fight against Mau
Mau.   He was a Specially Elected Member, 1957-59;
and again European Member for Rift Valley 1959-63.
Between 1955 and 1959 he was the Minister of Agriculture, and again in 1961-62.   He became the Leader of
the New Kenya Group, a multi-racial grouping of liberal politicians, mostly Europeans, in 1959 and remained
in charge until 1963 when the party was dissolved.

Besides farming and politics, Blundell held several directorships (14 by 1967) in multi-national corporations operating in East Africa.   He was Chairman of
the East African Breweries Ltd. from 1964; Chairman
of Uganda Breweries since 1965; Chairman of Saccone
and Speed Ltd. , the wine merchants associated with
Courage, Barclay and Simonds Ltd.   He also held directorships in Ind Coope Ltd. , Ind Coope African Investments Ltd. as well as in Barclays Bank.   He was
knighted in 1962.   He is the author of an autobiographical work, So Rough a Wind, first published in 1964.

BOMBAY AFRICANS.   These liberated Africans had been
rescued from Arab dhows by British naval cruisers pa-
trolling the Indian Ocean and sent to India in 1847.
They were later settled at a Christian Village at Shar-
anpur, near Nasik, where they were given industrial
training.   Others were trained as catechists, evangel-
ists and teachers.   Over 150 of these Bombay Africans
were returned to Kenya in 1875 to settle at Freretown
at the Coast.   Before then many of them had played a
leading role in exploration and evangelistic work in Africa.   In 1865, nine of them accompanied David Livingstone to East and Central Africa where they worked as
interpreters and negotiators.   John Rebman had also
recruited some Bombay Africans to help him with evangelistic work at Rabai.   David George was a Bombay
African who worked as a catechist at the CMS station
at Rabai from 1841 to 1874.   In 1873, five of them--
Mathew Wellington, Jacob Wainwright, William Benjamin, Kalos, and Legget--left Bombay to accompany
H. M. Stanley in his search for Livingstone.   Mathew

Wellington later went to Freretown in 1874; Wainwright
and Kalos settled in Zanzibar; and Legget and William
Benjamin returned to their homeland in Mozambique
where they became missionaries. From 1874 to 1904,
the Bombay Africans played leading roles as catechists,
readers, and pastors in the spread of Christianity in
the coast region of Kenya. Their numbers had increased
to about 3,000 by 1880, and they were concentrated at
the two mission stations of Rabai and Freretown. The
freed slaves as a distinct group gradually disappeared
in Kenya following the abolition of slavery in the country in 1907.

BONI.   The Boni live in the area between Lamu and the
    Somali border.   Together with the Somali and the Ren-
    dille they constitute the group that the linguists have re-
    cently referred to as "Sam-speaking" people.   The name
    is derived from the root "sam," meaning "nose," a
    term which is shared by the languages of the three
    groups. They migrated originally from the Ethiopian
    Highlands across northern Kenya to the coast, and thence
    northwards towards modern Somalia. Originally pas-
    toralists, they later changed to a hunting-gathering ex-
    istence for reasons that are still unclear. They hunt
    with large bows and arrows, although a few of them
    have been forced by the southward infiltration of the
    Somali to adopt agriculture.

BORANA.   The Borana are the extension of the Ethiopian
    Borana who are said to have descended from the high-
    lands between 1660-1720, abandoned agriculture and then
    adopted pastoralism.   In Kenya they number over 36,000
    and are thus the largest Oromo-speaking group in the
    country.   "Borana" is said to mean "free."   Unlike their
    relations the Oromo, who have remained cattle-keepers,
    the Borana have been forced by the progressive dessi-
    cation of their land to change to a predominantly camel-
    herding economy.

BROMHEAD'S SITE.   A burial site on the south bank of the
    Makalia River, south of Lake Nakuru.   The site was
    discovered by W. S. Bromhead in 1918, and rediscov-
    ered by Dr. L. S. B. Leakey and B. H. Newsam in
    1927.   Skeletons belonging to about 30 individuals have
    been identified in these Mesolithic burials.   Most of the
    skeletons were tall with long faces, while others were
    short, with broader heads and faces.   The culture as-

sociated with these remains belongs to the Elementeitan
industry.

BURJI.   The Burji live in the Marsabit District, in the
    North-Eastern Province.   They originated from Ethi-
    opia, where they formerly lived on the Burji Moun-
    tains between Lake Chew Bahir and Lake Abaya, grow-
    ing mostly cotton and coffee.   The Ethiopian Emperor
    Menelik (1889-1913) conquered the Oromo territories in-
    cluding the land of the Burji between 1890 and 1900.
    The Emperor treated the Burji as serfs, allocating them
    among his generals and soldiers as free labor.   This
    led to a mass migration of the Burji into Kenya between
    1906 and 1930.

BUSAIDI DYNASTY.   Originated in Oman, where it ousted
    the Yarubi dynasty from power in 1741.   They intensi-
    fied their commercial links with East Africa; and in
    1840, Seyyid Said moved his capital to Zanzibar.   In
    1861, the dynasty was split into two independent dynas-
    ties, one ruling Oman and the other one ruling Zanzi-
    bar and the coastal region.   They maintained "govern-
    ors" at several of the coastal towns.   In Kenya, the
    overlordship of this dynasty over a ten-mile coastal
    strip was formally recognized by according protector-
    ate status over this area until 1963, when it was re-
    absorbed into independent Kenya.   The dynasty was
    finally overthrown by the Zanzibar revolution of 1964
    led by John Okello.

- C -

CAPRICORN AFRICA SOCIETY, THE.   Founded in Salisbury,
    Southern Rhodesia, by David Stirling in 1949.   Basically,
    the movement represented a reaction of liberal Euro-
    peans to the nationalists' demands in East and Central
    Africa.   It aimed at establishing a British Dominion
    covering the area between the Equator and the Tropic
    of Capricorn (hence the name Capricorn Africa Society).
    The power structure model envisaged was that Africans
    who had attained certain European standards should be
    admitted into the colonial power structure.   As more
    Africans accepted European economic and social norms
    (or "civilized standards") they would be admitted into
    the power structure and one day be in the majority.   The
    Society operated as a multi-racial pressure group led by

Europeans. It was condemned by the conservative white
settlers in Kenya, Tanganyika, Northern and Southern
Rhodesia as over-liberal and by the African nationalists
in these countries as elitist and a camouflage for white
domination.

The Society campaigned vigorously for the Central
African Federation from 1951. Rhodes' dictum of "Equal
rights for all Civilized Men" was adopted by the Society.
Stirling published a booklet called, Greater Rhodesia:
The London Proposals Examined (n.d.), in which he
stated the aims of the Society: "The objects of the
Capricorn Society are, first, to establish western civilization in Africa, or at least in that part of Africa
which can take white settlement; second, to make Capricorn Africa as much an offshoot and [bulwark] of Western European, Christian, liberal civilization as are the
United States and Canada, [because without these Europeans and their values] the labor of Africans would cer-
tainly not suffice to develop the potential wealth of the
area and turn (it) ... into a great community, with a
thriving industrial activity."

When it was discovered that Africans in this region were opposed to any form of federation dominated
by Europeans, the Society decided to concentrate its
efforts on improving race relations. Branches of the
Society were formed in East and Central Africa, as
well as in London. The London Committee was chaired
by Air Vice Marshall Sir John Slessor and included Sir
Charles Ponsonby (Chairman of the Joint East Africa
Board, an influential committee of the unofficials concerned with trade between Britain and East Africa), F. S.
Joelson (editor of East Africa and Rhodesia), Air Com-
modore Benson, and Laurens Van der Post. In February 1954, the "Capricorn Manifesto" was published. It
encouraged the formation of "Citizenship Committees" in
the six territories whose main function was to formulate
a "common loyalty to Capricorn Africa."

In June 1956, a race relations Convention met
at Salima on the shores of Lake Malawi to ratify a Capricorn Contract. All branches were represented, Kenya being represented by 43 delegates consisting of 13
Africans, 9 Asians and 21 Europeans. As the political
tempo quickened in this region, the Capricorn platform
rapidly became obsolete and conservative. In 1958,
Stirling resigned as President of the Society for personal reasons, and was succeeded by the Chairman of the
Kenya Branch, Michael Wood. Three meetings were

held in December 1958 and in October 1959 in London,
and in January 1961 in Kenya, where members of all
the branches were represented. However, the activities
of the Society in Africa continued to decline, and by
1960 only two branches remained, the Kenyan and the
Central African. In December 1963, the Capricorn African Society was formally closed.

CARTER LAND COMMISSION. One of the Commissions that
had been requested by the Parliamentary Joint Select
Committee in 1931. It was composed of Sir Morris
Carter, former Chief Justice of Uganda and Tanganyika,
Captain F. O'B. Wilson, a Kenya settler, and Mr. Ru-
pert W. Hemsted, a former administrative officer in
Kenya. With such a membership, which included two
white settlers, it is little wonder that the Africans
showed a mistrust of the Commission. The Commission
had two major tasks: 1) to consider the needs of the
African population present and prospective, and 2) to
delimitate the so-called "White Highlands." It took evidence from all parts of Kenya, which were faithfully re-
corded and published in several volumes of the Report,
under the title of Kenya Land Commission: Evidence
and Memoranda, Col. 91 (1934). The Report itself was
published in 1934 (Report of the Kenya Land Commission, Cmd. 4556). The Commissioners recommended
that additional land should be added to the so-called
"native reserves" (an increase of some 3 percent) and
they defined the boundaries of the so-called "White Highlands." The report of the Carter Land Commission thus
marked the limit of European land aspirations.

CAVENDISH-BENTINCK, SIR FERDINAND, KBE, CMG, MC.
Born in 1889. He began his career in East Africa as
private secretary to the Governor of Uganda from 1925
to 1927. He moved to Kenya where he became a tough-
liner in European politics and a strong defender of the
concept of Kenya as a "White Man's Country." He became Secretary of the Convention of Association and then
a European Elected Member in the Legislative Council
representing the Nairobi North Constituency. He was
appointed Secretary of the European Elected Members
Organization of that Council. In 1945, when Sir Philip
Mitchell, the Governor of Kenya, introduced the "Membership" system, (whereby leading unofficial members
of the Legislative Council resigned their constituencies
and joined the Government as nominated Members in

charge of portfolios) Cavendish-Bentinck became the
Member for Agriculture, Forests and Water Develop-
ment--the first settler Minister. His appointment marked
the first political advance for the unofficial communities
in Kenya. From 1955 to 1960, he was the Speaker of
the Kenya Legislative Council. He resigned in March
1960 to form the Kenya Coalition Party whose policies
aimed at protecting European interests which, according to Cavendish-Bentinck, had been betrayed by the
British Government's decision to grant political independence to Kenya. In 1977, at the age of eighty-eight,
he became the eighth Duke of Portland following the
death of his cousin. This meant that he became a member of the British House of Lords. He died in Kenya in
December 1980.

CENTRAL BANK OF KENYA. Kenya, Uganda, and Tanzania
continued to operate a regional currency for a few years
after independence. The regional currency was managed
by the East African Currency Board which had been in
existence since 1919. In February 1965, the government of Tanzania announced its decision to establish a
central national bank and to issue its own currency.
The other two East African countries had no alternative
but to follow. In Kenya, the Central Bank of Kenya Act
was signed on March 24, 1966, with an authorized capital of K. Shillings 26 million. The Bank is a key institution in economic management of the country. It is
charged with managing the money supply and foreign reserves of the country. It also advises the Kenya government on financial matters.

CENTRAL ORGANISATION OF TRADE UNIONS, KENYA,
THE (COTU). A federal body to which twenty-eight
trade unions are affiliated. Despite strong effort to
have one central trade union organization, it was evident by 1965 that the trade unions were deeply divided
along ideological lines. There were two central organizations: the Kenya Federation of Labour, which was
regarded as pro-West, and the Kenya African Workers
Congress, which leaned to the East. The government
decided to de-register both organizations in 1965, and
to establish COTU, thus increasing government control
of trade union activities.

CHIEF. In most societies in Kenya, the institution of chief-
tainship was a colonial creation. For administrative
purposes, the British divided Kenya into provinces, which

were divided in turn into districts and locations. This
three-tier system constituted and still constitutes, the
provincial administration on which Central Government
has heavily relied since 1902. During the colonial period, the provinces and districts were under the jurisdic-
tion of British officials, and the locations were the responsibility of the chiefs. The chiefs were thus colonial agents, whose authority derived from the 1902 and
1912 Chiefs Ordinances. These ordinances gave the
chiefs three areas of responsibility: the maintenance
of public order; the encouragement of development projects through labor recruitment for various purposes;
and minor judicial functions. The office has continued
into the post-independence period without much change.

CHIEF SECRETARY. Formerly known as the Colonial Secretary, the Chief Secretary was the chief executive officer and the head of the colonial civil service under the
Governor. He was the link between all departments and
the government. He was advised by two senior Commissioners: the Commissioner for Local Government,
Lands and Settlement who was in charge of the "White
Highlands" and the Chief Native Commissioner, a post
created in 1918, who was the advisor on African affairs.
The post was re-established in 1980.

CHURCH MISSIONARY SOCIETY. The Kenya Mission of the
Church Missionary Society for Africa and the East,
which had been founded in 1799, was started in East
Africa in 1844 by the Rev. J. Krapf. For the next
thirty years, the CMS was represented in East Africa
by German missionaries, especially Johann Ludwig
Krapf (until 1855) and Johann Rebmann (until 1875).
From Mombasa and Rabai centers, the CMS, whose
early history is the same as that of the Anglican Church
in Kenya, expanded into Mijikenda and coastal area:
Jilore station among the Giriama (1890), Sagalla on
Taita Hills (1883), Taveta (1892). By 1914, the CMS
had established sixteen resident mission centers in
coastal, eastern and central Kenya: Nairobi Kabete
(1900), Weithaga (1903), Kahuhia (1903), Kathukeini,
Kabare (1910) and Kigari (1910). In Western Kenya,
mission stations were established at Kisumu, Maseno
(1906), Ng'iya, and Butere. In 1921, Nyanza was removed from the Diocese of Uganda and transferred to
Diocese of Mombasa. In 1927, Northern Tanganyika
was removed from the Diocese of Mombasa, which now
covered Kenya only. It was not until 1955 that the first

African Bishops of the Anglican Church in Kenya--Festo Olang' and Obadiah Kariuki--were consecrated.

CHURCH OF SCOTLAND MISSION. Founded in 1891 by a number of the Directors of the British East Africa Company under the Chairmanship of Sir William Mackinon. Dr. Steward of Lovedale established the first center of the Mission at Kibwezi in 1891. The site was found to be an unhealthy one, and the Mission was then transferred to Kikuyu. In 1900 the Mission was handed over to the Church of Scotland, and was endowed with the sum of £38,000 by the friends of Sir William Mackinnon and Mr. A. L. Bruce as a memorial. The Mission aimed at promoting the spiritual and material development of the African through evangelical, medical, educational, and industrial agencies on the broad lines of Lovedale, Blantyre, and Livingtonia. From Kikuyu, other centers were established in different parts of Central Kenya: Tumutumu in Nyeri 1909, St. Andrew's Church, Nairobi, 1910, and Chogoria 1922. This was the beginning of the present Presbyterian Church of East Africa which is still, on the whole, largely a Central Kenya ecclesiastical institution.

CHYULU HILLS. A large, waterless volcanic range of hills, south-west of the Nairobi-Mombasa road. The Masai call the hills lldoinyo Lolkirosin, meaning "mountains of dwarfs." According to Masai tradition, the hills were formerly inhabited by a people of very short stature.

COCKAR, SAEED RAHMAN. Born in 1926 in India. Educated at Duke of Gloucester School (now Jamhuri School), Nairobi 1936-42; Barrister-at-Law, Lincoln's Inn 1947 and in the same year started practicing as Advocate of the High Court of Kenya. He was appointed first Judge of Kenya Industrial Court in 1964, a post he still holds. The Court operates in accordance with the Trade Dispute Act of 1964 as amended in 1965 which aims at encouraging parties to trade disputes to settle them amicably and responsibly. Under his able chairmanship, the Court has earned a high reputation in the Third World, and his awards are regularly reported in the international newsletters and are used in other industrial courts. He has managed to win the confidence of both employers and workers, and in this way has contributed enormously towards industrial peace in Kenya. He was a Kenya

tennis champion for four years and represented Kenya
at the first All Africa Games in Brazzaville 1965, winning a silver medal in doubles. He has also represented
Kenya in hockey and cricket.

COFFEE.   The largest single cash crop in Kenya, employing over 200,000 full- and part-time workers.   It is
also the major export producing industry.   Kenya produces the "Colombian Mild" variety of coffee, which is
used for flavor blending with other varieties.   About
85-90 percent of the coffee estates are owned by individuals or private companies, the rest being owned by
public companies.

COMMERCE.   Since independence several basic changes in
the pattern of internal trade, in terms of ownership as
well as content and character, have been effected.   The
two most important changes have been the transfer of
distribution activities from foreign to Kenyan hands; and
secondly, the shift from the semi-subsistence type of
production to market-oriented production.   The Government has encouraged Kenyans to enter the commerce
sector through various measures, incentives and extension services.   The most notable of these measures
was the 1967 Trade Licensing Act which empowered the
Government to limit the number of trading licenses giv-
en to non-citizens.   As a result, almost all businesses
in rural centers are in Kenyan hands today.   Non-citizens are still free to operate in the urban general business areas, leaving the other business centers in the
urban areas to citizen traders only.   The total wage
employment in the formal commerce sector is expected
to increase from 39,000 in 1976 to 51,000 in 1983.   Besides the formal section, there is a growing informal
commerce sector which is providing self-employment
opportunities to a large number of rural and urban people.

COMMONWEALTH.   "A voluntary association of independent
sovereign states, each responsible for its own policies,
consulting and cooperating in the common interests of
their peoples and in the promotion of international understanding and world peace."   This was part of the
Declaration of Commonwealth Principles approved at
the Singapore meeting of Commonwealth Heads of Government on January 22, 1971.   The history of this association goes back to 1931, when the relationship be-

tween Britain and her former white colonies--now renamed Dominions--was defined in the Statute of West-
minster. These countries formed the British Commonwealth, and they owed common allegiance to the British
Crown. In 1947, India became the first non-white member of, as well as the first republic in, the association.
In 1949, it was decided to drop the word "British" from
the title. All former British colonies in Africa, including Kenya, are members, with the exception of the Sudan, which declined to join, and South Africa, which was
forced to withdraw in 1961 because of its racial policies.
It has a Secretariat established in 1965 in London at
Marborough House, which is headed by the Secretary
General and which is responsible to all member governments. The Secretariat administers the Commonwealth
Fund for Technical Cooperation which was established
in 1971.

COMMONWEALTH DEVELOPMENT CORPORATION, THE.
Established in 1948 as the Colonial Development Corporation, a British subsidiary to make investments in
colonial territories. In 1963, it became the Commonwealth Development Corporation and operated in independent Commonwealth countries. Since 1969, its activities have been extended to all developing countries.
The CDC is an investor in Kenya with a total investment of some K. £30 million, spread over twenty projects which include the Development Finance Company
of Kenya, the Kenya Tea Development Authority, the
Tana River Development Authority, the Kenya Power
Company and the National Housing Corporation. The
regional office for East Africa is housed in the Commonwealth House, Moi Avenue, Nairobi, Kenya.

COMMUNICATIONS AND TRANSPORT. Comprises rail,
road, maritime, and air transport as well as postal
and telecommunications systems.
     Railways: The rail network consists of 1,086
kilometers of the main line between Mombasa and the
Uganda border, a total of 1,028 kilometers of branch
lines and the inland water-ways systems. Railway transport is the second major mode of transport of goods and
people, particularly bulky goods over long distances.
Railway services deteriorated between 1972 and 1977
largely due to the political wranglings within the former
East African Community. No new locomotives, rolling
stock, equipment, nor spare parts were acquired. How-

ever, with the establishment of the Kenya Railways Corporation in 1977, a total of over K. £50 million was invested in the Corporation from 1977 to 1979 to provide it with capital for the above items. See also UGANDA RAILWAY.

Roads: Historically, the development of the road network in Kenya was subsidiary to that of the railway. Restrictive measures were imposed to protect the railway, but were lifted in 1959. Since that time, expansion of road network has been rapid. At the time of independence, there were some 1,811 kilometers of bitumen roads. By 1978 this figure had gone up to 4,331 kilometers. The road system is divided into classified and unclassified roads, both totalling 150,600 kilometers. Of this, 50,600 kilometers are classified. The Mombasa-Lagos Transafrican Highway is also under construction.

Marine Transport: Kenya Ports Authority was established in 1977 as a wholly-owned Government Corporation to take over from the East African Harbours Corporation. The Authority is responsible for operating other minor ports along the coast of Kenya. Mombasa is Kenya's major port and it also caters for the trade of several Eastern African countries. The coastal trade and fishing activities are served by several small ports such as Kilifi, Lamu, Malindi, Mtwapa, and Shimony. In 1979, the Authority employed 3,000 people.

Air Transport: Kenya has two large international airports in Nairobi and Mombasa, medium-sized aerodromes in Kisumu and Malindi, plus Wilson Airport in Nairobi, which caters to Charter flights and also provided flying training services. Kenya Airways is wholly owned by the Government and was established in February 1977 as a national air carrier serving international routes to Europe, Asia, and the Middle East; regional routes within Africa; and domestic services in Kenya. The airline has two subsidiary companies: Flamingo Airways, which operates cargo services abroad, and Kenya Airfreight Handling Company Ltd., which provides cargo handling services in Nairobi and Mombasa. By 1979, a total of K. £15.6 million had been invested in the airline, which had a fleet of seven medium- and long-range jets, employing a staff of 2,640.

The Kenya Posts and Telecommunications Corporation: Provides postal and telecommunications services both within Kenya and to foreign countries. The telecommunications services have been greatly expanded to meet the needs of commerce and industry. By June

1978, the local telephone network had 54 automatic and 185 manual exchanges and 64,656 subscriber exchange lines.   The telephone services have also been expanded into the rural areas.   Since independence, 77 new exchanges have been opened in the rural areas.   In the urban areas, the introduction of the Subscribers Trunk Dialling (STD) facility has improved the quality of telephone service by enabling subscribers to dial their trunk calls directly.   By 1979, 80 percent of all subscribers in urban areas had this facility.   The introduction of international semi-automatic switching facilities and high quality satellite circuits have facilitated the growth of international traffic, which has been generated by the rapid development of Kenya's economy.   Most of the incoming traffic is now connected automatically through the International Subscriber Dialling (ISD) facility with foreign countries.

      Kenya External Telecommunications Company (Kenextel).   A wholly owned Government Corporation established in 1977.   It is geared towards the improvement and expansion of telecommunications facilities to meet the needs of the expanding economy for increased telephone, telex, telegram, photo-telegraph and television services.   Arrangements are afoot to include provision for data services for big business organizations in Kenya, in the Kenextel program.   Existing equipment is also to be modified so as to introduce international direct dialling system.

CONVENTION OF ASSOCIATIONS, THE.   This was the Kenya settlers' most important organization and popularly known as the "Settlers' Parliament."   It was founded in 1910 to merge Delamere's Colonists Association and the Pastoralists' Association.   It aimed at maintaining the sanctity of the "White Highlands" and racial purity and at securing greater European influence in the government.   The colonial Government regarded it as the most representative body of the European settlers. Though it spoke for all Europeans, it drew most of its support from the farmers and most of its leaders were farmers: Ewart Grogan, the first Chairman; T. H. Harper, Chairman of the Ruiru Farmers Association; Lord Francis Scott; and C. O. Oates.   The only Chairman of the Convention who was not a farmer was George Nicol, head of Smith Mackenzie, 1958-59.   By 1940, the Convention's position was increasingly being challenged by other organizations in which commercial and indus-

trial interests among the European community played
a greater role, e.g. Chambers of Commerce.   In 1944,
the European Electors Union was formed to represent
all local political organizations.   By the 1950's, the
Kenya National Farmers Union was founded and it dealt
with most of the agricultural problems that used to form
the core of the Convention's work.   But from 1957, with
the approach of political independence, a split occurred
within the European community between the die-hards
who wanted to resist change and the so-called moderates
who worked hard to persuade the Europeans that they
had a place in an independent Kenya.   It was among the
former that the Convention was revived for a short
time, first headed by George Nicol and secondly by
C. O. Oates.   With the attainment of independence in
1963, the Convention died a natural death.

CO-OPERATIVE MOVEMENT.   Co-operative societies in
Kenya were/first started as voluntary organizations before World War I for the purpose of marketing the farm
produce and processed products of European farmers.
The first society to be registered was the Kenya Creameries (Cooperative) and the Kenya Planters Cooperative
Union.   Both of them were registered under the original
ordinance enacted in 1931.   A new ordinance was passed
in 1945 setting up the Department of Cooperative Development, although it was not until 1952 that staff was
provided to assist in the development of the Cooperative
societies.   For the first time, Africans were allowed
to form Cooperative societies.   The introduction of the
Swynnerton Plan in 1954 stimulated the development of
the cooperative movement.   The turnover of societies
in 1952 was K.£9,520,000 of which about K.£20,000
represented African-owned produce.   In 1964, the turnover of the societies was K.£30,000,000, and most of
it was from African societies.   A new Co-operative Act
was introduced in December 1966 which aimed at streamlining the movement and introducing greater government
supervision and control through the Commissioner for
Cooperatives.   The need for training Committee members and employees was recognized and in May 1967
the Co-operative College of Kenya was opened in temporary accommodation and transferred to Lang'ata in
1971.   On January 1, 1969, the Cooperative Bank
was launched.   By the end of 1970, there were 1,859
active co-operative societies in Kenya of which 1,000
were agricultural.   There total sales turnover was over
K.£50 million.

The last ten years have witnessed the consolidation of the cooperative movement. The cooperatives
have been transformed from being mere collecting centers for agricultural produce into multi-functional institutions providing a variety of services to the farmers.
All these services are coordinated by the Kenya National Federation of Cooperatives Ltd. (KNFC), which was
established in 1964. It was instrumental in the formation of the Co-operative Bank of Kenya, the Kenya Union
of Savings and Credit Co-operatives, and more recently,
the Co-operative Insurance Ltd. which is a private insurance company owned by the KNFC and the Co-operative movement in Kenya. It also operates a printing
press which prints all standardized accounting stationery
for the movement. The total number of cooperative societies registered in 1978 had been reduced to 1693 as
part of a streamlining process. These catered to
1,137,422 members, who had bought shares worth
K.Shs. 2,161, 216, 100 which represents a large per-
centage of total commercial activities in the country.

CORYNDON, SIR ROBERT THORN. Born in 1870 in South
Africa and educated in South Africa and in England. He
marched with Rhodes' pioneer column when it occupied
Mashonaland. Became Resident Commissioner of Swaziland from October 1907 to 1916. Later served in Rhodesia and Basutoland, before being appointed Governor
of Uganda. Was Governor and Commander-in-Chief of
Kenya from 1922 to 1925. His period is remembered
for the introduction of the Local Native Councils in
1924, which were to act as a link between the chiefs
and the people and to provide an outlet for the political
ambitions of young and educated Africans. He died
early in 1925, following an operation.

CORYNDON MEMORIAL MUSEUM see KENYA NATIONAL
MUSEUM

COUTTS REPORT, THE. Officially known as Report of the
Commissioner Appointed to Enquire into Methods for the
Selection of African Representatives to the Legislative
Council (Nairobi, 1955), this report was produced by
Sir Water Coutts, who had been appointed in 1955 as a
Commissioner to advise on the best method of electing
African representatives to the Legislative Council. The
report insisted that the vote is a public privilege, not
a political right. It introduced the system of multiple

voting: an African could vote if his age was 21 years
or over; had completed intermediate schooling; had an
annual income of £120 and over; was worth £500; had
long service in government service or the armed forces;
had legislative experience or meritorious service. Each
person got a vote for each such qualification up to a
maximum of three. However, the African leaders were
opposed to these recommendations although they agreed to
contest the first African elections in 1957 under them.

COUTTS, SIR WATER, GCMG, MBC. Born in 1912, he
later became Chief Secretary of Kenya in 1958; Governor and Commander-in-Chief, Uganda 1961-62; and
Governor General, Uganda in 1962.

- D -

DAHALO. A small group living in the lower Tana River
region. Formerly hunter-gatherers, today they are
only partially so. Linguistic research reveals that
they originally spoke a language with clicks before
adopting the present Dahaloan tongue introduced into
Kenya by Dahaloan-speaking Southern Cushites.

DAILY NATION. The newspaper with the largest circulation
in East Africa. Established by H.H. The Aga Khan in
March 1961, "to produce the leading African Newspaper
edited and staffed by Africans containing news of specific interest to Africa and expressing an African point
of view to a predominantly African readership." Appointed its first African Editor-in-Chief, Mr. Hilary
Ng'weno, in 1964.

DELAMERE, LORD (Hugh Cholmondeley). Born on April
28, 1870, at Vale Royal in Cheshire, England. Hugh
Cholmondeley was educated at Eton, and he became
third Baron Delamere on the death of his father when
he was only seventeen years old. He made several
trips abroad--to Corsica, New Zealand, Australia--be-
fore visiting Africa, starting with Somaliland in 1891.
He made six hunting trips to Somaliland between 1891
and 1896. Between 1896 and 1897 he travelled through
Gallaland, eventually arriving in East Africa Protectorate (Kenya) in 1897. He returned as a settler in 1903.
He soon became the chief exponent of the idea of transforming Kenya into a "White Man's Country." He built

Nakuru hotel in 1908. Delamere also played a leading
role in breeding rust-resisting wheat. He founded Unga
Ltd. in 1908 and was its first Managing Director. The
Company still controls over 50 percent of flour milling
business in Kenya. Besides demonstrating that wheat
could be grown succesfully in Kenya, Delamere also
contributed substantially towards sheep-rearing and dairy
farming in Kenya. He started a Cooperative Creamery
at Naivasha in 1925--the present Kenya Cooperative
Creameries. He was the first president of the Farmers' and Planters' Association founded in January 1903.
It changed its name to the Colonists' Association in
1904. Delamere soon emerged as the Settlers' leader,
a position he retained until his death on November 13,
1931. At various times between 1907 and 1931 he was
a Member of the Legislative and Executive Councils.

DESAI, MANILAL AMBALAL. Born in 1879 at Gotalvadi
near Surat in India. Educated at the Mission High
School in Surat. Worked with a firm of solicitors in
Bombay for over ten years. Arrived in Kenya from
India in October 1915, while still single. Desai got
work with a Nairobi legal firm of Harrison, Solmon
and Creswell. They soon disagreed about salary and
he resigned in 1917. He tried his hand at business
by opening a general shop on River Road, but he had
to close it because he devoted most of his time to politics. Henceforth, he lived on the charity of his political supporters such as A. M. Jeevanjee and Hus-
seinbhai Suleman Verjee. He soon emerged as the Indian Leader through his force of personality, sacrifice
and dedication.

A few European settlers led by Lord Delamere
and Grogan were striving to turn Kenya into another
South Africa. Desai led the struggle against these un-
just demands. He worked tirelessly to organize various
Indian Associations throughout the country under the ban-
ner of the East African Indian National Congress. He
extended his work to include safeguarding African interests. In 1917, he became a member of the Nairobi Municipal Council. By 1923, he had become President of
the Indian Congress. In that position he contended that
African interests should come before the interests of
either Europeans or Indians.

Desai founded his own newspaper, The East African Chronicle, to champion the cause of justice. This
is the paper that gave publicity to African grievances by

working closely with Harry Thuku (who was accommo-
dated in its offices) and other African leaders. Desai
was suspected of assisting Harry Thuku, but this did
not deter him. He was elected to the Legislative Council in 1925, where he moved several motions dealing
with injustices practiced against Indians and Africans.
On July 15, 1926, while on a tour of East Africa to
collect subscriptions for Achariar's paper, The Democrat, he suddenly fell ill and died. "The Uncrowned
King of the Masses," as he was known, died a pauper.
All sections of the Indian Community combined to collect
funds to erect a lasting memorial to him. The Desai
Memorial Hall on Tom Mboya Street in Nairobi was
built with these funds.

DEVELOPMENT FINANCE COMPANY OF KENYA, THE.
Incorporated in 1963 as a private company with an authorized share capital of K. Shs. 80 million, all of which
has been issued. The Government, through the ICDC,
owns 37.5 percent and the other partners in the venture
are three foreign development companies: the German
Development Company (25 percent), the Commonwealth
Development Corporation (12.5 percent) and the Nether-
lands Finance Company for Developing Countries (25 percent). DFCK facilities are primarily geared towards the
development of manufacturing and agricultural processing enterprises. It also undertakes investments in the
tourist industry through hotel development and in forestry and fisheries projects. The company also con-
ducts field surveys and offers consultancy services.

DEVONSHIRE PAPER OF 1923 (officially known as Indians
in Kenya, Cmd. 1922). From the beginning of white
settlement in Kenya, attempts were made by the local
colonial government and the settlers to exclude Indians
from having a say in policy and administration of the
country. This was resisted by the Indians. In the
early 1920's, this controversy became an imperial issue which the colonial office was called upon to resolve.
The colonial office answer to the question was contained
in the famous Devonshire declaration. The paper resolved the conflict between the two immigrant races
(Europeans and Indians) by reminding both that in fact,
Kenya belonged to neither of them. "Primarily, Kenya
is an African territory," it stated emphatically, "and
His Majesty's Government think it necessary definitely
to record their considered opinion that the interests of

the African natives must be paramount, and that if, and
when these interests and the interests of the immigrant
races should conflict, the former should prevail." Coming in the year in which a few Europeans in Southern
Rhodesia were granted internal self-government, this
was an important constitutional document in the history
of Kenya. However, it took another forty years before
the declaration could be turned into reality.

DINESEN, ISAK see BLIXEN OF RUNGSTEDLUND, BAR-
ONESS KAREN

DINI YA MSAMBWA. A religious cult started by Elija Masinde and Benjamin Wekuke in 1943. Most of the followers were ex-mission converts who had rebelled
against missionary distortion and undermining of African culture. Their slogan, "Africa for the Africans,"
frightened the colonial government. They promised to
drive out the Europeans and to replace the colonial government with an African one. Christianity was de-
nounced as the religion of the imperialists, and Africans were urged to go back to the religion of their ancestors. They also attacked Asian businessmen as ex-
ploiters. The chiefs were condemned as oppressive
agents of imperialism; and civil disobedience was advocated. From Bungoma district, where it started,
the cult had spread to the Trans Nzoia and Uasin Gishu
districts of Kenya and the Mbale districts of Uganda by
1948. In 1950, the Kolloa Affray occurred. Pokot adherents of the cult clashed with government forces at
Kolloa in Baringo district. Lucas Pkiech, leader of
the Pokot, and 28 of his followers were killed and about
50 others were wounded. Although the cult had been
proscribed in 1948, it continued underground. During
the Emergency, there is evidence that the cult followers
worked closely with the Mau Mau leaders. During the
post-independence period, after several government warn-
ings had gone unheeded, the sect was finally banned on
October 25, 1968, as a "society dangerous to the good
government of the Republic."

DISTRICT COMMISSIONER. The title of the chief administrative officer of each of the forty-one districts of Kenya. Besides his law and order responsibilities, he also coordinates and promotes development.

DOROBO (see also OKIEK). The term "dorobo" is derived

from Masai and it means a hunter and therefore "a poor
person." The Dorobo have few or no cattle and therefore are poverty-stricken in the eyes of the Masai. It
is the Swahili version of the Masai term "Il Torobo"
("ol toroboni," singular), meaning a person who has no
cattle and who therefore lives on the meat of wild animals. It was gradually adopted to apply to virtually
anyone who lives by hunting in a wide area stretching
from northeastern Uganda to northern Tanzania. The
Dorobo generally have no distinctive language of their
own, and the majority of them speak Masai or Kalenjin
languages, thus indicating a long history of contact with
these peoples if not actual derivation from them. Ling-
uistically, the Kalenjin-speaking Dorobo are the most
widespread, stretching from Mt. Kenya to northern Tanzania.

- E -

EAST AFRICAN ASSOCIATION, THE. An urban-based militant political association founded in 1921 by African ac-
tivists in Pangani, Nairobi. Led by Harry Thuku, it
was multi-ethnic in composition, including Africans from
the Coastal, Central and Western regions, as well as a
few Uganda Africans living in Nairobi. It also included
both Christians and Muslims at a time when most African organizations tended to be organized on a religious
basis. The issues it articulated included land, forced
labor, settler power, taxation, Kipande, wages etc.
Harry Thuku attempted to extend the movement first into Kiambu--where he was less succesful due to opposition from the more Conservative Kikuyu Association--
and then into Murang'a where he achieved a major success. On March 14, 1922, Harry Thuku was arrested
and deported to the coast. A major and bloody demon-
stration in Nairobi followed. The EAA, at least in Murang'a, went underground, and was later in 1924, to be
transformed into the Kikuyu Central Association.

EAST AFRICAN COMMUNITY. A common market formed
by Kenya, Uganda and Tanzania whose origins go back
to the beginning of this century. The cooperation, under British colonial rule, started in an ad hoc way without any formal constitutional framework, particularly in
the form of the Uganda Railway and the arrangements
for the allocation of customs revenue between Kenya and

Uganda instituted in 1917.   Tanganyika joined the customs union in 1927.   A Court of Appeal, postal services, a common currency together with a common
transport and communications system and a customs
union were administered by a permanent Secretariat of
the East African Governors' Conference established in
1926.

The Governors' Conference, however, had no
legal constitutional standing.   Hence, the three countries decided to establish the East African High Commission through an Order in Council of 1947.   The
High Commission, which came into being in 1948, consisted of the three Governors and a Central Legislative
Council, which was empowered to enact legislation in
respect of the common services including transport and
communications, inter-territorial research services, customs and excise, and civil aviation.   The High Commission remained in existence until 1960.   The approach-
ing era of independence called for a review of the cooperation arrangements.   The Raisman Commission was
therefore appointed in 1961 by the British Government
and the recommendations contained in its Report formed
the basis for the East African Common Services Organization which was subsequently established in December
1961.

In spite of this highly formalized type of economic cooperation, EACSO experienced many problems
between 1964 and 1967, mainly because the Member
states were undermining the arrangements through uni-
lateral decisions.   Consequently, the Member states
agreed to re-examine the organizational structure and
other matters pertaining to EACSO.   The first significant but abortive step in this direction was the Kampala
Agreement whose main objective was to rectify and reduce the imbalances of inter-territorial trade based on
proposals for the allocation and re-allocation of industries and their productive capacities.   The situation
was further aggravated by the break up of the common
East African currency in 1966 and the consequent trade
restrictions.   To arrest the situation, the three governments appointed the Philip Commission (named after
Professor Kjeld Philip, its Chairman), whose Report
led to the signing of the Treaty for East African Cooperation in Kampala on June 6, 1967, establishing the
East African Community.   It had its own Legislative
Assembly, Central Secretariat located in Arusha, Tanzania, four jointly owned Corporations: East African

Harbours, East African Railways, East African Airways and East African Posts and Telecommunications. It also had over twenty service organizations, covering economic, scientific, industrial and university fields. Between 1972 and 1976, the Community experienced difficulties similar to the 1960's, with the difference that the Heads of State in Uganda and Tanzania were not on speaking terms. In 1976, a Treaty Review Commission under Mr. William Demas tried in vain to salvage the Community. It disintegrated in early 1977--thus collapsed one of the longest established and most far-reaching examples of economic integration in developing countries.

EAST AFRICAN INDIAN NATIONAL CONGRESS.   Founded in 1914 to demand equality with the Europeans: they demanded that so-called "White Highlands" be opened to Indian farmers; that election to the Legislative Council should be based on a common roll of Europeans and Indians; and that Indian immigration into Kenya should be encouraged. The Congress championed the Indian cause until 1952.

EAST AFRICAN ROYAL COMMISSION 1953-1955 REPORT (Cmd. 9475).   The East Africa Royal Commission, under the Chairmanship of Sir Hugh Dow, was appointed in January 1953 and reported two-and-a-half years later. The other members of the Commission were Sally Herbert Frankel, Arthur Gaitskell, C. M. G. , Rowland Skeffington Hudson, C. M. G. , Daniel Thomson Jack, J. P. , Kidaha Makwaia, Sir Fredrick Seaford, C. M. G. , C. B. E. , Frank Sykes, with J. H. Ingham, M. B. E. as Secretary. The terms of reference were based on an aide-memoire prepared by the then Governor of Kenya, Sir Philip Mitchell (his dispatch to the Secretary of State No. 193 of 16th November 1951), who was concerned about the effect of agrarian policies and about the pace and direction of social and economic policies in East Africa. The Commission was to pay particular attention to the economic development of the land already in occupation, the adaptation or modifications in "traditional, tribal systems of tenure necessary for the full development of the land"; the opening for cultivation and settlement of land at present not fully used; the development and siting of industries; employment conditions in industry, commerce, mining, plantation agriculture, with special reference to social conditions and the growth

of large urban populations; and the social problems
which arise from the growth of permanent urban and
industrial populations. But the Commission was to re-
strict its inquiry to economic and social problems only,
and had no power to examine or report on political questions. Also, it was enjoined to take account of existing
obligations relating to the security of land reserved for
the different races and groups. Its Report, which was
482 pages long, is a major historical document. Evidence was taken from 1,300 persons and groups, more
than half of them from Kenya. The Report was unani-
mous on several points:

1) Traditional methods of production and exchange
had to be transformed, if new income necessary to raise
the living standards of the African was to be created;
and money, skill and knowledge had to be expended where
they will be most effective.

2) Greater specialization in production was seen
as requiring expanded markets; restrictions and controls must therefore be re-examined and those that per-
petuate area self-sufficiency or sectional interests dis-
carded. The re-organization and development of agriculture will enlarge the domestic industrial market.

3) Foreign help will be needed for some time,
but a bigger contribution from Africans than had been
the case was necessary, partly to dispel their fears
about undue external influence and partly because their
help was needed for effective development.

4) A settled labor force, both rural and urban,
was regarded as being essential and to achieve this an
adequate income either from the land or from urban
employment had to be obtained.

5) The improvement of agriculture was seen as
the most important factor in East Africa's development
and to that end a new land law was necessary to ensure
that private interest in land was recognized and to accept the principle of willing-seller, willing-buyer. In
other words, every effort was to be made towards the
individualization of ownership and registration of African land. Policies which maintained customary tenures
or sectional land reservations were to be abandoned.

EAST AFRICAN SAFARI RALLY. This is a motor rally
which first set off from Nairobi in 1953 when it was
organized as the "Coronation" Safari to mark the crown-
ing of the British Queen. It was spread over 1,961
miles. Until 1967, it was mainly a local event involving

only "Group I" cars, that is, ordinary saloon cars man-
ufactured for general use. Since 1967, the Safari has
counted towards the World Constructors' Rally Champ-
ionship and the cars entered comply with the international formulas of Group I, II, III and IV. Large numbers of overseas drivers now regularly enter the Safari,
which is recognized as perhaps the most demanding motor rally in the world and which is now confined to Kenya.

EDUCATION. Enrollment of primary school-age children
has risen from less than 50 percent in 1963 to over 85
percent in 1978. Enrollment in 1979 and 1980 was
3,274,000 and 3,409,000 children respectively. The
objective of free primary education was also achieved
in 1979. Secondary education has also expanded considerably since independence. Enrollment has increased
from 30,000 in 1963 to 350,000 in 1978. More than
half of these students are enrolled in non-government
schools. For instance, in 1977 there were 444 government aided secondary schools with a total enrollment of
128,324 as opposed to 1,042 unaided secondary schools
with a total enrollment of 191,986. Total enrollment
in Government secondary schools in 1979 and 1980 were
138,459 and 140,116 children respectively. In addition,
technical education is provided in secondary technical
schools, polytechnics and Harambee Institutes of technology. The expansion of the secondary school education has led to a serious bottleneck at the university
level. Kenya has only one university--the University
of Nairobi which incorporates Kenyatta University College. Enrollment there in 1978/79 was 6,250; in 1979/
80--6,625; and in 1980/81--7,170. This means that
many Kenyans who would otherwise benefit from a university education have no hope of ever doing so within
the country. Plans are underway to start a second university by 1983.

ELDORET. A town in the Rift Valley which began as a
post-office in 1910. By 1908 the Government had realized that it was no longer possible for the Uasin Gishu
region to be administered from Kapsabet as part of Nyanza Province. In 1910, J. Gosling, the Postmaster
General, made a tour of inspection of the area resulting
in the establishment of post offices at Sergoit, Farm 45
and Farm 64, which Gosling called Edlare River. With
the completion of the first building on 64, the history of

Eldoret begins. In December 1911, Governor Sir Percy
Girouard went to tour the region with a view to select-
ing a site for the district center. At a meeting at 64,
the Governor asked the farmers to choose a name for
their future town: Sosiani, Sirikwa, Girouardfontein,
and Bado Kidogo were suggested names. Eventually,
Eldare was agreed upon, but the Governor suggested
that a "t" should be added to the name to make it sound
like a Nandi word. From Eldaret it eventually became
Eldoret, though some say through a printer's error.
On January 1, 1912, it was declared in the Official
Gazette that "the Administrative Station on the Uasin
Gishu Plateau formerly known as Farm 64 will for the
future be officially styled Eldoret. On November
14, 1912, Eldoret, with an area of 2,770 acres, was
declared a township. It became an administrative station and a trading center for the local farmers. When
the railway reached Eldoret in 1924, a new era began
for the town. Goods could be imported cheaply and
regularly and farm products could be transported to
distant markets at competitive prices, instead of by
the wearisome wagon journey to Londiani. Today Eldoret is a fast growing town (the fifth largest) with
several major industries.

ELECTORS' UNION, THE. A European political organization formed in 1944 with the aim of bringing together
the farmers and businessmen; and thereby expressing
the essential unity of the European community.

"ELGIN PLEDGE." Lord Elgin had become Secretary of
State in 1905 after the transfer of the administration
of the East African Protectorate (Kenya) from the Foreign office to the Colonial office. In 1908, he issued
a Despatch containing the afterwards famous "Elgin
Pledge" which ran as follows:
It would not be in accordance with the policy of
H. M. Government to exclude any class of His Subjects from holding land in any part of a British
Protectorate, but that, in view of the comparatively
limited area in the Protectorate suitable for European colonization, a reasonable discretion will be
exercised in dealing with application for land on
the part of natives of India and other non-Europeans. With regard to paragraph 4 of your Despatch, I have to inform you that I approve of your
adhering to the principle acted on by your prede-

cessors, viz. that land lying outside Municipal
limits, roughly lying between Kiu and Fort Ternan, should be granted only to European settlers.
This Despatch, dated March 19, 1908, Sections 8 and
20 Cmd. 4117 of 1908, marked the official genesis of
the policy of "White Highlands."

ELGON, MOUNT. A vast extinct volcano situated on the
Kenya-Uganda border. Its height is 14,178 feet, and
its name is derived from the Masai words "Oldoinyo
lLgoon," meaning "mountain shaped like breasts." The
diameter of the base of the mountain is about 80 miles,
and of the summit crater, about four miles. The caves
on the southern slopes of the mountain were still inhabited by the El Kony in 1883 when J. J. Thomson visited
the area.

ELIOT, SIR CHARLES. A brilliant scholar and a career
diplomat who was appointed Commissioner and Consul-
General of the British East Africa Protectorate in December, 1900. Prior to his appointment in East Africa, he had served at St. Petersburg, Russia, as 3rd
Secretary in 1887; in the Near East; and at Washington,
in the United States as First Secretary in 1898. During
his tenure as Commissioner, the Eastern Province of
Uganda was transferred to the East Africa Protectorate
on March 5, 1902, and the Uganda Railway reached Port
Ugowe, shortly renamed Kisumu, on Lake Victoria. Eliot had little confidence in the ability of the Africans
and strongly affirmed the idea of Kenya being a "white
man's country." He was forced to resign in 1904 over
disagreement with the Foreign Office about the need to
safeguard African interests. From 1905 to 1911, he
was Vice-Chancellor of Sheffield University. In 1912,
he became the Vice-Chancellor of Hong Kong University;
from 1920 to 1926, he was Ambassador to Japan. Author of The East Africa Protectorate (1905), Eliot was
awarded K.C.M.G. and C.B.

ELMENTEITA, LAKE. Small soda lake which lies between
Lake Naivasha to the south and Lake Nakuru to the
northwest, in the Rift Valley region. Near it are several famous archaeological sites. It has been suggested
that the strand lines above the lake show that during an
earlier, moister phase, it stood very much higher than
it does today.

EL MOLO. The El Molo are the smallest ethnic group in

Africa today. They live on the southeastern shores of
Lake Turkana and in 1975 they numbered 230. More
than half of them were under 16 years of age. Their
early history is still unknown although some writers believe they are related to the Rendille. Their diet is
composed almost entirely of fish. They spend most of
their lives in the water. Originally they spoke an East
Cushitic language, whereas today some of them are
Maa-speakers.

EMBU. A group of the Central Bantu-speakers living in the
Embu district in the Eastern Province. They are closely related to the Gikuyu and the Meru. The early history of some sections of these three groups are similar.
They were great hunter-gatherers who later adopted agriculture and grew millet, sorghum, arrowroot, cassava and pulses. Later still bananas, sugarcane, and
maize were introduced. Today the Embu, who number
about 130,000, grow coffee, tea, pyrethrum, and maize.
They also keep cattle, goats and sheep.

ENERGY. About 85 percent of commercially traded energy
in Kenya is derived from imported petroleum. About a
quarter of the nation's foreign exchange earnings is used
for petroleum imports. The rural population still re-
lies almost exclusively on firewood, a dependency which
results in deforestation and soil erosion. On the other
hand, Kenya has already developed one third of the total estimated hydroelectric potential of 700 megawatts.
Geothermal potential is estimated at about 500 Mw, and
the first geothermal station producing 15 Mw is scheduled
to come into operation in 1981. Two power alcohol factories in Western Kenya will also come into production
in 1981.

EUROPEANS. In Kenya, Europeans number almost 60,000
and they comprise several nationalities. Only about
four thousand are citizens, the rest being businessmen,
professionals and bureaucrats. The first Europeans to
come to Kenya were the Portuguese, who dominated the
East Coast from the 16th century to the beginning of
the 18th century. The period of European dominance
in Kenya started in the second half of the nineteenth
century with the colonization of Africa by Europe. Although the colonial period in Kenya ended at the end of
1963, European dominance has continued, especially in
the fields of ideas and economy.

- F -

FARSY, SHEIKH ABDULLA SALEH. The Chief Kadhi of
    Kenya, Farsy was born on February 12, 1912, in Zan-
    zibar. From 1924 to 1929, he attended the Central
    Primary School in Zanzibar, after which he entered the
    Zanzibar Teachers' Training College. On completion
    he became a primary school teacher in Zanzibar in
    1933. He was later appointed to several posts starting
    with inspector of primary schools in Zanzibar and Pem-
    ba, principal of the Muslim Academy secondary school,
    and headmaster of the Arabic-speaking school which
    catered for all races. The last post he held in the
    Ministry of Education in Zanzibar was that of tutor at
    the teachers' training college. In 1960, he became the
    Kadhi of Zanzibar; on May 29, 1968, he became the
    Chief Kadhi of Kenya, and soon afterwards, he became
    a Kenya citizen. He has travelled widely in East and
    Central Africa and has visited Egypt, Iraq and Mecca.
    A broadcaster and a writer of biographies and religious
    books, his major work is the translation of the Holy
    Quran into Kiswahili, Qurani Takatifu, which runs into
    805 pages and which took him sixteen years to complete.

FOREIGN RELATIONS see specific countries, e.g., SO-
    VIET UNION-KENYA RELATIONS; ISRAEL-KENYA RE-
    LATIONS

FORT JESUS. Built at Mombasa by the Portuguese at the
    end of the sixteenth century to safeguard their position
    on the east coast against Turkish and Arab attacks. It
    was designed by an Italian architect and engineer, Joao
    Batista Cairato, the leading architect of the Portuguese
    in India. The plan consists of a central court with bas-
    tions at the four corners and a rectangular projection
    facing the sea. It covers an area of about two acres.
    The fort was built by Mateus Mendes de Vasconcelos,
    who was the last Captain of Malindi and the First Cap-
    tain of Mombasa. The great siege of the fort by the
    Omani Arabs began on March 13, 1696, and ended on
    December 13, 1698. During the Zanzibar period (1837-
    1895), the Fort was used as a barracks for the soldiers
    of the Sultan. On July 1, 1895, the British Protector-
    ate was proclaimed, and the Fort was converted into a
    prison. It was used as such until May 1958 when, with
    a financial grant from the Gulbenkian Foundation of
    £30,000, Fort Jesus was restored as a historical monu-

ment and a museum was built. On October 24 in the
same year, Fort Jesus was declared a National Park.
In January 1961, it was transferred to the custody of
the Museum Trustees of Kenya.

FORT TERNAN.   Situated in the Nyando Valley in Nyanza.
The fort was named after Brigadier-General Trevor
Ternan who was sent to Kampala in 1894 to strengthen
the protectorate forces and to reorganize the Uganda
Rifles.   Ternan had commanded one of the Sudanese
battalions of the Egyptian army.   During his service
in Uganda he participated in campaigns in Bunyoro and
against the Nandi and the Tugen.   Fort Ternan is also
a famous miocene fossil locality which has yielded the
oldest probable member of the family of man (the Hom-
inidae) thus far found in Africa.   Tests by the potassium-
argon technique have yielded dates of about 14 million
years for the volcanic tuffs at the site.

FRANCE-KENYA RELATIONS.   The cultural, scientific and
technical cooperation agreement was signed between
France and Kenya in 1971.   It defined the framework
and forms of bilateral cooperation between the two countries.   Since that time, five Franco-Kenyan joint commissions have been held to define directions and programs of cooperation.   From 1973 to the first half of
1980, Kenya has received French aid worth K. Shs. 72
million in the form of cultural, scientific and technical
assistance.   This makes Kenya second after Nigeria in
terms of aid received from France in the English-speak-
ing African countries.   The teaching of French has an
important place in this aid program, although also included are technical assistance and the organization of
training courses in such fields as water development,
road techniques, the sugar agro-industry, telecommunications and meteorology, teledetection, administrative
data processing, and forestry.   Relations between the
two countries have grown from strength to strength.
They were particularly reinforced by the first state visit by a Kenyan President made by Daniel arap Moi in
October 1978--his first state visit after assuming power.
With regard to bilateral trade ties, France is relatively
a newcomer on the Kenya market.   But already Kenya's
exports to France are gaining momentum and France
will soon be among Kenya's ten major importers.   In
1979, for instance, Kenya's exports to France amounted
to 135 million French francs.   Agricultural products

make up the bulk of Kenya's export to France with coffee topping the list.   Horticultural products such as
green beans and fruits are also in great demand.
France's main exports to Kenya are vehicles, electrical and industrial machinery, engines, and communications equipment.

FRANCIS, EDWARD CAREY.   An eminent educationist,
    Francis was born in Hampstead London, September 13,
    1897.   Educated at William Ellis School, London 1904-
    16; Cambridge University, 1919-1922.   Obtained an
    M.A., elected Fellow of Peterhouse Cambridge.   Dur-
    ing the First World War, he was in the Honourable Ar-
    tillery Company, 1916-1919, and became a Lieutenant
    and mentioned in Despatches.   At the end of the war,
    he went back to Cambridge University as Fellow and
    Lecturer 1922-1928.   Was Bursar Peterhouse 1924-28.
    Worked as a C.M.S. Missionary in Kenya from 1928
    to 1962.   In that role, he was Principal of Maseno
    School, 1928-40 and Headmaster, Alliance High School,
    Kikuyu 1940-1962.   He thus helped to lay a firm foun-
    dation for two of Kenya's major secondary schools.   On
    retirement, he took a job as an Assistant Master at
    Pumwani Secondary School, Nairobi, where he died
    teaching on July 27, 1966.   He was made Honorary
    Fellow of Makerere University College in 1961; and he
    was awarded Royal African Society Medal in 1929.   Au-
    thor of a succesful series on school mathematics.

FRERETOWN.   Located just outside Mombasa Island across
    the Nyali Bridge.   It was founded in the 19th century
    by Sir Bartle Frere as a colony for freed slaves.   He
    had been sent on a special mission to Zanzibar in 1872
    to negotiate a more effective treaty for the suppression
    of slave trade.   On his return he urged the C.M.S. to
    provide a refuge for the reception of freed slaves and
    in 1874 the settlement at Freretown was established by
    the Rev. W. S. Price.   Although it fulfilled its purpose
    and housed 500 freed slaves within a year of its incep-
    tion, it proved a continual matter of contention with the
    slave owners.   The settlement is still largely inhabited
    by the descendants of the freed slaves.   It also has one
    of the oldest Christian Churches in East Africa built at
    the end of the 19th century.

FRIEND'S AFRICA MISSION.   Formerly known as Friend's
    Africa Industrial Mission.   It was established in East

Africa in August 1902 under the direction of the American Friends' Board of Foreign Missions, whose headquarters was at Richmond, Indiana, America. It established five stations in Western Kenya, the most important being Kaimosi.

- G -

GABBRA. Oromo-speakers who live mainly in the Marsabit District in North-Eastern Kenya, although some are
found near the Kenya-Ethiopia border and around Lake
Turkana. They are camel nomads who number about
26,000. Originally, they were probably a sub-group
of the Borana who later emerged as a distinct people.

GAMA, VASCO DA. The Commander of the first Portuguese fleet to round southern Africa to India via Kenya.
Born in about 1460, he was sent by King Manuel I in
1497 to complete the route to India which had been
started by Bartolomeu Diaz in 1492. Travelling via
the Cape of Good Hope, he reached Mombasa in April
1498, where he clashed with the rulers. He was, however, well-received at Malindi, where he met the pilot
Ibn Majib, who led him to Calicut. He made another
journey to India in 1502. In 1524, he was appointed
Viceroy of India, but died shortly after arrival.

GAMBLE'S CAVE. A rock shelter near Lake Nakuru which
is the scene of important discoveries of archaeological
remains. It is on a farm that formerly belonged to
Mr. Gamble. The cave deposit was discovered by Dr.
L. S. B. Leakey and members of his 1926-27 expeditions, and was excavated by them in 1927, 1928, and
1929. Recently, G. Isaac has re-excavated the rock
shelter. The culture represented at this site has been
identified as Upper Palaeolithic which is widespread in
the Rift Valley region of Kenya. Charcoal from the
lower part of the deposit has been dated to less than
10,000 years before the present.

GATU, JOHN GACHANGO. At present Gatu is the Moderator of the Presbyterian Church of East Africa. Born
in Kiambu, Central Province in 1925 and educated at
Kiambu Mission, 1931-40; St. Paul's United Theological
College, 1951-55; and University of Pittsburgh, U.S.A.,
1963. Served in the Army (1941-47), where he trained

as wireless operator in the corps of signals. Worked
as an instructor at Karen and Nanyuki depots. After
the war, he trained in business administration at the
Ex-Servicemen's Institute (later Kenya Institute of Administration), Kabete. Worked as a wireless operator
for the Royal Air Force, Eastleigh, Nairobi. Joined
Henry Muoria as his editorial assistant on the Kikuyu
newspaper Mumenyerere. He then went to work with
the colonial film unit of the regional information office,
where he studied documentary film making and became
a cutting room editor. From here he went back to
Kambui to work as an administrative clerk at the Church
Mission. After his training at St. Paul's United Theological College, Gatu was given his first Parish at Kia-
mathare, in Kiambu (1955-1958). In 1958, he was sent
to Scotland for further studies at the New College at the
University of Edinburgh, and was an assistant Pastor
at St. Ninian's Parish, Greenock. From 1960-63, he
was the Deputy General Secretary of the Presbyterian
Church of East Africa; and General Secretary from 1964
to 1979, when he became the Moderator.

GECAGA, BETHUEL MAREKA. Lawyer and business executive. Born at Kahuhia, Murang'a and educated at
Kahuhia School (1931-39), Alliance High School (1940-
43), and Makerere University College (1944-45). Barrister-at-Law Middle Temple. Junior Executive in a
Commercial firm in Nairobi 1946-48. He then joined
the Government as Administrative Assistant, 1949-52;
Ministry of Legal Affairs 1957-60. He became Chairman and General Manager of B.A.T. (Kenya) Ltd. in
1967, the first African to be appointed Company Chairman of this international tobacco company. Gecaga has
been a key figure in the University administration for
many years, having served without interruption as Chairman of the Governing Council of the former Royal College, University College, and University of Nairobi from
1963 to 1980.

GEDI. A site about nine miles south of Malindi on the
Kenya coast. About seven hundred years ago, a city
was founded in the forests which are adjacent to the
present village of Gedi. The origin of this city and
the source of its development are questions that historians have not yet been able to answer satisfactorily.
About forty-five acres of land were covered with stone
buildings including a large palace, several mosques and

many prosperous private houses. These prosperous inhabitants imported trinkets from Persia and India, Arabic pottery, and Ming ware from China. After about three hundred years of prosperity, Gedi suddenly died and was probably evacuated peacefully by its inhabitants. What lies behind this mysterious death of Gedi is again a historical puzzle, nor do we know what happened to the inhabitants. Today it is a National Park with a small museum.

"GENERAL CHINA" see ITOTE, WARUHIU

GICHURU, JAMES SAMUEL. Born in 1914 at Thogoto village in Kiambu district. Educated at a Church of Scotland Mission school, the Alliance High School, Kikuyu, and Makerere College, Uganda, (1933-34). From 1935 to 1940 he taught at the Alliance High School. For ten years, until 1950, he was headmaster of the Church of Scotland Mission School at Dagoretti. It was during this period that he began to take an active interest in politics. He was a founder of the Kenya African Union and its first President from 1944 to 1947, when he resigned in favor of Kenyatta. In 1948, he became Vice-President of the Kiambu District Council.

From 1950 to 1952, Gichuru was Chief of Dagoretti location. He resigned just before the Emergency because he disagreed with the government policy. From 1955 to January 1960 he was placed under a restriction order and restricted to Githunguri, in the Kiambu district. On his release from restriction, he taught for a time at the Githunguri Roman Catholic Secondary School, but gave this up to concentrate on politics. He was appointed president of the Kenya African National Union at its inception in March 1960; in January 1961, he stood for election to the Legislative Council as the KANU candidate for Kiambu and was returned unopposed. In October 1961, he resigned as President of KANU in favor of Kenyatta. Gichuru was elected by the Legislative Council as one of Kenya's nine representatives to serve on the newly constituted Central Legislative Assembly of the East African Common Services Organization in January 1962. In April 1962, when the Coalition Government was formed, he became Minister for Finance. He was elected unopposed to the Limuru seat in the House of Representatives in the 1963 General Election and retained the portfolio of finance, his title being changed to Minister for Finance and Economic

Planning. He was elected Vice-President of KANU in
Central Province at the KANU national elections in 1966.
In 1969, he was returned as member for Limuru in
Parliament and appointed Minister for Defence. The
same applied to the 1974 General Election. Re-elected
to Parliament in 1979 as Member for Limuru, and was
appointed Minister of State in the President's Office.

GIKUYU (KIKUYU). The Gikuyu form the largest group of
Central Bantu-speaking peoples, numbering over two
and a quarter million. They emerged as a single group
in the Kirinyaga region from diverse groups such as
the Thagicu, the elements from Igembe and Tigania, the
Acheera and the Agachiko clans which are probably of
Kamba origin from the 15th century. As the proto-Ki-
kuyu expanded westwards and northwards, they assimilated the Gumba, the Athi and the Masai, especially in
the Mathira and Tetu divisions of Nyeri District in the
Central Province. Today they inhabit the Central Province of Kenya and they have also expanded into the Nakuru District in the Rift Valley Province. They practice mixed agriculture, growing coffee, tea, pyrethrum,
maize, potatoes and keeping cattle, goats and sheep.

GIKUYU, EMBU AND MERU ASSOCIATION (GEMA). Formed
in March 1971, its main objective was the promotion of unity, welfare and the spirit of brotherhood among Gikuyu, Embu and Meru people. It is also charged with the task of pre-
serving, promoting and refining the cultural heritage of the
above peoples. Its formation seems to have been inspired by
politicians who wished to forge a larger political unit. Since
1973, Mr. Njenga Karume, a successful businessman and
from 1974-1979 a Nominated Member of Parliament, has
been the Chairman of GEMA. Associated with the organization is Gema Holdings, which by August 1977 already owned
property worth more than three million shillings. Together
with other ethnic organization in Kenya, it was wound up in
1980 as a result of a Government decision.

GIROUARD, COLONEL SIR PERCY. An army officer with
wide experience of railway construction and administration. He was a French Canadian, born in Montreal.
He had entered the army in 1888. He served in the
Sudan: Dongola Expedition 1896, Nile Expedition 1897
and Director of Sudan Railways, 1896-98. From 1898-
99, he was Director of the Egyptian Railway Board.
He was then transferred to South Africa, where he was
Director of Railways from 1899-1902--a period which

coincided with the Boer war. Girouard was one of "Milner's Young Men." After the war he gained experience in the Transvaal and the Orange River Colony where he worked as Commissioner of Railways, 1902-04. He then succeeded Lugard as High Commissioner and Governor of Northern Nigeria from 1907 to 1909. From 1909 to March 1912 he was Governor and Commander-in-Chief of the East African Protectorate. In Kenya, he is best remembered for the notorious Masai move from Laikipia to Narok and Kajiado districts, contrary to the Masai Agreement of 1904. Perhaps because of his Nigerian experience, he was able to reorganize and systematize the Provincial administration in Kenya. He also reorganized, with the assistance of his Treasurer, Mr. Bowring, the country's finances and did away with the grant-in-aid within three years. It was paid for the last time in 1912. Following his resignation, he became managing director of Armstrong-Vickers.

GITHUNGURI TEACHERS COLLEGE. Founded on January 7, 1939, by Mbiyu Koinange, the first Kenya African to obtain a degree in a foreign university, who had come back in 1938 with an M.A. from Teachers College, Columbia University in New York. In a sense it marked the culmination of the Independent school movement in Kikuyuland and it was initially intended to be an independent teacher training college. But as the demand for education was very great, it soon established a primary school, a teachers college, and later, secondary and adult education sections. It was financed from voluntary contributions from the public. When Jomo Kenyatta returned from England in 1946, he joined Mbiyu at the College. They had staff recruitment and equipment problems. By 1950, there were about 1,000 students mostly from Central Province, although a few came from Nyanza and Rift Valley provinces as well as from Tanzania. The college was closed in 1952 due to the declaration of the State of Emergency.

GOSPEL MISSIONARY SOCIETY, THE. One of the organizations that developed from the evangelical and revival movement in late nineteenth-century America, under the leadership of Reverend M. S. Anderson. The first representatives of the Society arrived in Kenya in 1899 and opened their first station at Thembigwa, in Kiambu district, where they acquired a 600-acre farm. Two of

its leading personalities were Reverend and Mr. W. P.
Knapp. The GMS never established any stations outside
Kikuyu area. Two other important stations that the
Knapps founded soon after 1900 were Kambui and Ngenda, both of them in Kiambu. Among its leading converts were Harry Thuku and Waruhiu wa Kungu, an
important colonial chief. After selling Thembigwa, the
mission had only two stations (Kambui and Ngenda) serving about twenty outstations and running several hospitals
and schools. The death of W. Knapp in 1940 and of
his wife in the following year virtually killed the mission. In 1946, it was incorporated into the Church of
Scotland Mission.

GOVERNMENT LAND. Comprises all the land which, prior
to December 12, 1963, when Kenya attained independence, was known as Crown land and includes all the
urban land within municipalities and townships in the
former so-called "White Highlands."

GREAT BRITAIN-KENYA RELATIONS. After Nigeria, Kenya is Britain's best market in black Africa, buying
about £125 million sterling worth of British exports in
1979. The total British aid to Kenya from independence
to end of 1979 amounted to £200 million sterling, the
highest of any African country. Since 1964, over half
of this aid has been concentrated in agriculture, especially land transfer, settlement, and adjudication. In
addition, Kenya has received eight to nine million pounds
per year from Britain for technical assistance in the
form of technical experts and scholarships to Britain
for Kenyans. March 1979 saw the completion of the
Land Transfer Programme begun in 1961 to settle African farmers on the previously exclusively European-
owned "White Highlands." This program cost altogether
£33 million sterling, which was converted into a grant
in 1978. Other areas into which British aid to Kenya
has been channelled have been irrigation schemes, rural
and road programs, and cash crop production of such
commodities as sugar, coffee, tea, pyrethrum, fruits
and vegetables. Kenya's major exports to Britain are
also agricultural products, with tea and coffee in the
lead. On the other hand, Britain has been since 1963,
and still is, Kenya's largest overseas supplier. Kenya's
imports from Britain are dominated by capital plant,
machinery and transport equipment. In 1978, for instance, the total import from Britain was £195.7 million sterling.

Political relationships have been cordial. Between 1895 and 1963, the Anglo-Kenyan relations were colonial and therefore sour. But since independence, firm friendship developed between the two countries during the office of Jomo Kenyatta, who displayed great tolerance and who promoted reconciliation through his policy of "forgiving, and not forgetting" or "suffering without bitterness." This friendship was reinforced by the recent state visit of President Daniel arap Moi—Kenyatta's successor—to Britain from June 12 to June 19, 1980, which was indeed a historic occasion because this was the first state visit by a President of the Republic of Kenya. Many people of British origin also live and work in Kenya, and many Kenyans go to Britain for training, study and business. Furthermore, Britain and Kenya are members of the Commonwealth, an association that provides a unique forum for informal consultation and cooperation between sovereign states.

GRIFFIN, GEOFFREY WILLIAM. Born in 1933 at Eldoret, Kenya. Educated at Prince of Wales School, Nairobi 1945-50. Served in the army 1953-55. He was appointed Deputy Commandant of Wamumu Youth Camp, 1955-57 and was Youth Advisor to the Kenya Government from 1957 to 1964. Griffin has been Director of National Youth Service since 1964 and founded Starehe Boys' Center of which he has been the Honorary Director since 1959. He was appointed Honorary Administrator in Kenya of the Save the Children Fund in 1963.

GRIGG, SIR EDWARD (later Lord Altrincham). Governor of Kenya from October 1925 to 1930. He was one of the followers of Lord Milner and had worked closely with L. S. Amery, another disciple of Milner, on the staff of The Times, 1903-10. He had also been a soldier, a civil servant, and a Liberal Member of Parliament for Oldham. He was appointed by Amery who was now Secretary of State for the Colonies to bring about closer Union in East Africa. Grigg, however, failed in his mission, partly due to stiff opposition by Governor Cameron of Tanganyika and partly because of the general reluctance of the metropolitan to hand over political power to European settlers in Kenya. He was keen on improving the standard of architecture in the country, especially as regards government buildings. He invited Sir Herbert Baker from South Africa who had designed several buildings in Pretoria, to design the Government House (now State House) in Nairobi.

Baker also designed the Government House in Mombasa,
which was built by Grigg. He also built the Prince of
Wales School, now Nairobi School. Wrote Kenya's Opportunity: Memories, Hopes and Ideas (1955).

GROGAN, EWART SCOTT, LT. COL. Born in 1874 and
educated at Winchester and Cambridge University. Became financial editor of the Financial Times before mi-
grating to Africa. Made the famous journey from Cape
to Cairo in 1898-99. Arrived in East Africa Protectorate (Kenya) in 1903 and acquired considerable land property interests. He opened up the port of Kilindini in
Mombasa, developed the forest industry in the interior,
became a large sisal and coffee farmer and a prominent
property owner in Nairobi. He saw military service
in both World Wars. A great orator, Grogan represented European settlers in the Legislative Council at
various times, besides serving as the second President
of the Convention of Associations after Lord Delamere.
Throughout his public life in Kenya, he held reactionary
and somewhat rigid political views which made him popular amongst Conservative white settlers but notorious
amongst non-Europeans. He built Gertrude Garden
Children's Hospital in Nairobi as a memorial to his
wife. Retired to South Africa where he died in 1964.
Author of From the Cape to Cairo, 1900.

GUSII. A Bantu group that lives in the Kisii district in the
Nyanza Province. They number about 800,000 and their
history covers the last 500 years. Like many Western
Bantu groups, they apparently reached their present
home, the Kisii highlands which are 2,000 meters above
sea level, from the Elgon region. They are keen mixed
farmers, growing pyrethrum, tea, millet, maize, cassava and bananas, as well as keeping cattle. Their
district is one of the most densely populated areas of
Kenya.

- H -

HABWE, RUTH. A pioneer women's leader. Born at Ma-
seno and educated at Maseno Junior School and Butere
Girls' School, where she later taught for eight years.
She was one of the first African women to take a teach-
er's training course at the Kabete Teachers' Training
College in 1945. In 1948 she married and moved to

Dar-es-Salaam in Tanzania with her husband, who went
there to train post office workers. She taught at Kich-
wele Government Girls' School in Dar-es-Salaam for
two years, before returning to Kenya to teach at her
home town, Maseno. In 1960, she took an upgrading
course at Siriba Teachers' College, specializing in domestic science as well as in arts and crafts. In 1962,
she joined the Kenya-Israel School of Social Studies at
Machakos. In the following year, she was sponsored
for a leadership training course in welfare work in New
York by the African-American Institute. In 1964, she
was a member of the Kenya Education Commission and
later in the same year she was a member of the Kenya
delegation to the 19th Session of the U.N. General Assembly in New York. She remained behind to attend a
two-year course in arts and crafts at the Riverside
Church College, where she learned weaving, rug making, designing and silk screening. On her return, she
worked with the Ministry of Home Affairs as technical
instructor in the Prison Industry. Habwe was one-time
Chairman of the Maendeleo Ya Wanawake, the grass-
roots women's organization in Kenya. Today, she is
the Managing Director of the African Culture Industry,
which she started in 1969 and which trains young boys
and girls in arts and crafts.

HALL, FRANCIS GEORGE. A pioneer British administra-
    tor in Kenya. Born at Saugor in India in October 1860.
    He was the third son of Col. Edward Hall of the 52nd
    Bengal Native Infantry, and a nephew of Lord Goschen.
    Educated at Sherborne and Tornbridge. Worked as a
    clerk for the Bank of England until 1880, when he went
    off to seek his fortune in South Africa. Did a variety
    of jobs during the twelve years he spent in South Afri-
    ca, including teaching, shop-keeping, farming and taxi-
    driving. He also volunteered for active service in the
    Kaffir Rising of 1881, the Basuto Campaign and Bechu-
    analand Field Force. Went back to England in 1891.
    Came out to East Africa in 1892 as a junior officer
    with the Imperial British East Africa Company. With
    the declaration of a British Protectorate over the future
    Kenya, he was appointed Collector at Fort Smith (1895-
    1899), Machakos (1899-1900) and Mbiri (1900-1901),
    which was subsequently renamed Fort Hall in recogni-
    tion of his contribution towards the founding of the sta-
    tion, which since independence is known as Murang'a
    town. He died in Kenya in April 1901.

HALWENGE, EDWARD. Born in 1921 at Kisumu, Central
Nyanza. Educated at C. M. S. Maseno School, Cambridge
University, where he studied administrative law (1956-
57). Worked for a time in the Tanganyika Civil Service, starting with Clerk/Chief Clerk, Tanganyika Civil
Service, 1940-41; Secretary/Treasurer, Binza Local
Treasury, Sukumaland, 1945; Government Cashier, Sukumaland Federation Headquarters (1946-47); Secretary/
Treasurer, North Mara District Council (1949-51); Assistant District Officer (1950-57); Assistant Secretary
in the Treasury (1957-60); District Commissioner (1960-
61); Senior District Commissioner 1961; Deputy Permanent Secretary, Ministry of Commerce and Industry
(1962-64). In 1964, he was transferred to the East African Railways and Harbours as Assistant to Chief Ports
Manager, 1964-65. In 1966, he became the General
Manager of the East African Cargo Handling Services,
a post he still holds.

"HARAMBEE". On the achievement of political independence
in 1963, Kenya adopted "harambee" (meaning "let us
pull together") as the national watch-word and it was
incorporated into the national coat-of-arms. One of
the concrete aspects of harambee is participation in
self-help effort to generate a spirit of self-reliance.
This is done both at the national and at the local levels. At the national level, "harambee" means a policy
which does not rely for development finance entirely on
foreign sources. Domestic resources must be mobilized.
For instance, in 1963/64, 82 percent of the total development budget originated in external sources; in 1972/
73, this proportion had fallen to 46 percent. At the
local level, harambee consists of self-help activities
such as educational institutions, water projects, public
health schemes, community institutions, etc. These
self-help activities are an expression of the extent to
which the people of any area are willing to make available resources for projects which will be of direct benefit to them. These resources are in the form of voluntary unpaid labor as well as cash contributions.

HARDACRE COMMISSION. Following the collapse of Regionalism and the voluntary dissolution of the Kenya African Democratic Union (KADU) at the end of 1964, the
Government appointed a Commission in 1965 to review the structure, composition and functions of local authorities and their relationship with the cen-

tral government.   The Commission was chaired by
W. S. Hardacre, a local government expert from
Britain.   The Commission Report, Local Government
Commission of Inquiry, 1965, Report, strongly favored
greater control of local authorities by the central government to ensure co-ordination of all local government
matters in the country, fair allocation of staff and finance, and the establishment of ties between local authorities and Parliament.   The aldermanic system,
which was designed to enable municipalities to retain
or acquire the services of people who had special experience but who could not for various reasons stand
for election, was abolished and so were the reserved
seats.

HARDINGE, SIR ARTHUR.   Hardinge started his diplomatic
career as 3rd Secretary in Madrid in 1883.   He moved
to Constantinople as Second Secretary in 1888 and to
Cairo as Acting Consul-General in 1891.   He came to
East Africa in 1894 as Agent and Consul-General in
Zanzibar.   It was in this capacity that on July 1, 1895,
at Mombasa, he proclaimed a British Protectorate over
the territory between Uganda and the coast.   In 1896,
he became the first Commissioner and Consul-General
for East Africa Protectorate, a post he held up to October 1900.   He then held a series of ministerial posts
in Iran (1900-06), Belgium (1906-1911), and Portugal
(1911-1913) before being appointed Ambassador to Spain
in 1913.   Hardinge wrote A Diplomatist in the East
(1928).

HAVELOCK, SIR WILFRID BOWEN.   Born in 1912 in Trinidad and educated at Imperial Service College Windsor
1925-29.   Havelock was a member of the Legislative
Council 1947-63; Chairman of European Elected Members, Kenya Legislative Council 1950-54; Minister for
Local Government 1954-61; Minister for Agriculture
1961-63; and Director of Companies.

HEALTH.   In 1978, the Government operated 191 health
centers, 34 sub-centers and 536 dispensaries, compared with 131 health centers, 56 sub-centers and 416
dispensaries in 1973.   Most of these are located in the
rural areas, and the decline in the number of sub-centers was due to the up-grading of a number of them to
full health centers.   In addition, there were 316 other
rural health institutions, most of them dispensaries

managed by Church organizations. In the same year,
there were 33 districts and provincial hospitals and 24
sub-district hospitals run and managed by the Government, providing a total of 6,568 hospital beds. There
were also 42 Church hospitals providing about 30 percent of the total number of beds available in Government and Church hospitals. Most of the Church hospitals are located in the rural areas. In terms of personnel, the number of doctors and dentists employed by
the Ministry of Health increased from 412 in 1974 to
564 in 1978. It is planned to have 960 by 1983. It
should be noted that the number of doctors in Kenya is
much higher than those engaged in Government service.
For example, doctors in Kenya for the years 1962,
1965, 1967, and 1970 numbered 904, 910, 970, and
1437 respectively. Of these, about 70 percent were in
private practice in urban centers. The ratio of private
to government doctors of about 7:3 has remained more
or less constant.

HILTON YOUNG COMMISSION (1927-1929). This was the
    second British Commission appointed to look into the
    question of closer Union in East and Central Africa.
    Specifically, it was to make recommendations as to
    whether, either by federation or by some other form
    of closer union, more effective co-operation between
    the different Governments in Eastern and Central Af-
    rica might be secured, more particularly in regard to
    the development of transport and communications, cus-
    toms tariffs and customs administration, scientific re-
    search and defense. The Commission was also to con-
    sider what form of constitution was suitable for the ter-
    ritories in which non-African immigrant communities
    had become permanently domiciled. It was composed
    of Sir Edward Hilton Young (Chairman), Sir Reginald
    Mant, Sir George Schuster, and Mr. J. H. Oldham.
    It was appointed in November 1927 and was in Africa
    from December 1927 to May 1928. It published its re-
    port in January 1929.
        The Commission concluded that the time was not
    yet ripe for federation or closer union of all the ter-
    ritories between the Limpopo and the Nile, but that the
    time had come for a Central Unified Government for
    the three territories of Kenya, Tanganyika and Uganda--
    essentially a unit. In this connection, the Commission
    noted that there was an urgent need for the co-ordination
    of policy on "Native Affairs" and all matters concerning

the relations between Africans and immigrants; that
there is need for the co-ordination, and so far as possible, central direction of certain services of common
interest to the three territories such as communications,
customs, defense and research. The publication of the
Report marked the beginning of the East African Common Services Organization which was later to evolve into the East African Community.

In Kenya, the Commission recommended that
some rearrangement of the constitutional position was
immediately desirable. It proposed the Appointment
of a High Commissioner for the three territories. The
High Commissioner was to have full executive powers
and control over legislation and "native" policy. At the
same time they rejected any advance in political power
of the European Unofficial Community of Kenya in toto
as unsound while agreeing to give Kenya European Unofficial majority in the Legislative Council subject to
the special legislative powers which would enable the
High Commissioner to enact (contrary to the vote of
the majority of Council) any legislation that he regarded
as essential.

Sir Samuel Wilson, Under-Secretary of State for
the Colonies, was sent on a special mission to Kenya
in 1929, as a direct result of the Report to "ascertain
on what lines a scheme for closer union would be administratively workable and otherwise acceptable." He
secured agreement in Kenya from the Unofficial community of 1) a scheme of central control over Railways,
Customs, Post and Telegraphs, Defense and Fundamental Research; and 2) a modern reform of the Kenya Legislative Council which provided for an unofficial but not
an elected majority. The Governors of Kenya and Uganda agreed. The Governor of Tanganyika did not agree
over "Native" policy. Following Wilson's report, the
British Government issued its conclusions on Closer
Union, and asked for the appointment of a Joint Select
Committee of Parliament to consider them. The Committee was formed in November 1930 and concluded its
work in September 1931. The main finding of the Committee was that "for a considerable time to come the
progress and development of East Africa as a whole can
best be assured by each of the three territories continuing to develop upon its own lines."

HINDOCHA, DEVJIBHAI KARAMSHI. Industrialist, plantation, land and property owner and one of the pioneers

of the sugar and cotton industries in Uganda, Tanzania
and Kenya. Born at Modhpar, India, in 1890, Hindocha
came to East Africa in 1909 at the age of eighteen, with
one rupee in his pocket. Worked for Messrs. Vithal-
das and Company for thirteen years after which he became a partner. In 1930, they established the Kakira
Sugar Industry in Uganda and afterwards several cotton
ginneries and mills not only in Uganda, but also in Kenya and Tanzania. The Company was dissolved in 1946
and Hindocha took over the Kenya interests. In 1947,
he bought the Victoria Nyanza Sugar Company Ltd.,
which had been established in 1919 by Mr. Meyers, an
Australian who died in that year. The Company owned
4,500 acres of sugar cane and produced 75 bags a day.
Hindocha renamed the company the Miwani Sugar Mills
Ltd. and by 1963 it had 15,000 acres under cane and
was producing 20,000 tons of sugar a year with a staff
of 4,300, most of them Africans. Hindocha was also
a great philanthropist and donated large funds for the
establishment of schools, colleges, hospitals, and sports
facilities, as well as awarding educational scholarships
to deserving students.

HOBLEY, CHARLES WILLIAM. A pioneer British administrator. Born in July 1867 in London. He was educated
at Mason Science College, Birmingham. Seeing no pros-
pects in Britain, he secured an appointment in 1890
with the Imperial British East Africa Company where
he was employed mainly in geological work and exploration. In 1894, he became an administrative officer in
the then Eastern Province of Uganda, where he was
largely responsible for introducing British rule in what
is now Western Kenya. He was appointed Assistant
Deputy Commissioner for East African Protectorate in
1902, Acting Deputy Commissioner, 1903-04 and Acting
Commissioner in 1904. During the First World War
and in the post-war period up to 1921, he was Provincial Commissioner of the Coast Province.
        Hobley was a keen student of the flora and fauna
of East Africa and was a co-founder of the East Africa
and Uganda Natural History Society, and for many years
editor of its Journal. He wrote three major works--
The Ethnology of the Akamba and Other East African
Tribes (1910), Bantu Beliefs and Magic (1922), and Kenya: From Chartered Company to Crown Colony (1929)--
together with several articles, most of which were published in the Journal of the Anthropological Institute,

London. He was a member of the Royal Anthropological
Institute, London. He got the Uganda Mutiny medal,
1897-8, the Nandi medal, 1900, and clasp in 1906. He
was created C.M.G. in 1904.

HOLLIS, ALFRED CLAUDE. Born at Highgate, London on
May 12, 1874. Educated at Highgate, St. Leonards, in
Switzerland, and in Germany. Arrived in Kenya in
March 1897 and appointed Assistant Collector. He became Collector (later District Commissioner) in June
1900. From April 1900 to February 1901, he was Acting British Vice-Consul for German East Africa. He
then became Secretary to the Administration in Kenya
from 1901 to June 1907, when he was appointed Secretary for Native Affairs. He rendered assistance to the
Transport Department during the Uganda Mutiny, 1897-
98, and was for a short period Acting Director of Transport. He took part in several expeditions: the Jubaland Expedition, 1900-01, the Nandi Expedition, 1903
and the Nandi Expedition 1905-06. He published two
books, The Maasai, Their Language and Folklore (1905)
and The Nandi, Their Language and Folklore (1909), as
well as several academic papers on African culture.
He was a Corresponding Fellow of the Royal Anthropological Institute and a Fellow of the Royal Colonial Institute. In 1912, he was appointed Colonial Secretary
in Sierra Leone; and in 1916 he became Secretary to
the Provisional Administration in German East Africa.
In 1919, he was appointed Chief Secretary in Tanganyika and in 1924 he became British Resident in Zanzibar. From 1930 to 1936, he was Governor of Trinidad
and Tobago in West Indies.

HOPE-JONES, SIR ARTHUR. Born in 1911 in Britain. Educated at Cambridge University and Columbia University, U.S.A. He was Fellow of Christ College Cambridge
1937-48; and University Lecturer at Cambridge 1937-39.
He was in the War Service, 1939-45, and Economic and
Commercial Advisor to Kenya 1946-47. He was Member, and later Minister, for Commerce and Industry
1948-60.

HORSE RACING. In Kenya this sport started in 1904 at
Kariokor, now a densely populated area of Nairobi. In
1954, the Ngong Race Course in Nairobi was opened at
the edge of the Langata Forest. Racing is carried out
under the rules of the Jockey Club of Kenya. Four

meetings a year are held at the Limuru Race Course, which is 32 km. from Nairobi. The other 40 meetings a year are all held in Nairobi. Racing is popular, and the average attendance at each meeting is about 5,000.

HUXLEY, ELSPETH JOSCELINE. A British author, born July 23, 1907, London. Daughter of the late Josceline and Eleanour Grant who were settlers in Kenya for over thirty years. She married Gervas Huxley in 1931, with whom she had one son. Educated at Reading and Cornell Universities. Best known for her writings on Africa, especially Kenya. She worked as Assistant Press Officer for the Empire Marketing Board, 1929-32. She extensively travelled with her husband in America, Africa and elsewhere. She is Justice of the Peace for Malmesbury; was member of the Monckton Commission on Central Africa in 1960. Among her publications are White Man's Country, Lord Delamere and the Making of Kenya (2 volumes) 1933; Red Strangers (novel) (1939), depicting the coming of the White Man to Kenya; The Walled City (novel); Race and Politics in Kenya: A Correspondence Between E. Huxley and Margery Perham (1946); The Sorcerer's Apprentice: A Journey Through East Africa (travel) 1948; Four Guineas: A Journey Through West Africa (travel) 1952; A Thing to Love (novel) 1954; The Red Rock Wilderness (novel) 1957; The Flame Tree of Thika (autobiography), dealing with her childhood experiences at Thika, Kenya, 1959; A New Earth (travel) 1960; The Mottled Lizard (1962); The Merry Hippo (1963); A Man from Nowhere (1963); Forks and Hope (1964); Back Street New Worlds (1964); Brave New Victuals (1965); Their Shining Eldorado (travel) 1967; Love Among the Daughters (third volume of autobiography) 1968; The Challenge of Africa, 1971; Livingstone and His African Journeys, 1974; Florence Nightingale, 1975. Nellie: Letters from Africa (1980), letters written by her mother in Kenya from 1933-1965.

HYRAX HILL PREHISTORIC SITE. Located just outside the town of Nakuru. Hyrax Hill itself is a mound that commands good views of Lake Nakuru and the surrounding countryside. It is likely that at one time the Lake extended to the foot of the mound. The site is full of evidence of what were probably shore settlements--villages, burial sites and holes carved out in the rock for the games of bau or ajua.

- I -

IMPERIAL BRITISH EAST AFRICA COMPANY. The new
imperialism of the nineteenth century led Britain to re-
vive the system of chartered companies that had worked
well with the early companies such as the East India
Company or the Merchant Adventurers. Sir George
Goldie's Royal Niger Company in West Africa and Cecil
Rhodes' South Africa Company were such chartered companies, which were regarded as useful instruments of
colonial expansion. In East Africa, the Imperial British
East Africa Company (IBEA Co.) filled such a role.
This company was founded by Sir William Mackinnon,
Chairman of the British India Steam Navigation Company in 1888, with a subscribed capital of £240,000, a
sum which was to prove inadequate for the big task
ahead. It fought battles over Witu, Manda, Patta and
Lamu against the German East Africa Company before
sending Captain Fredrick Dealtry Lugard to Uganda to
establish the company's position there. Uganda cost
the company between £30,000 and £40,000 a year. It
was also spending about £150,000 a year on caravans
and £330,000 on steamers, launches, lighters, etc. In
early 1893 the Company had to sell out. Its assets
were bought up for £250,000, of which the Sultan of
Zanzibar paid £200,000 for his recovery of his con-
cession for the ten-mile coastal strip. As Dame Margery Perham has said, "Britain secured East Africa at
the bargain price of £50,000."

INDIA-KENYA RELATIONS. India's relations with East Africa, including Kenya, go back to ancient times. During the colonial period, many people of Indian origin
came to Kenya as traders, employees of the colonial
civil service, professionals, and artisans. Many of
them became Kenya Citizens at independence. On the
other hand, many Kenyans have received their training
and higher education in India. In the field of trade,
Kenya was an important trade partner of India from the
1950's. For instance, 29 percent of imports from and
15 percent of exports to Africa were with Kenya. This
changed between 1960 and 1972. Kenya's share in the
import trade with India declined by 50 percent while
Kenya's export trade remained at 2.7 percent during the
same period. The main reason was that textiles had
formed about 76 percent of imports from India. As
Kenya developed her textile industry, the value of im-

ports from India declined correspondingly. The other
important imports had been jute manufactures, but even
these were gradually replaced by sisal production in
Kenya. India, however, began to produce new exports--
chemicals, pharmaceuticals and cosmetics from 1968.
By 1974/75, Kenya absorbed 28 percent of these exports to Africa. The other exports developed during
this period were chemicals and allied products: paints,
varnishes, plywood and plywood products. Engineering
goods have also been exported to Kenya in large quan-
tities since 1969. These include auto and auto-parts,
railway wagons and parts, industrial plant and machinery, steel structures and electric wires and cables,
aluminum collapsible tubes, bicycles and parts, hand
tools, diesel engines, punps and compressors, telephone
equipment and electrical manufactures. Export of engineering goods to Kenya rose from 28,000,000 rupees in
1970-71 to 76,300,000 rupees in 1974/75, and the figure has
continued to rise. On the other hand, Kenya's export
trade to India has declined considerably since 1960/61.
It is concentrated on a few primary commodities such
as raw cotton, cashew nuts (raw), wattle extract, and
sisal fibre. To strengthen Indian-Kenyan trade relations several joint industrial ventures have been established. After Malaysia in Asia, it is in Kenya where
India has launched the largest number of joint ventures
in Africa. These cover a wide variety of industries
such as textiles (cotton, wool, synthetic and allied products), cork and cork products, paper products, chemical and chemical products, basic metal and allied industries. The system started in 1968 with the establishment of MS H.L. Malhotra, a light engineering complex for the manufacture of safety razor blades, safety
razors, wood and metal cutting saws, and agricultural
implements. In the same year, the Birla Brothers submitted a feasibility study for setting up a multi-million
shilling papermill. This led to the establishment of the
Pan-African Paper Mill Ltd. (E.A.) at Webuye. Today
it is the leading successful joint-venture between India
and Kenya.

INDUSTRIAL AND COMMERCIAL DEVELOPMENT CORPOR-
ATION, THE (ICDC). Incorporated as a statutory body
in 1964 to facilitate industrial and commercial development. It also promotes Africans in commerce and industry directly and to this end has incorporated a wholly-
owned subsidiary, the Kenya Industrial Estates Ltd. which

has set up industrial estates in Nairobi, Mombasa, Nakuru, and Kisumu. The ICDC also participates in the
equity capital of enterprises it wishes to promote, in
an auxiliary capacity without being a sole shareholder.
In addition, through the investment participation of a
subsidiary company, the ICDC Investment Company, the
ICDC organizes finance from Kenya citizen shareholders.
In this way, it has been able to promote African equity
participation in such important local companies as Block
Hotels, Union Carbide Kenya Ltd. , East African Industries Ltd. , and Raymond Woollen Mills (Kenya) Ltd.
Furthermore, the ICDC provides commercial and industrial loans to citizens.   Finally, the ICDC promotes
joint ventures with foreign investors.   Among the enterprises promoted by ICDC in this way are Firestone
East Africa (1969) Ltd. , Eltex Textile Mill, Flamingo
Textile Industries Ltd. , Kenya Engineering Industries
Ltd. , and Venus Easterbrook (E. A.) Ltd.   By June 1978,
it had sixty-four subsidiary and associate companies,
with a total investment of over K. Shs. 700 million.

ISLAM.   The religion of Islam reached Kenya in the 7th
century and until the 19th century was largely confined
to the urban centers along the coast.   Since the 19th
century it has extended inland partly to the new urban
centers and partly in the rural areas.   The Supreme
Council of Kenya Muslims, founded in the early 1970's,
is now a federation of over one hundred Muslim organizations.

ISRAEL-KENYA RELATIONS.   Close relations between the
two countries started in the 1950's when cooperation
was established between the labor movements of the two
countries--Israel's Histadrut and the Kenya Federation
of Registered Trade Unions.   Kenyan trade unionists
were among the leading participants in the first great
International Seminar on Labour and Cooperative Studies
called by the Histadrut's newly created Afro-Asian Institute in Tel Aviv from November 1958 to February
1959.   For the next fourteen years Kenyans attended
several courses and seminars in Israel, especially at
the Mt. Carmel Centre and the Afro-Asian Institute.
In Kenya itself, there were several joint ventures established by the two countries.   First the Kenya School
of Social Work was established at Machakos near Nairobi in October 1962 with money, equipment, and personnel,
including the director, from Israel.   It offered a two-

year course in social work. The school was handed
over to the Kenya Government in 1966. The second
project was the "Kenya-Netherlands-Israel Project for
Operations Research in Out-patient Service" (KNIPOROS),
which was set up in 1971 as a tripartite, inter-govern-
mental project to design a model clinic program for
Kenya. It was located at Kiambu, 25 miles north of
Nairobi. Kenya's severance of diplomatic relations
with Israel and the subsequent departure of the Israeli
resident staff in 1973 slowed down the work of the clinic.
Contact was, however, maintained between the Israeli
and the Dutch teams, and the head of the Israeli staff
came back to Kenya regularly for consultation with his
Kenyan and Dutch colleagues.

Israeli experts were also involved in the training
of pilots for the Kenya Air Force and in the setting up
of a chain of consumer cooperative stores. Since 1973,
Israeli interests in Kenya have been looked after by the
Danish Embassy, and Israel also has a Permanent Representative to the United Nations Environment Programme
(UNEP) and Habitat resident in Nairobi. Despite the
severance of diplomatic relations, it is evident that practical relations between the two countries, especially in
the economic and training fields, have remained cordial.
Israel's exports to Kenya in 1978 were valued at US.
$7.8 million, in 1979 US. $10.4 million and in the first
three months of 1980 US. $3.5 million. The main ex-
ports were pipelines, chemicals, fertilizers, agricultural
machinery, electronics, chicks, and fruit plants, especially oranges and apples. The main Kenya exports
to Israel are coffee, soda ash, and pineapples valued
at between US. $3 and 4 million per year.

There are also several Israeli firms operating
in Kenya. The main companies are Solel Boneh, a
building construction company; H. &Z., a road construction company; Plassin, an agricultural company which
manufactures agricultural equipment and which has been
involved in several irrigation programs; Zevet Company,
the architects of Nairobi Hilton, Coffee House in Nairobi
and other buildings; Amiran, an export-import company;
Asea, a pharmaceutical company; Continental Develop-
ers, specialists on housing projects, and manufacturers
of solar energy heaters and housing furniture. El Al,
the Israeli airline, also has offices in Nairobi and lands
in Kenya. As far as training is concerned, there were,
for example, 100-150 Kenya students in Israel during
1978/79 studying various subjects such as bee-keeping,

cattle-breeding, irrigation, fisheries, preventive medicine, social work, handicraft and community development. Kenya still sends the largest number of overseas students to the Afro-Asian Institute for Labour Studies and Cooperation.

ITESO. A Plains, Nilotic-speaking group who live in Busia District of Western Province. They are part of the Teso of Uganda, and they reached their present home during the second half of the nineteenth century.

ITOTE, WARUHIU (popularly known as "General China"). One of the few former Mau Mau forest leaders who are still alive. Born in 1921 at Kaheti in Nyeri district. Ran away from school to look for work. He worked as a farm laborer and a houseboy before he turned to business in Nairobi. In 1941, he joined the Kenya African Rifles (KAR) in Nairobi, from where he was posted to the 36 KAR in Tanzania. From there they went to Ceylon and thence to Burma to fight in the Second World War. He learned much about guerrilla warfare in the forests of Burma. In 1945, Itote returned to Kenya and resigned from the army. He started business as a charcoal burner and after a few years he joined the East African Railways and Harbours as a fireman.

In 1951, he resigned from the Railways and joined the Forty Group. He became an oath administrator in Nyeri District. In August 1952, Itote assumed the name of General China and led a group of forest fighters into the Hombe area of Mt. Kenya. He established a forest camp from which he organized and carried out raids. He was assisted by General Tanganyika and General Kariba. More forest camps were established under General China following the declaration of the State of Emergency. On January 15, 1954, General China was wounded and captured near Karatina by a platoon of the 7th Kenya Batallion of the KAR. On February 1, 1954, he was charged at Nyeri Emergency Assize Court with consorting with persons carrying firearms and being in possession of two rounds of ammunition without lawful authority or excuse. He was found guilty and sentenced to death. This was postponed following his agreement to assist the government in organizing cease-fire talks with forest fighters. The Governor, Sir Evelyn Baring, commuted his death sentence to life imprisonment on March 4. At the first of such

meetings on April 7, twenty-five freedom fighters were
killed and seven captured. The peace talks had to be
abandoned. He was released from prison on June 14,
1962. He was nominated by the leaders of the Kenya
African National Union for military training in Britain.
On his return he was admitted to Lanet for further training, from where he graduated with the rank of Second
Lieutenant in the Kenya Army Reserve. In 1964, he
joined the National Youth Service as Section Commander,
later rising to the position of Deputy Director of the
Service, a position he still holds.

- J -

JACKSON, FREDERICK JOHN. A pioneer British administrator in Kenya. A Yorkshireman born at Oran in
1860. Educated at Shrewsbury School and Jesus College, Cambridge. He first came to East Africa in 1889,
when he commanded an important caravan sent to Uganda by the Imperial British East Africa Company. He
became First Class Assistant in the Uganda Protectorate in July 1894 and was Vice-Consul in May of the following year. He became Deputy Commissioner in 1896
and Acting Commissioner, Uganda Protectorate, 1897-8
and 1901-2. In 1902, he was appointed Deputy Commissioner, East Africa Protectorate and was Lieutenant-
Governor, East Africa Protectorate in 1907. From 1911
to 1917, he was Governor of Uganda. He got the East
and Central Africa medal, with clasp, Uganda, 1897-98;
Luba and Africa General Service medal, Uganda, 1900;
Nairobi, 1905-06. He was a keen ornithologist and an
authority on East African fauna. Author of Early Days
in East Africa. He received the C.M.G. in 1902 and
the C.B.

JEANS SCHOOL, THE. Established in 1926 at Kabete, just
outside Nairobi, as a result of the Phelps-Stokes Commission. The Phelps-Stokes Fund sponsored two educational Commissions in the 1920's to investigate and report on African education. The Commissions consisted
largely of British and American officials. The Second
Commission visited Kenya in February and March 1924.
It supported mission education and recommended cooperation among all interested groups, so as to provide
appropriate and relevant education to the African. The
School was financed by a grant from the Carnegie Foun-

dation in the United States. The purpose of the school
was to produce teachers who would supervise the work
in rural schools so as to improve standards. It was
to be free from settler influence, and the hope was that
its graduates would bring better sanitary, health, educational, and agricultural techniques to rural Kenya. Its
curriculum was to be adapted to the rural environment.
The rural schools had been condemned by the Phelps-
Stokes Commission, and it believed that the Jeans School
teachers would transform them into modernizing centers
in rural Kenya. The Jeans School teacher played a significant role in improving the quality of life in rural Kenya.

JEEVANJEE, SETH ALIBHOY MULLA. A prominent pioneer
Indian businessman in Kenya. Born in 1856 in India, he
was already an established trader in India and from 1886
in Australia, where he established an agency for the import of Eastern goods at Adelaide. In 1890, he obtained
a contract from the Imperial British East Africa Company to recruit Indian labor--artisans and police--for
the company's territories. He opened a branch of his
Karachi-based firm in Mombasa, working as a contrac-
tor. His firm was hired by the Uganda Railways in
1896 to recruit Indian workers, construct buildings, do
earth-works and provide food to Indian railway workers.
        In 1899, he was commissioned to build John Ains-
worth's house in Nairobi--the beginning of his business
activities in Nairobi. His firm was later commissioned
to build government offices and residences, post offices
and railway stations between Mombasa and Kisumu. He
soon became a major land owner in Nairobi and Mombasa. He started a newspaper, the African Standard in
Mombasa, which he sold in 1903. It was renamed the
East African Standard. He also sold a sister paper
called the Mombasa Times and became an importer-
exporter and a shipowner, operating steamships between Bombay and Mauritius and Bombay and Jedda.
He laid the first public gardens in Nairobi (the Jeevanjee Garden) and helped with the construction of
the first Nairobi Club, a charitable act which earned
him honorary membership of the Club--the only Indian
Member of the Club until 1961. Jeevanjee was President of the Indian Association, Mombasa, 1905-06 and
was the unofficial Indian member in the Legislative Council from 1910 to 1911. In 1912, he published a document entitled An Appeal on Behalf of Indians in East

Africa, condemning racial discrimination against Indians
and demanding equality of treatment with the Europeans.
He died in 1934.

                              - K -

KAGGIA, BILDAD.   Born in 1922 at Dagoretti near Nairobi.
He was educated at Kahuhia School in his home district
of Murang'a.   With B. M. Gecaga, he qualified to go
to the Alliance High School, Kikuyu, but Kaggia could
not raise school fees.   He instead went to work as a
clerk in the District Commissioner's office at Murang'a
until 1940 when he joined the army.   He saw service in
Kenya, the Middle East and Britain before returning to
Kenya in 1946 as a revolutionary.   He declined to join
the Kenya African Studies Union (precursor of the Kenya African Union) claiming that it was elitist, conservative and urban.   Instead he started a religious sect that
aimed at interpreting Christianity through the African
idiom.   His sect rapidly spread throughout the Central
Province and into Ukambani and the Nyanza Province.
Kaggia and many of his followers were arrested and
jailed for holding unlicensed meetings.   In 1947 Kaggia
joined the KAU, then led by Jomo Kenyatta, who had
just returned from a long exile in Britain.   He got a
job as a clerk in the National Bank of India in Nairobi.
He formed the Clerks and Commercial Workers Union,
later becoming its president.   His Union joined Makhan
Singh's Labour Trade Union of East Africa.   When Singh
was arrested, Kaggia became the President of the
L. T. U. E. A.
         With Fred Kubai, Kaggia organized a trade union
take over of the Nairobi branch of KAU and turned it
into a radical and revolutionary movement.   In 1952,
he was arrested under Emergency regulations on October 20.   Together with Jomo Kenyatta and other nationalists, he was tried at Kapenguria and sentenced to
imprisonment.   From April 1953 to 1959, he was at
Lokitaung prison, from where he was restricted at Lodwar until November 1961.   From November to December 1961, he was restricted at his home in Murang'a.
In the 1963 General Election, he was elected to the House
of Representatives as KANU Member for Kandara and
was appointed Assistant Minister for Education.   He disagreed with Government's land policy and was removed
from office in 1964.   He continued to criticize various

aspects of government policy as a backbencher. Kaggia
was elected by the backbenchers as Chairman of the
East African Federation Committee. He was also Secretary of the backbenchers. In 1966, he was replaced
by Dr. J. G. Kiano as the branch Chairman of KANU
in Murang'a district. Later that year at the famous
KANU Conference at Limuru, the radicals in the party,
who included Oginga Odinga and Kaggia, were routed.
They resigned to form a new party, the Kenya People's
Union (KPU) with Kaggia as its Vice-President. During
the "Little General Election" in 1966, he lost his seat
in Parliament.

In 1968, Kaggia was arrested in South Nyanza
and charged with the offence of addressing a meeting
without a license. He was sentenced to one year's imprisonment, although it was later reduced on appeal to
six months. Towards the end of 1969 he resigned from
the KPU complaining that it had failed to deliver goods
to the masses. In the 1969 election, he stood on a
KANU ticket at Kandara but lost to Mr. Mwicigi. In
April 1970, he was appointed Chairman of the Cotton,
Lint and Seed Marketing Board and in April of the following year, he was transferred to another statutory
board--the Maize and Produce Board--as Chairman.
He is the author of Roots of Freedom 1921-1963 (1975),
an autobiographical work.

KALENJIN. The word "kalenjin" means "I tell you," and
was adopted in the 1940's as a name for the large number of groups who lived in the Western highlands of
Kenya in the Rift Valley Province. The Kalenjin comprise the Kipsigis, Nandi, Terik (or Nyang'ori), Keiyu
(Elgeyo), Tugen, Marakwet, Pokot, Sabaot (Kony, Pok
and Bungomek), Sebei (who live mostly in Uganda), and
a section of the Okiek. The Kalenjin language belongs
to the Southern (or Highland) branch of Nilotic languages,
which also includes Tatoga in northern Tanzania. Like
other Nilotic-speakers, they are supposed to have
emerged as a distinct group in the general area between Lake Turkana and the Southern Ethiopian highlands and in the direction of southeastern Sudan about
a thousand years ago. Today they number about one
and a half million people.

KALI, JOHN DAVID. Born in 1924 at Machakos. Educated
at Nairobi Government School and Kenya Teachers' College, Githunguri, which he left in 1940 to join the army.

He served with the 21st East African Brigade in Ceylon
in 1942, and with the 11th East African Division in India and Burma in 1944-46. He joined the Kenya African
Union on his return. He was elected a member of the
African District Council, Machakos in 1947. In the
same year he enrolled for a teaching course at the
Jeans School, Kabete, although he ended up as a Social
Welfare Assistant. It was at the Jeans School that he
first met Tom Mboya. On leaving the Jeans School, he
joined the East African Command Headquarters, where
he worked for a year. He worked on the KAU party paper Sauti ya Mwafrika. He later started his own newspaper, Kiliocha Mfanyi Kazi. He also became Vice-
President of the then East African Trade Union Congress,
Assistant Secretary of the KAU, Nairobi Branch, Secretary-General of the Akamba Union, and editor of the
Akamba paper Mukamba.

On the declaration of a State of Emergency, Kali
was arrested together with 90 other leaders on October
20, 1952, and detained at a camp near Kajiado. He
was later transferred to the island of Manda where he
spent seven years with people like Achieng' Oneko,
Chokwe, Pio Pinto, and the three Koinange brothers.
In March 1959, the group was divided into two: one
section went to Marsabit and a second section was sent
to Hola--the hell camp. He was one of those sent to
Hola, where the infamous Hola massacre later occurred.
Eleven detainees were brutally beaten to death by the
wardens. He was released from Hola in November 1961.
Kali accompanied Kenyatta on a visit to Ethiopia and
then went to England and spent about a year there. He
was elected KANU Member for Nairobi East to the House
of Representatives in 1963. In the same year, he was
appointed Government Chief Whip. He lost election in
1969, but was elected Member for Kilungu in 1974. In
1979, he was elected KANU Chief Whip, but he again
lost election later that year.

KALONDI, MENGO WORESHA see TAITA HILLS ASSOCIA-
TION

KAMBA. The Kamba are members of the Central Bantu-
speakers living in the two districts of Machakos and Kitui in the Eastern Province. They probably moved to
their present homeland from the region around Mount
Kilimanjaro (Kiima Kya Kyeu, the Mountain of Whiteness),
where they were living by the 15th century. Their mi-

gration route included the Chyulu Hills, the Kibwezi
Plains, Nzaui Rock, and the Mbooni ("the place of the
buffalo") Hills. By the 18th century, they began to settle in their present homeland, and by the end of that
century, they had extended into Kitui and Machakos
Hills. By the beginning of the 19th century, long-distance trade had emerged as a major pursuit amongst
the Kamba. Today, they form the fourth largest ethnic
group in Kenya, numbering about 1.3 million. They
practice mixed farming, although a large part of Ukambani is semi-arid.

KANAM.   A famous prehistoric locality in South Nyanza at
the foot of a dissected volcano, Homa Mountain.   This
area has yielded a fossilized human jaw fragment and
a Late Upper Pliocene or Early Pleistocene mammalian
fauna.

KANJERA.   A famous prehistoric site at the foot of Homa
Mountain, South Nyanza, at which fossilized bones, including human remains and stone implements have been
found.   The first fossils were found in 1911 by Dr. Fe-
lix Oswald.   In 1932, Dr. L. S. B. Leakey's expedition
found human skull fragments and Acheulian hand-axes.

KARANJA, JOSPHAT NJUGUNA.   A diplomat and administrator, Karanja was born on February 5, 1931.   Educated at Alliance High School, Kikuyu, Makerere College, Uganda, University of Delhi, India, and Princeton University, U.S.A., where he obtained his Ph.D.
in History and Political Science.   For one year he was
Lecturer in African Studies at Fairleigh Dickinson University, New Jersey, U.S.A. 1961-62; Lecturer in African and Modern European History, at the Royal College, Nairobi 1962-63.   He was appointed High Commissioner for Kenya in the United Kingdom in 1963,
where he remained until 1970.   He was also accredited
to the Holy See, 1966-70.   In 1970, he was appointed
Vice-Chancellor of the University of Nairobi, a post he
held until 1979.

KARIANDUSI.   A prehistoric site, just outside Gilgil, on
the Gilgil-Nakuru Road.   It was probably on the shore
of what must have been a huge Rift Valley lake.   There
is a small museum at the site.

KARIUKI, JOSIAH MWANGI.   Born on March 21, 1929, at

Kabati Forest in the Rift Valley Province of Kenya
where his parents had migrated and settled from their
home in Nyeri, Central Province in 1928. He was educated at Karima and Kerugoya Schools before going to
the King's College, Budo in Uganda. At the outbreak
of the Mau Mau uprising, Kariuki was a member of the
Kenya African Union (KAU), and though young, was already active in politics. In 1953, he started a lucra-
tive hotel business in Nakuru. From 1953 to 1960 he
was detained under the Emergency Regulations in various camps. On being released from detention, he went
to Oxford University where he wrote his succesful autobiographical book, Mau Mau Detainee, first published in
1963. On returning to Kenya, he became Mzee Kenyatta's private Secretary, and in the general election of
that year, he contested the Aberdare's Constituency (the
present Nyandarua District) seat and won with a big
majority. When the National Youth Service was formed
in 1964, he became its leader. He also became the
Chairman of the Betting and Lotteries Licensing Board.
On July 1, 1968, he was appointed an Assistant Minister for Agriculture. After the 1969 General Elections
he became an Assistant Minister for Tourism and Wildlife. After the 1974 General Elections, he was dropped
from Government probably because of his controversial
stand on basic political issues. On the night of March
2, 1975, he was ruthlessly murdered, and his body left
in Ngong Hills about thirty miles from Nairobi.

KARUME, NJENGA. A self-made man born at Elementaita
in 1929. He decided, at an early age, to try his hand
at business after spending some time at Riara Catholic
Mission. In 1950, he entered the timber business at
Elburgon. In 1953, he found it impossible to operate
his business in the Rift Valley because of the Emergency situation. He accordingly moved to Kiambu where
he opened a small retail shop with the money he had
saved up from his timber business in the Rift Valley.
From 1954 to 1955, Karume was detained at
Langata Detention Camp, leaving his wife Wariara to
manage the shop. When he was released he opened a
small bar in Kiambu town--the first African owned bar
in the whole of Central Province. Besides his bar business, Karume did sub-contracting work and transport
business. In 1958 the East African Breweries appointed
him their agent in Kiambu to distribute beer. Later,
he was appointed BAT distributor in Kiambu. He holds

directorships in many firms including Credit Finance
Corporation, Guiness East Africa, United Transport
Company and East African Road Services. When the
Gikuyu Embu Meru Association (GEMA) was formed in
1970, Njenga Karume became its first national Chairman. He is also Chairman of Gema Holdings Ltd. In
1974, he was appointed a Nominated Member of Parliament by the President to represent Central Province.
He was elected to Parliament in 1979 as Member for
Kiambaa, and appointed Assistant Minister for Home Affairs.

KAVIRONDO TAXPAYERS WELFARE ASSOCIATION, THE.
In early 1923, Archdeacon Owen persuaded the leaders
of the Young Kavirondo Association, a political organization, to transform their Association into a welfare
body, which was renamed the Kavirondo Taxpayers Welfare Association. Intellectual, social, and spiritual advance was to precede political development. Racial cooperation was stressed, with Booker T. Washington's
philosophy adopted as the right approach. Owen himself became the first President and the Provincial Commissioner and District Commissioner were made Vice-
Presidents, thus formalizing the cooperation between
provincial administration and the leaders of the people.
Later on, the chiefs were also appointed Vice-Presidents
in order to avoid a rift developing between the younger,
educated people and the more conservative elders.
        Most of the original leaders of the Young Ka-
virondo Association such as Jonathan Okwiri, Simon Nyende, Benjamin Owuor Gumba, Ezekial Apindi and Daniel
Odindo, continued to lead the reconstituted body. Nyende and Apindi, for example, later became presidents
of the Association. It organized the first Agricultural
Show in Nyanza in 1923 at Maseno; gave evidence before
the Phelps-Stokes Commission in 1924; published a
health primer; employed a development officer in 1925
to assist members in self-improvement; built water-
powered maize mills for its members and by 1930, the
Association had collected 10,000 shillings to provide sixteen bursaries annually to needy pupils at Maseno School.
We thus see that self-help projects, christened harambee
projects during the post-independence period, were an
important aspect of African development during the colonial period.
        The Association also demanded a school of Ad-
ministration where Africans could be trained in modern

methods of administration and of development and it
continued to discuss political issues.   The Association
produced a Memorandum for the Hilton-Young Commission in 1927.   The grievances expressed in this Memorandum were similar to the 1921-22 grievances.   In
1930, Ezekiel Apindi effectively represented the Association before the Joint Select Committee in London.
With the rising prosperity in the 1930's, the Association increasingly functioned as a Chamber of Commerce,
representing the interests of the African traders.   In
1936, Owen relinquished his presidency of the KTWA.
It had become an entirely Luo association, with the formation of the Abaluhya Central Association.   With almost all African associations proscribed in 1940 because of war conditions, Owen was persuaded to re-
sume the leadership of KTWA in order to save it from
being banned.   Owen died in 1945, and despite attempts
to revive the KTWA later, a new generation of leaders
had emerged in Nyanza who were more interested in
national political organizations than in welfare bodies.

KENEXTEL see COMMUNICATIONS AND TRANSPORT

KENYA AFRICAN DEMOCRATIC UNION.   Formed at a con-
    ference held at Ngong, near Nairobi, on June 25, 1960,
    attended by representatives of the Kalenjin Political Al-
    liance led by Daniel arap Moi, Kenya African People's
    Party (a new name for Muliro's former Kenya National
    Party), the Masai United Front, Coast political associ-
    ations led by Ronald Ngala, and representatives of the
    Somali.   Ngala and Muliro became Leader and Deputy
    Leader respectively.   The main philosophy of the party
    was regionalism, which viewed the "Westminster model"
    as inappropriate for Kenya.   It demanded the devolution
    of powers to the regions.   The party formed a short-
    lived government before Kenyatta was released.   It was
    the official Opposition Party from 1963 to end of 1964
    when it was voluntarily dissolved.

KENYA AFRICAN NATIONAL UNION.   Founded in May 1960
    at Kiambu, Central Province.   It was determined to use
    Jomo Kenyatta, who was still in detention, as a symbol
    around which to build a mass movement.   Kenyatta was
    therefore elected President of the Party in absentia,
    with James Gichuru as Acting President; Oginga Odinga
    and Tom Mboya were elected Vice-President and Secre-
    tary-General respectively; and Ronald Ngala and Daniel

arap Moi were elected in absentia Treasurer and Deputy
Treasurer respectively. The latter two leaders de-
clined, and decided to form a rival political party, the
Kenya African Democratic Union. This split in the nationalist movement had already emerged amongst the
African elected members of the Legislative Council,
where in July 1959, one group had founded the Kenya
National Party led by Masinde Muliro, Ronald Ngala,
Daniel arap Moi and Taaitta arap Toweett; and a second
group responded with the Kenya Independence Movement
led by Oginga Odinga, Tom Mboya and Dr. Julius Kiano.
At the end of 1964, KADU was dissolved, and its members joined KANU, which has been the ruling party since
independence, and the only political party since 1969.

KENYA AFRICAN UNION, THE. This group represents the
first serious attempt to mobilize the African masses
for the nationist struggle. Originally called the Kenya
African Study Union when it was formed in 1944, it
changed its name to the Kenya African Union in 1946.
The Union also wanted to demonstrate to the other communities in Kenya and to the Colonial government that
Mr. E. W. Mathu (the first, and at that time the only,
African Member of the Legislative Council), had a united
community to represent. It started its own newspaper,
Sauti ya Mwafrika, edited by Mr. W. W. W. Awori.
Following his return from a long sojourn in Britain in
1946, Mr. Jomo Kenyatta became its President in 1947,
taking over from Mr. James Gichuru. The main problem facing the Union was to gain support from areas
outside central Kenya. Despite strenuous efforts, especially in Nyanza where Messrs Oginga Odinga and
Achieng' Oneko tried to mobilize the Luo in support of
the organization, the Union remained largely concentrated in Nairobi and the surrounding region. By 1952,
before the Mau Mau uprising, it claimed a membership
of 100,000, each paying five shillings annually.

KENYA ASSOCIATION OF MANUFACTURERS, THE. Formed
as a co-operative body in 1959. It is a representative
organization of industrialists in Kenya whose aim is to
encourage investment and develop the industrial potential
of Kenya. It is a non-political and non-profit-making
organization entirely dependent upon the subscriptions
of its members for its finances. Its ordinary membership is restricted to individuals, firms, companies or
other bodies directly engaged in manufacture, processing

or other productive undertakings within Kenya. It has
also an associate membership of others who by the very
nature of their business have a direct interest in the expansion of the industrial potential of the country.

KENYA COALITION, THE. Formed following the First Lancaster House Conference in London at which political
power was transferred to the Africans in Kenya. Sir
Ferdinand Cavendish-Bentinck, an old settler tough-
liner, resigned as Speaker of the Kenya Legislative
Council on March 4, 1960, to found the party. They
accused the British Government of betraying the Kenya
Europeans. The party was formed on March 30 to protect European interests, especially over land. It worked
in alliance with the Convention of Associations until
1963 which saw the demise of both organizations.

KENYA COMMERCIAL BANK, THE. The leading commercial bank in Kenya. Its history goes back to 1896,
when the National Bank of India Ltd. opened a branch
in Mombasa. In 1904, the bank extended its activities
to Nairobi. In 1958, the Grindlays bank merged with
the National Bank to form the National and Grindlays
Bank Ltd. In 1970, the Government of Kenya acquired
60 percent of the National and Grindlays Bank business,
the remaining 40 percent being retained by Grindlays
Bank Ltd. In 1976, the Government purchased the remaining 40 percent of the shares to obtain complete control of what had already become the largest banking institution in the country. By 1980, the Bank operated
43 branches, 37 sub-branches and 130 mobile units.
The bank is thus playing a vital role in the economic
development of this country.

KENYA CO-OPERATIVE CREAMERIES. One of the biggest
co-operative organizations in Kenya as well as being
one of the oldest. The dairy industry in its modern
form was started in Kenya in 1901 by Mr. and Mrs.
Sandbach-Baker who farmed at Muthaiga and sold their
butter in Nairobi. By 1911 farmers up-country had
realized the necessity of organized production and marketing and had opened up a creamery at Lumbwa. This
was a co-operative effort. In 1926, the Kenya Co-operative Creamery opened at Naivasha. In 1928 another
creamery was opened at Nanyuki and in 1931 these
three were united and became Kenya Co-operative Creameries Ltd. It is owned by the farmers of Kenya and

manufactures butter, ghee, cheese, milk powder, condensed milk and also processes milk for consumption. These products are also exported to many countries overseas. Through KCC, Kenya was the first African country to adopt the modern Tetrapak method of packing milk. This paper and polythene pack is of Swedish origin and KCC was one of the pioneers in its use. In 1961, the KCC, in conjunction with Cow and Gate of England, opened a plant to manufacture whole milk powder.

KENYA EDUCATION COMMISSION REPORT, 1964-65 (often known as the Ominde Commission Report). One of the areas to which the independent Government of Kenya turned its attention almost immediately was education. It appointed a National Commission consisting largely of Kenya citizens and chaired by Professor S. H. Ominde, an eminent Kenya educationist and geographer, to "survey the existing educational resources of Kenya and to advise the Government of Kenya in the formulation of national policies for education." The Report of the Commission appeared in two volumes, the first volume being published in December 1964, while the second one followed in July 1965. It provided a thorough survey of Kenya's educational resources and a comprehensive analysis of the country's educational problems. The Report was, however, too general about the fundamental issue of how to restructure the country's education system. It recommended gradual development of primary education, restriction of self-help secondary school expansion and warned that in the former non-African schools (the so-called high-cost schools) the racial factor could easily change into a social one. Many of its recommendations were implemented by the Government. It remains a basic document for an understanding of educational problems during the post-independence period.

KENYA EPISCOPAL CONFERENCE. An organization of the Catholic Bishops of Kenya, the highest decision-making body of the Catholic Church. It meets twice a year to coordinate the services of Catholic dioceses, with the Kenya Catholic Secretariat as its executive body.

KENYA EXTERNAL TELECOMMUNICATIONS COMPANY see COMMUNICATIONS AND TRANSPORT

KENYA EXTERNAL TRADE AUTHORITY, THE. A government body established in 1976, with the aim of promoting, coordinating, and developing Kenya's export trade. It coordinates the activities of the public and private sectors that participate in export trade; identifies incentives for export trade development; and assists the Government in the formulation and implementation of trade policies. It also publicizes Kenya products abroad and carries out surveys of foreign markets for Kenyan products.

KENYA INDUSTRIAL COURT, THE. Established in June 1964 by the enactment of the Trade Disputes Act. Its scope and powers were considerably enlarged by a new Trade Disputes Act of 1965. About seven years later, a new Trade Disputes (Amendment) Act was passed in 1971. The Court consists of a President (a judge of the High Court of Kenya), and four independent members. It has powers to create or modify contractual obligations between employees and employers. It has earned a reputation of being an impartial tribunal in which the workers, the employers, and the Government have faith and confidence. In this way, it has contributed significantly towards the creation and maintenance of good industrial relations and peace in Kenya.

KENYA INDUSTRIAL ESTATE LIMITED. Established by the government in 1967 to accelerate the rate of industrial development by setting up industrial estates in the large towns, and to encourage indigenous businessmen to play an increased role in industrial production. In 1971, the company was entrusted with the running of the Rural Industrial Development Program whose purpose is to stimulate industrial development in the rural sector by setting up rural development centers in the smaller towns. With an authorized share capital of K. Shs. 50 million, it promotes and finances small scale industrial projects, with preference given to those projects that promote African entrepreneurship, generate or save foreign exchange, provide substantial opportunities and make use of local raw materials. By 1980 it was operating five industrial estates at Nairobi, Mombasa, Nakuru, Kisumu, and Eldoret and eleven rural industrial development centers at Nyeri, Kakamega, Embu, Machakos, Kisii, Malindi, Voi, Kericho, Homa Bay, Meru and Murang'a. The KIE has been described as "a model for industrial promotion in Africa."

KENYA LAND FREEDOM ARMY (KLFA). Formed in mid-

1958 in Murang'a district, by former leaders of Mau
Mau, with Mbaria Kaniu, a famous forest "general,"
as Chairman. It aimed at 1) uniting the Africans for
the purpose of achieving independence; 2) ensuring that
independent government was not in the hands of loyal-
ists; and 3) securing the land in the Kenya Highlands
for the landless who had fought the imperialists. From
Murang'a, the movement extended to Nairobi, and by
early 1959 the Rift Valley Province had become the
main area of operation. The Batun Oath, which had
been used during the Mau Mau, was adopted for recruitment purposes. With the formation of KANU and
KADU in 1960, the KLFA decided to join the former as
the party that represented African interests. The KLFA
was apparently joined by a few non-Kikuyu Africans such
as Zephenia Adholla and Wasonga Sijeyo--both of whom
had been Luo militants involved in Mau Mau and detained. On July 8, 1961, the Government proscribed
the organization under its five aliases: "The Kenya
Land Freedom Army," "Kenya Land Freedom Party,"
"Kenya Parliament," "Rift Valley Government," and
"Rift Valley Parliament."

KENYA NATIONAL CHAMBER OF COMMERCE AND INDUS-
TRY. Established in 1965 to replace the racial chambers of commerce which had hitherto been a feature of
the commercial and industrial life of Kenya. Before
the amalgamation, there were the Nairobi Chamber of
Commerce, the African Chamber of Commerce, and
the Mombasa Chamber of Commerce and Agriculture.
Such racial organizations were incompatible with the
policies of independent Kenya. The then Minister for
Commerce and Industry, Dr. J. G. Kiano, accordingly
ordered their dismantling and replacement by a single
national chamber. The Chamber derives its membership from large multi-national companies in the country as well as from small individual traders. Any
business organization, large or small, can join the
Chamber as the sole representative of business interests. It has branches in all parts of the country.

KENYA NATIONAL FARMERS UNION, THE. Formed in
1948 to represent the interests of the European farmers.
It was actively supported by the then Member for Agriculture, Sir Ferdinand Cavendish-Bentinck. By 1954,
it had 1700 members. It demanded increased European
immigration, recognition of the "White Highlands" as the

focus of agricultural production in Kenya, long term
credit on easy terms for farmers, guaranteed prices
for produce, and more money for agricultural research.
In March 1957, the rules of the Union were amended to
allow farmers of any race to join the Union, but by
1962, very few African farmers had joined, largely because the Africans had their own organization: the Kenya African Farmers' Union.   Between 1962 and 1964,
however, as a result of active recruitment campaigns,
over 1700 African members joined.   In 1968, one of
the two Vice-Presidents, Mr. P. N. Sifuna, was elected
President of the Union--the first African President.   The
rival organization--the Kenya African Farmers' Union--
had also been dissolved in 1967, and the President of Kenya,
Jomo Kenyatta, had also accepted the invitation of the Union to become its Patron.   The takeover by the African
farmers was complete, and the Union could legitimately
claim to represent the Kenya Farmers' interests.

KENYA NATIONAL MUSEUM, THE.   One of the largest and
most important of its kind in tropical Africa.   Formerly known as the Coryndon Memorial Museum, the Kenya National Museum is situated on a small hill (formerly known as Ainsworth Hill) by the Nairobi river, and
is only two and a half kilometers from the city center.
The Museum is famous primarily for its natural history
collections, with vast study collections of mammals,
birds, reptiles, amphibia, fishes, molluscs, and insects.
It also houses a wide variety of other exhibits including
ones on archaeology, palaeontology and ethnography.
There are two extensions, a snake park and the National Herbarium.
        The Museum's history goes back to 1910, when
a number of enthusiastic amateur naturalists met at the
home of Sir Fredrick Jackson, Governor of Kenya (and
himself an authority on birds), and decided to form the
East Africa and Uganda Natural History Society.   To
make available to a wider public material collected by
the society, it was decided to rent a room in the center
of Nairobi in 1910, and this marked the beginning of the
Museum.   In 1914, Arthur Loveridge, who later became
world famous as Curator of Herpetology at Harvard, became the first full-time curator of the Museum, having
resigned from the National Museum of Wales.   From
then on the Museum grew rapidly in size and reputation
and was soon attracting the attention of leading scientists
from all over the world.   It was, however, not until the

time of Governor Robert Coryndon that a proper Government-subsidized museum scheme was introduced. He stressed the educational value of a museum and envisaged it as developing eventually into a large central museum with a scope wider than that of Natural History alone. When he died in 1925, it was decided to erect a Museum and research institution bearing his name as a memorial to his initiative. The Coryndon Memorial was completed in 1929, although it was not until 1937, when the Museum became known as the Coryndon Memorial Museum. The Museum was also lucky in attracting capable Curators: Loveridge 1914; Dr. V. G. L. van Someren (1929-1940); Dr. L. S. B. Leakey 1940-1961; Mr. R. H. Carcasson 1961.

In December 1964, in keeping with the new status of Kenya, the Museum changed its name to The National Museum. When L. S. B. Leakey resigned from his job as Curator, he set up the center for prehistory and palaeontology situated behind the main Museum, which he directed until his death in 1972. The center contained collections of prehistoric stone implements and fossils, including casts of the remains of Early Man. All these collections have now been moved to the new Louis Leakey Memorial Institute for African Prehistory, which was formally opened in 1977 with Professor B. A. Ogot as its first Director.

KENYA NATIONAL TRADING CORPORATION. Established in March 1965 as a non-profit-making organization to "Kenyanize" both the wholesale and retail trade. It is owned by the Kenya Government through the Industrial and Commercial Development Corporation. It participates in the export of Kenya's agricultural products as well as in the importation of items intended for consumption by Africans. It acquired shares in a Mombasa clearing and forwarding company, Wafco-Sutherland Ltd. in 1966, and in the Kenya Shipping Agency Ltd. in 1967. It controls trade in sugar, rice, salt, cotton seed oils, soaps, matches, cement, bicycles, nails, wines and spirits, and certain textiles.

KENYA NEWS AGENCY, THE. Established by an act of Parliament in 1963 to co-ordinate and speed up the free flow of international and national news. Its function is therefore to gather and disseminate news on a national basis. For the reception of international news, the Kenya News Agency has acquired interception and distribution rights from UPI, Reuters, AFP, Tass, and Tanjug. For local news, it is linked by telex circuits to all Provincial Information Offices, the national broadcasting station, Voice of Kenya, newspaper subscribers, and Kenya's diplomatic offices in the major cities of the world.

KENYA PEOPLE'S UNION (KPU). Formed by the radical wing of the Kenya African National Union (KANU) after the Limuru KANU Conference of 1966. It was registered on May 20, 1966, with Oginga Odinga as its Leader and Bildad Kaggia as Deputy Leader. Its aims were socialist, promising national control over the means of production, the distribution of free land to the landless, and free primary education. In Parliament, after the Little General Election in 1966, the KPU was represented by nine members, although the support outside the House was greater than is suggested by this number. KPU was proscribed in October 1969.

KENYA POSTS AND TELECOMMUNICATIONS CORPORATION see COMMUNICATIONS AND TRANSPORT

KENYA TEA DEVELOPMENT AUTHORITY. Established in January 1964 to take over the work and operations of the then Special Crops Development Authority. Its main objective was defined as the expansion of tea cultivation by smallholder growers. At that time, there were only 2270 acres planted with tea and owned by some 2400 growers. The scheme was widely criticized as likely to fail since small-scale agricultural development had failed in most developing countries. But thanks largely to the work of the KTDA, the Kenyan experiment has been a great success. By the beginning of 1980, there were 120,900 acres of tea owned by 126,000 small-holder tea growers, distributed in twelve tea growing districts. It operates 28 factories and about 85 percent of Kenya's tea is exported.

KENYA TOURIST DEVELOPMENT CORPORATION, THE (KTDC). This is a parastatal organization created by an Act of Parliament in 1965 and became operational in 1966. The Corporation's main task is to promote and develop tourism in Kenya, and it is the organ through which Government financial participation in the tourist industry is chanelled. Already the KTDC's investments in various projects amount to over K.Sh. 100,000,000.

KTDC is also responsible for the Kenyanization of the hotel industry. It helps Kenyans to own and manage tourist enterprises.

KENYATTA, JOMO. Born in 1890 at Gatundu in Kiambu district. He was educated at the Church of Scotland Mission, Kikuyu, outside Nairobi. From 1921 to 1926 he was employed by the Nairobi Municipality and was known as Johnstone, a name which he relinquished in favor of Jomo in 1938. He was regarded not only as one of the founders and leaders of the nationalist struggle in Kenya, but also widely recognized and respected in many African countries as one of the fathers of African nationalism. He joined the East African Association in 1922, and when this became the Kikuyu Central Association in 1924, he joined it and was elected General Secretary and editor of the association's magazine Muigwithania in 1928.

In February 1929, Kenyatta left for England as a leader of a delegation to present the Kenya African case to the British Government. He later submitted evidence to the Carter Land Commission on the Kikuyu land problem. His stay in Europe lasted fifteen years. During that time, he studied at Selly Oak College, and London School of Economics. He also studied at Moscow University and attended the International Negro Workers' Congress in Hamburg. He travelled extensively in Europe; and in 1945 attended the Pan-African Congress at Manchester as an East African representative. He returned to Kenya in September 1946 and immediately assumed the Presidency of Kenya African Union, which had been formed in 1944 under the title of the Kenya African Study Union. He took an active part in broadening the basis of its membership until October 20, 1952, when a State of Emergency was declared in Kenya and he, together with other leading nationalists, was arrested. Kenyatta together with Achieng' Oneko, Bildad Kaggia, Fred Kubai, Kungu Karumba and Paul Ngei were charged with managing Mau Mau. The trial which was held at Kapenguria court developed into one of the longest in Kenya's legal history and provoked worldwide interest and concern. Following the Privy Council's rejection of an appeal, Kenyatta and the other nationalists commenced a period of seven years' imprisonment at Lokitaung in North-Western Kenya. Later, Kenyatta was moved from Lodwar to Maralal, where he remained until August 1961.

On August 14, 1961, he was allowed to return
to his home at Gatundu in Kiambu and later freed from
all restrictions on August 21, 1961, nine years after
his arrest. He assumed Presidency of the Kenya African National Union in October of that year and in January 1962, he entered the Legislative Council, following
the action of Kariuki Njiiri in resigning his seat in Murang'a to create a vacancy. In April of that year Kenyatta was appointed Minister of State for Constitutional
Affairs and Economic Planning in the Coalition Government, 1962-63. In the 1963 elections, he was returned
unopposed as KANU Member for Thika-Gatundu. KANU
had emerged victorious from the 1963 elections, Kenyatta was therefore sworn in as Kenya's First Prime
Minister during Internal Self-Government phase of Constitutional Development. On Kenya attaining independence on December 12, 1963, he was appointed Prime
Minister and Minister for Internal Security and Defence.
He became the first President of the Republic of Kenya
on December 12, 1964. In March 1966, he was re-
appointed unopposed President of KANU. On January
29, 1970, he was sworn in as President for the second
time, and on 5th November, 1974, he was installed as
President for the third time. Much of the political
stability Kenya had enjoyed during the post-independence
period can be attributed to his wise leadership. Kenyatta died on August 22, 1978 at Mombasa. He was
the author of Facing Mount Kenya (1938), My People of
Kikuyu and the Life of Chief Wang'ombe (1942), Harambee (1964), Suffering Without Bitterness (1968).

KENYATTA, MAMA NGINA. Born in 1933 at Kiganjo in
    Kiambu. Daughter of ex-Senior Chief Muhoho. Mar-
    ried Kenyatta in September 1951. During the Emergency
    she was detained for four years and in 1959 she was
    permitted to join her husband, Mzee Jomo Kenyatta, who
    was then detained at Lodwar. Mama Ngina remained
    with him thereafter, at Lodwar and Maralal, pending the
    return of the family to Gatundu in August 1961. She
    played a prominent part in public life as the Hostess at
    Gatundu and at State House. While devoting much of
    her time to her family of two sons and two daughters,
    Mama Ngina retained an active interest in the Presi-
    dential Farm. She undertakes many duties on behalf
    of women's organizations and those concerned with child
    care. She is the patron of both the Maendeleo Ya Wan-
    awake Organization and of the Kenya Girl Guides Asso-

ciation.   Mama Ngina accompanied her husband on many
official tours and at public engagements in Kenya.

KENYATTA, MARGARET WAMBUI.   Born in Nairobi in
    1928.   Educated at Ruthimitu Primary School, the
    Church of Scotland Mission School at Thogoto and Al-
    liance High School, Kikuyu.   She went to the boys school,
    because the Alliance Girls School was not yet established.
    Taught at the Kenya Teaching Training College, Githun-
    guri, 1948-52.
        With the declaration of a State of Emergency in
    Kenya, all independent schools were closed down by the
    colonial government.   Margaret Kenyatta went to Nai-
    robi, where she worked as a telephonist, a bookbind-
    er, and book-keeper.   Joined Nairobi People's Con-
    vention Party led by Tom Mboya and the Kiambu Free-
    dom Party, 1957-59.   Founder Member of the Kenya
    National African Union (KANU) in 1960.   Elected as-
    sistant Secretary of the party in Kiambu and leader of
    its Women's wing.   From 1961 to 1963, she was a mem-
    ber of the Kiambu County Council.   She was also the
    Chairman of the Kenya Women's Seminar which, be-
    tween 1958 and 1961, tried to unite women from all
    walks of life with a view to making them aware of their
    rights.   From 1963 to 1976, she was a Member of Nai-
    robi City Council and the Mayor of Nairobi from 1969
    to 1976.   Appointed the Permanent Representative to
    UNEP in 1976 and the United Nations Habitat in 1979-
    1980.

KENYATTA CONFERENCE CENTRE, NAIROBI.   Built as a
    monument to Mzee Kenyatta's leadership.   It has a ro-
    tating restaurant on the 28th floor, above which there
    is a helio-port.   Its electronic telecommunication sys-
    tem is one of the biggest and most sophisticated in the
    world.   It was built by Facta Construction Company Lim-
    ited, at a cost of K.£3,720,000 provided by the Kenya
    Government.   This most impressive 32-storeyed confer-
    ence, office and amphitheatre complex was designed by
    the world famous architect, Karl Nostvick.

KERIRI, JOHN MATERE.   Born in 1936 to a poor family in
    Kirinyaga District, Central Province.   Educated at Gov-
    ernment Secondary School, Embu (now Kangaru High
    School--1950-57 and Makerere University College, 1958-
    62, where he graduated with a Bachelors of Arts degree
    in Economics, History and Political Science.   Keriri

was posted to Kisumu as a District Officer from where
he was posted to the Treasury in 1963 as Assistant
Secretary under the Coalition Government. He became
Senior Assistant Secretary and then Under Secretary in
1964. In 1967 he was appointed Deputy Secretary in
the Treasury. Went to the Economic Development Institute of the World Bank in Washington to take a spe-
cialized six months' course on development. On his
return, he was appointed head of the Treasury Department of the Ministry of Finance. In 1972, he was appointed the General Manager of the Development Finance
Company of Kenya (D. F. C. K.)--one of the leading financial institutions in the country founded in 1963 which
has played a leading role in the development of Kenya's
industry and tourism--a post he still holds. He is a
major shareholder in Milimani Hotel, Nairobi.

KEYO (sometimes referred to as the Elgeyo). This group
   occupies a narrow strip of land on the western bank of
   the Kerio River. A Kalenjin group, numbering about
   120,000, which lives mostly in the Elgeyo-Marakwet
   District, an area that ranges in altitude from 3,500
   feet in the Kerio Valley to 8,500 feet at the top of the
   Tambach escarpment. They also practice mixed farming, growing maize, groundnuts, coffee, wheat and
   keeping cattle, goats, and sheep.

KHAMISI, FRANCIS JOSEPH. Born in 1913 at Rabai in the
   Coast Province. Educated at Catholic High School, Kabaa. Worked with East African Meteorological Service
   (1937-39). He was editor of Baraza, a pioneer Swahili
   newspaper, 1939-45, during which period the paper
   played a leading role in winning African support for the
   British at a critical time. General Secretary of the
   Kenya African Union (KAU), the first African national
   political party, 1944-47. Appointed Chief Clerk with
   African Mercantile, Mombasa, 1948-58. Was elected
   to the Legislative Council as Member for Mombasa area,
   1958-61. Appointed to the East African Central Legislative Assembly, 1957-61. When the Pan African Movement for East and Central Africa was founded at Mwanza, Tanzania in 1958, Khamisi became its first Chairman. He was also active in local government: member of Nairobi Municipal Council 1946-47 and Mombasa
   Municipal Board 1950-60. In 1961, he went back to full-
   time journalism, and was editor of Baraza from 1961
   until its demise in 1979.

KIANO, JULIUS GIKONYO. Born on June 1, 1926, at Ka-
huti in Murang'a. Son of a farmer, he went to school
at Kagumo and Alliance High School, Kikuyu, where he
edited the handwritten Saturday Evening Paper. From
Alliance, he went to Makerere College, where in 1947,
he abruptly interrupted his studies to make preparations
to go to the United States. He entered Pioneer Business College Philadelphia where Nigerian's "Zik" started his American education. Because there was much
racial discrimination in the area, he quit the place and
went to join Ohio's Antioch College from which he graduated as Bachelor of Arts with a major in Economics.
In 1950, he joined the United Nations Trusteeship Department under Ralph Bunche. Two years later he obtained his Masters Degree and won University Honours
Fellowship from the Stanford University. In 1953 he
joined the University of California first to do his Ph.D.
and then for a year to teach Political Science. Here
he met Earnestine, a registered nurse, who became
his first wife.

Kiano returned to Kenya in 1956 and became the
first African Lecturer at the Royal Technical College
which was later to become the University of Nairobi.
In 1958, when the number of seats for African elected
members in the colonial Legislature was raised from
eight to fourteen, he stood for the Central Province
seat and won it overwhelmingly. In 1960, he was appointed Minister for Commerce and Industry in the pre-
independence caretaker Government. When he was re-
elected to the Legislative Council in 1961, he became
Parliamentary Secretary to Jomo Kenyatta in the Coalition Government. In 1963 General Elections, he was
elected to the House of Representatives as Member for
Kangema. He was again appointed Minister for Commerce and Industry. In 1966, he became Minister of
Labour and in 1968 he was transferred to the Ministry
of Education. In the same year he presided over the
African Ministers of Education Conference in Nairobi.
At the 1969 General Elections, he was elected Member
for Mbiri and was appointed Minister for Local Government. In 1973, he became, for the third time, Minister of Commerce and Industry. In that capacity he presided over the Conference of the Commonwealth African
Ministers of Trade held in Nairobi in April, 1973. In
1976, he was moved to the newly-created Ministry for
Water Resources, a post he retained until November,
1979. He was awarded by the Government the honor

of Elder of the Golden Heart. His second wife, Jane,
whom he married after divorcing the first one, is a
prominent woman leader in Kenya, and is at the moment Chairperson of Maendeleo Ya Wanawake (Organization for Women's Progress). Kiano was appointed Managing
Director of the Industrial Bank of Kenya in December 1980.

KIBACHIA, CHEGE. Born in 1920 in Kiambu; educated at
the Alliance High School, Kikuyu 1939-42. He worked
with the Kiambu Chicken and Egg Sellers 1943-45, and
East African Clothing Factory, Mombasa. He became
President of African Workers Federation, Mombasa, in
1947. Because of his trade union activities which had
become anti-colonial, he was deported to Baringo 1947-
57. He was employed in the D. O.'s office at Maralal.
In 1964, he was appointed Industrial Relations Officer
in the Labour Department at Mombasa. By the end of
the same year he became Senior Labour Officer in Mombasa. Has been a member of the Industrial Court of
Kenya since 1979.

KIBAKI, MWAI. Born in Othaya, Nyeri District in 1931,
and attended the local Kirima Mission School and Nyeri
Boys' School before going to Mangu High School in Thika.
In 1951, he went to Makerere University College from
where he graduated in 1954 with a first class honours
degree in economics, political science and history. He
won a fellowship to the London School of Economics to
study public finance which he did not take up until 1956.
He obtained a B. Sc. in public finance in 1959, and came
back to lecture in Economics at Makerere. Early in
1960, he resigned from his post and came back to Kenya to help in forming the future ruling party, the Kenya
African National Union (KANU). He played a significant
role in drafting the original KANU constitution and manifesto. In 1961, he was appointed National Executive Officer of KANU, and his first task was to organize the
"Kenyatta Election" of 1961. This was the first national
election in which Africans in Kenya were allowed to participate. From 1962 to 1963, he was a Member of the
East African Central Legislative Assembly. In 1963,
Kibaki was elected an MP for Bahati in Nairobi, a Constituency which he served until 1974 when he went back
to his home area, Othaya. In 1963, he was again elected
as C. L. A. Member as well as being Parliamentary Secretary to the Treasury. In 1965 he was appointed Chairman of the Planning Commission in the Ministry, which
in 1964 developed into a full-fledged Ministry of Economic

Planning and Development under the late Tom Mboya.
Kibaki became Assistant Minister in the new Ministry.
In 1966 he was appointed Minister of Commerce and
Industry and his main job was to Africanize Commerce
and Industry. After the 1969 General Elections, Kibaki
replaced Gichuru at the Ministry of Finance which was
merged with planning again. Re-elected Member of
Parliament for Othaya in 1974, and re-appointed Minister for Finance Economic Planning. Appointed Vice-
President and Minister for Finance by President Moi
on October 11, 1978. Re-elected to Parliament as Member for Othaya in 1979, and re-appointed Vice-President
and Minister for Finance. He has thus been involved
in evolving the economic policies of Kenya since 1963.

KIKUYU see GIKUYU

KIKUYU ASSOCIATION. Following the end of the First
World War, Central Kenya, like other parts of the country, was faced with several disasters: drought, famine,
Spanish influenza. The demobilized Africans were ig-
nored and, instead, taxes were increased, the government planned massive recruitment of cheap labor for
white settlers, and, worse still, the Soldier Settlement
Scheme was formulated to encourage British war veter-
ans to settle in Kenya. The Kikuyu Association was
formed by Kiambu Chiefs in 1919 to protect their land
from further alienation. Chief Koinange was elected
President, Philip Karanja Secretary, and Josiah Njonjo
and Waruhiu were active members.
        Initially the Association worked closely with the
missionaries. It requested a survey of farms in Kiambu and the issuing of title deeds to landholders. They
also made representation to the government about other
grievances such as forced labor, registration, taxes
etc. Unfortunately, the Kikuyu Association increasingly
came to be associated with the Native Authority in Kiambu. The Government supported it because it was
moderate compared with the militant Kikuyu Central Association. The Association testified before two parliamentary commissions, the Ormsby-Gore Commission in
1924 and the Hilton Young Commission in 1928. Membership, though not confined to chiefs, was largely el-
derly and conservative. Most of them were also land-
owners.
        From 1925 the Association dominated the Kiambu
Local Native Council, which it turned into a modernizing

agency concerned with agricultural improvement, educational expansion and the abolition of customs that, in its view, retarded development. During the female circumcision controversy from 1929, the Association supported the missionaries who were under severe attack by the KCA. The reputation of the KA suffered considerably. But the good performance of Koinange in London when he gave evidence before the Joint Select Committee on Closer Union, angered the colonial government in Kenya. They threatened to proscribe the KA. In 1931, the leaders of the Association decided to change its name to "Kikuyu Loyal Patriots." In 1932-34, when the Kenya Land Commission was making their inquiry into African land grievances, the KLP and the KCA worked closely together.

KIKUYU CENTRAL ASSOCIATION, THE (KCA). A militant pan-Kikuyu political association which emerged from the ashes of the East African Association (EAA) in 1925 and dominated the inter-war period until it was proscribed in 1940 during the Second World War. Started in Murang'a, with the encouragement of the missionary H. D. Hooper of Kahuhia who, it is said, encouraged his African converts to abandon the pan-Kenyan approach of Harry Thuku's EAA and to alter the focus of their organization to a pan-Kikuyu one. The colonial government also demanded that they have a European as advisor as a condition of government support and recognition. Hence, Hooper did for the Kikuyu what W. E. Owen did in Nyanza in transforming the Young Kavirondo Association into Kavirondo Taxpayers Welfare Association.

From Murang'a, the KCA expanded into Kiambu and Nairobi, where they engaged Johnstone Kenyatta as general secretary and editor of its publication Muigwithania. On the whole KCA operated within the colonial framework and emphasized self-help activities more than self-government. Its other main objective was to unite the Kikuyu. As Kenyatta put it:

> The KCA seeks night and day for that which will cause all Kikuyu to be one mind, educated and uneducated, ceasing to ask each other what school or mission do you belong to or saying to each other, "you are not a reader." For if there could be an end to things like these, the country of the Kikuyu could go ahead in peace.

It sent Kenyatta to England to plead the cause of the

African.   The KCA used the female circumcision controversy of 1929 to mobilize the Kikuyu for political
goals.   The controversy also led to the founding of independent churches and schools as a means of assert-
ing cultural independence.

KIKUYU INDEPENDENT SCHOOLS ASSOCIATION, THE.   As
a result of the female circumcision controversy in Kikuyuland, which led to the missionaries' final ultimatum
on the issue in 1929, many Kikuyu leaders decided to
start their own schools.   In August 1934, the Kikuyu
Independent Schools Association was launched at Gituamba in Murang'a.   Johana Kunyiha from Nyeri and Hezek-
ia Gachui from Murang'a were later in the month elected
to be President and Vice-President respectively.   In
1935, Archbishop Alexander of the African Orthodox
Church based in South Africa visited Kenya under the
auspices of KISA.   He founded a seminary at Gituamba
where he trained candidates from the different districts.
In 1937, when Archbishop Alexander was leaving, having ordained Daudi Maina of Murang'a, Harrison Gachokia of Kiambu, and Philip Kiandi of Nyeri on June 27,
1937, a disagreement occurred between him and the
KISA leaders.   The Archbishop wanted the Kenya Church
to be subordinated to his African Orthodox Church and
to remit funds to him in South Africa.   This was unac-
ceptable to KISA leaders, who proceeded to establish
the African Independent Pentecostal Church under the
leadership of Maina and Gachokia.   The KISA developed
churches and schools in central Kenya.   After 1945
the Association extended its work to Kericho and Ukambani.   Over two hundred schools were started in this
self-help way.   With the declaration of the State of
Emergency in 1952, the independent schools were closed
down.

KIKUYU LOYAL PATRIOTS   see   KIKUYU ASSOCIATION

KIMATHI, DEDAN (known during the Mau Mau war as Field
Marshall Dedan Kimathi).   Born on October 31, 1920,
in Thegenge village of Tetu location in Nyeri.   He was
educated at Karunaini school in Tetu location.   He spent
a month in the army in 1941, and then did various jobs
such as clerk, trader, teacher and farm worker.   He
joined the Kenya African Union (KAU) in 1946, and soon
became an active member.   He joined the Forty Group
(the militant wing of the defunct Kikuyu Central Associa-

tion) in 1951. In the same year he became a youth
winger and organizer of KAU. In the middle of 1952,
he was elected branch Secretary of the KAU in the Ol
Kalou and Thomson's Falls area. He also became an
important oath administrator in the area.

Kimathi was suspected of being implicated in the
murder of Senior Chief Nderi Wang'ombe of Thegenge
location, Nyeri, on October 22, 1952. He was arrested, but managed to escape into the Aberdare forest with
a big following from North Tetu Division and other parts
of Nyeri. He superseded Stanley Mathenge as the leader of forest fighters. He formed the Kenya Defence
Council to coordinate forest fighting. He was elected
President of the Council and Field Marshall in the Kenya Land and Freedom Army. In 1955, the security
forces formed the pseudo gangs of freedom fighters who
had surrendered and had agreed to cooperate with the
government. Led by Ian Henderson, these gangs eventually traced the whereabouts of Kimathi. He was captured on October 21, 1956, after being severely wounded in the thigh. On November 19, 1956, he was charged
with being in unlawful possession of firearms and six
rounds of ammunition at the Supreme Court in Nyeri.
On November 25, 1956, he was found guilty on both
charges and was executed in a Nairobi prison on February 18, 1957. The greatest of the Mau Mau leaders,
Kimathi refused to accept defeat, and his name lives on
as one of the greatest freedom fighters of Kenya.

KINANGOP. A mountain in the Nyandarua range. It is
12,816 feet high. Its name is derived from the Masai
word "Ilkinopop" meaning "the owners of the land."
According to Masai tradition, the area originally belonged to the Laikipiak Masai, who were defeated and
dispersed by the Purko in about 1875. It was the Purko
who gave the name to the area.

KINYANJUI WA GATHIRIMO. Undoubtedly one of the leading colonial Kikuyu chiefs. He was born about 1867.
He was a hunter with no property and no traditional
standing. He owed his rise to power to British favor
and acted as a guide for the Imperial British East Africa Company (IBEA Co.). He worked with Captain
Smith to open a new station among the Kikuyu, and it
was in recognition of his services to the Fort Smith
garrison that he was made a chief in 1892. In 1908,
he was appointed Paramount Chief of the Kikuyu, although

his authority was only limited to Kiambu. Like many
Kikuyu colonial chiefs, Kinyanjui soon drew most of his
economic and political support from his landholdings.
He emerged as the largest landholder in Kiambu. These
properties gave him many tenants who depended on him
for their livelihood. He had sixty wives. Kinyanjui
died on March 1, 1929, at the hospital of the Scottish
Mission, Kikuyu, at the age of sixty-two.

"KIPANDE" SYSTEM. This system of personal registration
was introduced into Kenya after World War I, and was
applied solely to the African population. The system
then introduced--The Native Registration Ordinance, com-
monly referred to as the "Kipande" Ordinance--provided
for registration of movement, labor control, and statis-
tics. The system was rigidly applied and it was used
as a means of supervision and control in a manner in
which a civil registration system is not normally used.
The police had the right to demand the "kipande"--an
identity disc--at all times, even when a person was
patently on his lawful business; a high fee was imposed
for the issue of a duplicate "kipande," out of proportion
to its cost. The Africans were totally opposed to the
system.

        In May 1946, a Sub-Committee of the Labour Ad-
visory Board was appointed by the Government to investigate and report upon this matter. It consisted of the
Labour Commissioner as Chairman (the only official),
with two Europeans, one Asian and two Africans as
Members. After an exhaustive survey, including visits
to most parts of the country, where evidence was taken
from representatives of all communities, the Committee
came to the conclusion that the "kipande" system had to
be abandoned. It recommended the repeal of the Native
Registration Ordinance and its replacement by the Registration of Persons Ordinance, which was to apply to
all races. The "kipande" disc was to be replaced by
an identity document. The identification system for all
races was to be backed by finger prints and was to apply, as did the "kipande" system, only to male persons
over the age of sixteen years.

        The Government accepted these recommendations
which were embodied in the Registration of Persons Ordinance, enacted in December 1947. One other important aspect of the new identity cards was that no par-
ticulars of employment were to be entered on them. In
other words, Identity Records were to be divorced from

Employment Records. The Central Registration office was to be in charge of the former, while the Labour Department became responsible for employment records. Furthermore, the Identity Card was not to be carried at all times. This is the position which still holds, with the only major modification being that all persons over the age of sixteen, male and female, must now have identity cards.

KIPSIGIS. The largest of the Kalenjin groups, numbering about half a million. They occupy the highland region (altitude ranging from five to eight thousand feet) around Kericho town. The climate is cool and the rainfall is good; and they grow tea, pyrethrum and maize, besides keeping cattle. For the early history, see KALENJIN.

KISUMU. This town, whose local name is "Wi nam," meaning "the head of the lake," stands on the shores of Lake Victoria at an altitude of 3,725 feet. It was founded in 1900 largely as a railway terminus and a lake port. It is today the chief port on Lake Victoria and the third biggest town in Kenya, with a projected population of about 150,000. It is also the commercial center of the growing Western Kenya region which is a main source of grain supply and the main sugar growing region. For some years it was the terminus of Imperial Airways and with the switch over to flying boats it looked as if it would become the main airport for Kenya and Uganda. However, when airplanes replaced flying boats, Nairobi and Entebbe airports superseded Kisumu.

KITALE. This town is located to the east of Mount Elgon at an altitude of 6,200 feet. It is the center of the rich farmland of Trans-Nzoia district, which during the colonial period, was the home of Boer settlers in Kenya. The district produces coffee, dairy produce, pyrethrum, maize, wheat, and tea. It has a projected population of about 20,000 persons.

KIVOI. The most powerful merchant leader in mid-nineteenth century Ukambani. His early life remains obscure, but his rise to eminence was probably tied in with the general development of the Kamba long-distance trade in the 19th century. By the 1840's, he was being referred to as a "merchant prince" because he also exercised considerable political power in a wide region. He directed a large network of ivory caravans between central

Kenya, northern Tanzania and Mombasa. He operated
from his base at Kitui through agents. He was also
reputed to be a rain-maker and a ritual expert. He
met the German missionary Johann Krapf, whom he
took to see Mt. Kenya in 1849. He was killed in 1851
on the Tana River by rival traders in the company of
Krapf.

KOINANGE, MBIYU. Educationist and politician, born in
1907 at Njunu in Kiambu District. Educated at A.C.
Mission School Kiambaa; Kabete Primary School; Buxton High School; Mombasa Alliance High School, Kikuyu,
1926-27; Hampton Institute, Virginia, U.S.A., 1927-31;
and Ohio Wesleyan University, U.S.A., 1931-35, where
he obtained a B.A. degree in sociology and political
science. He then went to Teachers' College, Columbia
University, 1935-36, where he earned an M.A. degree.
From the U.S.A. he went to Britain, first to St. John's
College, Cambridge, 1936-37, where he did a Post-
Graduate Certificate in Education; and then, from 1937-
1938, he took a teaching diploma at the Institute of Education, University of London. Back in Kenya, he founded the Kenya Teachers' College, Githunguri in 1939,
and was its principal until 1948. He was a founder
member of the Kenya African Union (KAU) in 1946 and
its representative in Europe, 1951-1959. He then went
to Ghana at the invitation of Kwame Nkrumah to be Director for Eastern, Central and South Africa, Bureau
of African Affairs, Ghana, 1959-60. From Ghana he
moved to Dar-es-Salaam to become the Secretary-General for Pan African Freedom Movement for East, Central and South Africa (PAFMECA). With the approach-
ing independence of Kenya, he moved back to Kenya,
entered Parliament and was appointed Minister of State
for Pan-African Affairs, Kenya 1963-65; Minister for
Education 1965-66; Minister of State, office of the President, 1966-69; Minister of State for Foreign Affairs,
1969-71; Minister of State in the President's Office,
1971-78; Minister for Natural Resources 1978-79. He
is the author of People of Kenya Speak for Themselves.

KOINANGE WA MBIYU. Estimated date of birth is between
1878 and 1881. He belonged to mbari ya Njunu, a lineage that owned much land in southern Kiambu. In
1905, he was appointed headman under his father, Mbiyu,
who was Chief. In 1908, Koinange replaced his aging
father as chief, and was to remain in office until he

retired in 1949. He thus served the colonial government faithfully and with distinction for 45 years. He
became Senior Chief in 1938. He was converted to
Christianity by Canon Harry Leakey of the Church Missionary Society; provided land for a mission school at
Kiambaa.

    Though a colonial Chief, Koinange was deeply in-
volved in Kikuyu and African politics from 1919 to 1952.
He was particularly concerned about the alienation of
Kikuyu land to European settlers. In 1919, at a meeting of all the Kiambu chiefs, at Kinyanjui's home in
Riruta, the Kikuyu Association was founded with Koin-
ange as its President, Philip Karanja its Secretary and
Josiah Njonjo and Waruhiu as active members. The
Association also concerned itself with other grievances
such as forced labor, registration, taxes, and wages.
When the Local Native Councils were established in
1925, Koinange, through Kikuyu Association, dominated
the Kiambu Council. He was one of the African representatives from Kenya (the other two were Apindi and
Mutua) chosen by the government to testify before the
Joint Select Committee on Closer Union in London,
where he performed well. He demanded the restriction
of alienated lands, expansion of African education, and
the appointment of Africans to the Legislative Council.

    When the Kenya Land Commission was appointed
in 1932, Koinange played a leading role in co-ordinating
the evidence from Kiambu that was to be presented to
the Commission. The Report of the Land Commission,
published in May 1934, disappointed and disillusioned
him. He soon abandoned the moderate, constitutional
path for which he had been highly praised and joined
militant politics. His relationship with Kikuyu Central
Association became closer. He played a prominent
role in raising funds for the Teachers' College at Githunguri. He became a close friend of Kenyatta from
1946. He was appointed a member of the Executive
Committee of the Kenya African Union. In 1949, he
retired from the government and devoted the rest of
his life to politics. He was detained at Marsabit (1953)
and on March 22, 1958, was sent to Kabarnet township
to live in restricted residence. On June 30, 1960, he
returned to Kiambu, but was restricted to the house of
his son, Chief Charles Koinange, where he died in July
1960. A formidable Kikuyu and Kenya leader thus
passed away.

KRAPF, JOHANN LUDWIG. One of the most outstanding

missionary pioneers in East Africa. He played a leading role in the exploration and evangelization of the region in the 19th century. He was also an acute ob-
server of the African scene. Krapf was born on January 11, 1810, in the village of Derendingen in Germany. He was educated at the Basle Mission School,
1827-29, and in Tubingen, where he completed his theological studies in 1834. After working as Vicar in various places, he returned to Basle in 1836. In February
1837, he left Basle for Ethiopia. Remained in Ethiopia
until 1843 when he was refused entry into Shoa. He decided to follow the Galla--"the Germans of Africa," as
Krapf saw them--southwards into East Africa. In 1844,
he went to Zanzibar via Aden, Brava, Takaungu, Mombasa, Tanga, and Pangani. Took residence in Mombasa
in May 1844. He decided to learn something about the
geography and ethnography of East Africa as well as to
evangelize the coastal region.

Following the arrival of Johann Rebmann (another German missionary-explorer) in June 1846, Krapf
decided to establish a mission at Rabai in September
1846.   Between 1847-1849, he and Rebmann made six
major journeys inland. It was during this period that
they saw the snow-capped mountains of Kilimanjaro
and Kenya--the first Europeans to do so. Krapf
aimed at establishing a chain of missionary stations
between Rabai and Unyamwezi. His plan was accepted by the C.M.S. in 1850. He made his second
journey to Ukambani in July-September 1951. Because
of disagreement with his colleagues, the Rabai mission
did not succeed in its goal as envisaged by Krapf. In
1855, he returned to Germany via London, Jerusalem,
Massawa, Khartoum, and Cairo. He settled at Kornthal
near Stuttgart. Between 1855 and 1858, he worked on
a book about his life as a missionary in Africa.

Krapf returned with the United Methodist Free
Churches Mission to East Africa in January 1862. He
was still keen to go back to Ethiopia. In October 1867,
he joined Sir Robert Napier's expedition to Ethiopia as
a military interpreter. In February 1868, he was certi-
fied medically unfit for the job. He went back to Würt-
temberg where he remained for the rest of his life con-
centrating on linguistic work. He wrote over 25 books
including Travels, Researches, and Missionary Labours
During an Eighteen Years' Residence in Eastern Africa
(London, 1860); Outline of the Elements of the Ki-Swahili

Language (Tubingen, 1850); Vocabulary of Six East African Languages (Tubingen, 1850); Dictionary of the Swahili Language, ed. R. N. Cust (London, 1882). He died on November 25, 1881.

Several German missions were formed in response to his work: the Bavarian Evangelical Lutheran Society, which established three stations in Ukambani, Kenya, from 1886; the Leipzig Evangelical Lutheran Mission, which succeeded the B.E.L.S. in 1893; and the Berlin Evangelical Missionary Society, which established stations in German East Africa (future Tanganyika).

KUBAI, FRED. Born of a Kikuyu father and a Giriama mother on April 15, 1915, in Mombasa. Educated privately. He worked as a telegraphist with the East African Posts and Telegraphs Department 1931-46. He then turned his attention to trade unionism and it is as a pioneer trade unionist that he is largely remembered. He became Organizer of the African Workers Federation in 1946; Organizing Secretary of the Kenya African Road Transport and Mechanics Union (later Transport and Allied Workers Union) in 1947; Acting General Secretary in 1948. With the late Makhan Singh, he formed the East African Trade Union Congress in 1949 of which he became President. The Congress organized a boycott of the celebrations marking the award of a Royal Charter to the city of Nairobi in 1950. Kubai was arrested for the resulting disturbance and acquitted in 1950. He became Chairman of the Nairobi branch of the Kenya African Union (KAU) 1951, and editor of Sauti Ya Mwafrika, 1951. He was arrested, tried, and convicted with Jomo Kenyatta 1952-53; imprisoned and restricted up to 1961 when he was released. He tried and failed to take over the leadership of trade unionism in Kenya from Tom Mboya. In the General Election of 1963 he won the Nakuru East Seat for KANU. He was appointed a Junior Minister in the Ministry of Labour and Social Services. In the 1969 General Election he retained his Nakuru East Seat and was appointed Assistant Minister for Labour. He lost his seat in the 1974 General Election, and has since devoted his time to business.

KUNGU WA KARUMBA. Born about 1895 in Murang'a from where his father, Karumba wa Kungu, migrated to Ndeiya in Kiambu in the same year. His father died in 1905 and his two brothers, who had been conscripted

into the Carrier Corps in 1915 to assist British troops,
disappeared in Tanganyika. He spent most of his youth
looking after their goats and cattle. In 1912, he was
involved in a skirmish with Masai cattle raiders, as a
result of which he lost his left eye. He then became a
stock trader, travelling widely in Kiambu. In 1921, he
was one of the inhabitants of Ndeiya who was evicted to
make room for European settlement. He went to the
Rift Valley as a squatter and was employed on the farm
of a Major Stephenson, who was a mixed farmer. He
was given an acre on which he grew maize and potatoes.
It was in the Rift Valley that he first became interested
in politics, especially after attending a meeting in Naivasha addressed by Harry Thuku in early 1922. He also decided to learn how to read and write so that he
could read political letters that were being circulated
then. He was one of the laborers from the Rift Valley
who demonstrated in Nairobi on March 15, 1922, following the arrest of Harry Thuku on the previous day.
In 1930, he left Major Stephenson's farm and went back
to Kiambu to settle at Rireni in Limuru, where he continued with his old occupation of keeping cattle and goats.
        Kungu became a member of the Kikuyu Central
Association at this time and rose in 1935 to be the
Propaganda Secretary of the KCA in Kiambu. In 1940,
KCA was proscribed, although Kungu Karumba continued
to be active in politics. During the war, he became a
businessman, establishing a grocers' shop at Kikuyu
station. In 1943 he was appointed Councillor to the
Kiambu Local Council, Chura Division. At the same
time, he was appointed an elder of the Chura Tribunal
Court, which dealt largely with land disputes. Following the founding of the Kenya African Union, and especially the assumption of Presidency of the Union by Jomo
Kenyatta in 1947, many Kikuyu, including, Kungu Karumba, decided to join KAU. He was elected Chairman of
the Chura Division of KAU which covered Limuru, Kabete, Muguga, Dagoretti and Kiambaa areas of Kiambu.
On October 20, 1952, he was one of the KAU leaders
arrested and later charged with managing Mau Mau.
He was sentenced, together with Kenyatta, to seven
years imprisonment. He was released in June 1960
and returned to his home at Ndeiya. He was the only
one of the six detainees who were together with Kenyatta
who did not enter politics on his release, although for
a short time--December 1961 to June 1963--he was
Chairman of KANU's Ndeiya branch.

With a loan from the Kenya Government, Kungu
started the "Wanainchi Transport Company" of which he
became the Managing Director by virtue of owning majority shares.   The Company owned by 1974, twenty
buses, twenty trucks, and several bars and hotels in
Nairobi, Kisumu, Mombasa and Malindi.   The total capital stood at £100,000.   In June 1974, he disappeared
mysteriously.   Some people believe he was killed in
Uganda while others think he was killed in Kenya, possibly in the same way as J. M. Kariuki.

KURIA.   A Bantu group living in the South Nyanza District
in Western Kenya.   Today the majority of them live in
northern Tanzania.   They claim to have moved into Kenya from the Elgon region of Eastern Uganda, and evolved
into the present group between about 1500 and 1900.
They cultivate millet, maize, bananas and tobacco, and
keep cattle.   The section in Kenya numbers about 80,000.

- L -

LAIBON.   The term for a religious and ritual Masai leader
whose powers were normally advisory and consultative
rather than executive.   For instance, Mbatiany was a
powerful laibon in the late nineteenth century and he
was the father of Lenana and Sendeyu.

LAMU.   An ancient town on the East Coast with a long and
continuous history.   Famous for beautifully carved wood-
en doors and crafts.   It is also famous for elegant
mosques.

LAMWIA.   The highest and southernmost of the four distinct
peaks of the Ngong Hills which lie in the Rift Valley
about fifteen miles southwest of Nairobi.   The word is
derived from the Masai word "llemuya," which is another name for the famous Oloiboni (ritual expert) clan.
Indeed, the Masai name for Ngong Hills is Oloo-Laiserr,
which is a name for the descent group to which the Oloiboni clan belongs.   The hills feature prominently in
the Masai myths dealing with the origin of the ritual experts or the Oloiboni family.

LANCASTER HOUSE CONFERENCE 1960, THE.   The African Members of the Legislative Council had refused to
cooperate in the implementation of the imposed Lennox-

Boyd Constitution of 1958, and were demanding a constitutional conference to work out a political structure
for an independent Kenya. In October 1959, the Kenya
Government issued a Sessional Paper on the Report of
the East Africa Royal Commission 1953-55. According to the Paper, all racial barriers were to be removed including educational and land barriers. This
marked the end of the "White Highlands." In the same
month Ian Macleod succeeded Lennox-Boyd as Colonial
Secretary after a British General Election. In November 1959, he ended the State of Emergency.

The stage was now set for a Constitution Conference, which was held in January 1960. It was to be
attended by Members of the Legislative Council only.
The African members, led by Ronald Ngala as Chairman
and Tom Mboya as Secretary, demanded a common roll
on a one-man/one-vote basis and a majority in the
Council of Ministers. The European members were
divided into two groups: The New Kenya Group led by
Michael Blundell accepted the principle of multi-racialism and a common franchise, but with certain seats reserved for minority groups. It demanded constitutional
safeguards, especially those affecting private property.
The second group, the United Party, led by Group Captain Briggs, represented the die-hards, who were fighting for a rearguard action. They demanded "provincial
autonomy," a kind of regionalism. The majority of
Asian members were cautious, demanding safeguards
and special representation for minorities. The Arab
member wanted coastal autonomy and the Somali member demanded secession.

After one month of negotiations, during which no
agreement was reached, Macleod produced his own constitution. According to this, the Legislative Council
was to consist of 65 elected members, 53 of whom were
to be elected on a common roll, and 12 who were to be National Members (formerly known as Specially Elected
Members). Only elected members were to vote for National Members. Out of the 53 elected members, 20
were to be communally reserved: 10 for Europeans, 8
for Asians and 2 for Arabs. The rest were open to
contest by anyone. The Governor retained the right to
nominate members to the Legislative Council. The number of Ministers in the Council of Ministers was to be
reduced to twelve, of whom only four were to be officials. Out of the eight elected Ministers, four were to
be Africans, three Europeans and one Asian. The right

to appoint Ministers and allocate portfolios rested with
the Governor. Regarding safeguards, Macleod suggested a Bill of Rights. Property was not to be expropri-
ated without adequate compensation being paid. The independence of the judiciary was to be preserved through
the appointment of an independent Judicial Service Commission. Kenya was therefore to be an African country
and the Conference marked in a real sense the end of
an era.

LANCASTER HOUSE CONFERENCE 1962, THE. The Second
Lancaster House Conference took seven weeks, from
the middle of February to early April 1962. Its aim
was to draw up the independence constitution. The result produced after protracted and bitter negotiations
was the self-government Constitution. The office of
the Prime Minister, to be appointed by the Governor,
was created for the first time in Kenya. He was to
be the leader of the majority party in the House of Representatives. The Governor was to continue to be responsible for defense, external affairs, and internal security. The name and form of the legislature was
changed to the Central Legislature (later renamed Parliament at independence) consisting of the National Assembly and the Queen. The former became bi-cameral,
with the House of Representatives as the Lower House,
and the Senate as the Upper House. The constitution
also introduced regionalism (popularly known by the
Swahili word "majimbo") which divided the country into
seven regions, each with its own legislative and executive powers.

LANCASTER HOUSE CONFERENCE 1963, THE. This conference was held in London in September 1963 to final-
ize the constitutional arrangements for the granting of
independence. Procedures for amendment to the Kenya
constitution were reviewed. Specially entrenched provisions of the Constitution were to include chapters on
citizenship and fundamental rights, sections dealing with
the composition of, elections to, and the powers of the
Senate, the Structure of the Regions, provisions to alter
regional boundaries and transactions in tribal land. The
legislative and the executive authority of the Regions
were not entrenched, and this made it easy to whittle
down the powers of the Regions. The Conference also
decided to declare Kenya a dominion rather than a republic on December 12, 1963.

LAND AND AGRICULTURAL BANK OF KENYA. Established
by the Land Bank Ordinance, 1930 (No. 3 of 1931) and
came into operation on March 3, 1931. Its functions
were to invest public funds and provide credit for crops
and stock in Kenya. It was amalgamated with the Agricultural Finance Corporation in 1968.

LATHBURY, GENERAL SIR GERALD (GCB, DSO, MBE).
Born on 14 July, 1906. He was educated at Wellington
College and Sandhurst. In 1926 he was commissioned
into the Oxfordshire and Buckinghamshire Light Infantry;
seconded to the Royal West African Frontier Force in
1928 and then served with the Gold Coast Regiment from
1928-33. Between 1937-38 he was at the Staff College
and served in France in 1940, being made MBE for his
services. He then joined the Airborne Forces, serving
in North Africa, Sicily and Italy, and was awarded the
DSO in 1943. He commanded a brigade in the Arnhem
operation in 1944. He attended the Imperial Defence
College in 1948, from where he went to command the
16th Airborne Division (TA) as a Major-General. From
1951-53 he was Commandant of the Staff College. In
1954 he was appointed Vice Adjutant-General. Then in
1955 he came to Kenya as Commander-in-Chief, East
Africa to lead the colonial forces against the Mau Mau
movement. He was made KCB in 1956 for his work in
Kenya and on his return home in 1957, he was promoted
Lieutenant-General and appointed Director-General of
military training. In 1960 he was appointed GOC-in-C
Eastern Command and promoted General, and in 1961
he became Quarter-Master-General to the Forces. In
August 1965 he was appointed Governor and Commander-
in-Chief of Gibraltar at a time when Anglo-Spanish relations were strained. He retired in 1969. His main
hobbies were wild life conservation and ornithology. He
died on May 16, 1978.

LEAKEY, LOUIS SEYMOUR BAZETT. Born at Kabete,
Kenya in 1903. A scientific pioneer who spent nearly
half a century researching for the origins of man and
his close evolutionary kin. Leakey was educated at Wey-
mouth College 1920-22 and Cambridge University 1922-
26, where he obtained a B.A. and a Ph.D. in 1929.
He led a British Museum Expedition to Tanganyika in
1923 and East African Archaeological Expeditions 1926-
39. He was curator of Coryndon Museum, Nairobi 1940-
61, and Honorary Director, National Museum Centre for

Prehistory and Palaeontology 1962-1972. Leakey wrote
several books including The Stone Age Cultures of Kenya Colony (1931), Adam's Ancestors: The Evolution of
Man and His Culture (1934), The Stone Age Races of
Kenya (1935), Kenya: Contrasts and Problems (1936),
Stone Age Africa (1936), White African (1937), Olduvai
Gorge (1951), Defeating Mau Mau (1954), Mau Mau and
the Kikuyu (1955), The Progress and Evolution of Man
in Africa (1961), Olduvai Gorge, Volume I (1967), Animals of East Africa (1969), Unveiling Man's Origins
(with V. M. Goodall) (1969), By Evidence: Memoirs,
1932-1951 (1974), and A Social History of the Kikuyu
People in three volumes, written before World War II,
but published posthumously in 1978. He was awarded
honorary degrees by several universities: Hon. D. Sc.
Oxford (1958), Hon. D. Law (California) 1963; Hon.
D. Sc. University of East Africa 1965. Fellow of British
Academy. Died in October 1972.

LEGISLATIVE COUNCIL. In 1905 the British Imperial Government promulgated a new Order in Council which represented an important stage in the constitutional development of Kenya. The Order did two things: 1) it
changed the designation of the protectorate's chief officer from Commissioner to Governor and Commander-
in-Chief; and 2) it established two key institutions--the
Legislative Council and the Executive Council. The
main function of the former was to make laws for the
protectorate. This meant that the Commissioner (renamed Governor) could no longer make laws on his own.
The members were to be appointed by the Governor who
himself was to be the Chairman of the Council. From
its inception, the Council associated the unofficials in
the country with law-making. In this lay its great potential as an important and independent body--the body
that was to evolve into the National Assembly--the Parliament of an independent Kenya. Much of the debate
about Kenya politics and development from 1907, when
it was established, to 1963 when it was transformed into the National Assembly, took place in this Council.
The Constitutional development of Kenya also revolved
around the Council. It started with six official members and two unofficials, all of them Europeans and all
nominated. The elective principle was soon raised, although it was not until 1919, when it was granted to the
Europeans only. It provided for full adult white suffrage
--men and women. Kenya thus became the first place

in the British Empire (outside Britain) to give the vote
to women. Eleven elected seats were provided. Next
was the question of extending the franchise to the Indians, Arabs, and Africans. Closely tied to it was the
issue of whether communal or common rolls should be
adopted. The Europeans, on the other hand, were now
demanding a majority of unofficials in the Council in
order to entrench European influence in the country.
In 1924, provision was made for five Indian members
and one Arab member to be elected to the Council on
communal rolls. Africans were to be represented by
missionaries. This was not to change until 1944 when
Eliud Wambu Mathu was appointed to represent Africans.
The issue of the composition and powers of the Council
was not resolved until 1963.

LENANA (or Olonana). A Masai laibon or ritual leader.
A son of Mbatiany had a succession dispute with his
brother Sendeyo. Consequently, the Masai who had
been united under Mbatiany were now split into two
groups. The British who arrived at this time decided
to recognize Lenana as the official laibon. He signed
the Masai treaty of 1904 which gave some of the Masai
land to the white settlers and which was supposed to
safeguard the interests of the Masai in perpetuity. But
the agreement was abrogated in 1911, apparently with
the support of Lenana, and the Masai in Laikipia had
to be moved to Narok and Kajiado to make room for
European settlers.

LENNOX-BOYD, ALAN (later, Viscount Boyd of Merton).
Born in 1904. He was a Member of Parliament for
mid-Bedfordshire. Minister of State for Colonial Affairs 1951-52. Minister of Transport and Civil Aviation 1952-4. Secretary of State for the Colonies 1954-
59. It was at this time that he introduced the Lennox-
Boyd Constitution in 1958, which increased the number
of African elected members in Kenya from eight to fourteen and which introduced a special category of members known as Specially Elected Members.

LENNOX-BOYD CONSTITUTION, THE. Officially known as
the Kenya (Constitution) Order in Council, 1958 (S.I. 600),
it was named after the then British Colonial Secretary,
Alan Lennox-Boyd (later Lord Boyd). The previous
constitution--the Lyttelton Constitution--which had been
introduced in 1954, was meant to last until 1960. But

in 1957, the first direct election of African Members of the Legislative Council had taken place, bringing in a determined group of eight African legislators who were opposed to the constitution under which they had been elected.   The eight elected members (Mboya, Odinga, Ngala, Moi, Muliro, Oguda, Mate and Muimi) adopted a policy of non-cooperation, and refused to accept a post allocated to them in the Council of Ministers.   The Colonial Secretary Lennox-Boyd imposed a new constitution through an Order in Council.   According to the new constitution, the number of African elected members was to be increased from eight to fourteen, equal to the number of European elected members.   Secondly, a special category of members known as Specially Elected Members was introduced.   Four Africans, four Europeans, and four Asians (including Arabs) were to be elected by the Legislative Council--elected and nominated members--sitting as an electorate college.   This was regarded as a move away from communal rolls.   Also, no further seats were in the future to be established on a communal basis.   Thirdly, a Council of State consisting of a Chairman and ten members appointed by the Governor was set up in order to protect the racial communities against discriminatory legislation.   Its main function was to study new bills to ensure that none was discriminatory.   The constitution also enlarged the Council of Ministers to sixteen, half of whom had to be elected members.   The Executive Council was abolished.   The African members rejected the new constitution as not going far enough and demanded a constitutional conference, which was later held in 1960--the first Lancaster House Conference.

"LITTLE GENERAL ELECTION."   In March 1966, a KANU Conference, the first since October 1962, was called at Limuru to consider a new party constitution.   Elections for offices were also held in which the radical wing of KANU led by Oginga Odinga and Bildad Kaggia was defeated by the so-called "moderates."   Odinga and his supporters resigned from KANU and formed a new party --the Kenya People's Union (KPU).   Kenyatta retorted by summoning a special parliamentary session to pass a bill compelling those who resigned from the party for which they had been elected to seek re-election.   The election results confirmed Odinga's control of the Central Nyanza district.   All six Central Nyanza seats fell to the KPU.   Elsewhere the new party gained only three

seats: two in Machakos and one in Elgon West where
J. Nthula and S. M. Kioko in the former and Oduya
Oprong in the later, won. Both Achieng' Oneko in Na-
kuru and Bildad Kaggia in Kandara were defeated.

LIDBURY REPORT, THE. In 1953, the British Government
appointed a Commission, under the Chairmanship of Sir
David Lidbury, a retired assistant director-general of
the British postal services, to inquire into the salaries
of civil servants in East Africa. Over 7,000 people
were directly affected in Kenya. Racial salary scales
based on the three-fifth rule (an African with the same
qualifications as an Arab earned three-fifths of his salary; the Arab three-fifths of an Indian's salary; and the
Indian three-fifths of a European's salary) had been the
rule, especially in Kenya. The Lidbury Report, published in 1954, recommended the abolition of salary dif-
ferentials between local African, Asian, and European
civil servants. Grading by race rather than by responsibility had to disappear. "The limit of advance of any
serving member of a service must be set solely by his
qualifications and proved ability," said the Report. As
a temporary measure it recommended an expatriation
allowance for overseas civil servants. The Report thus
marked the end of the old dream of the white settlers
to make white rule safe by substituting local European
civil servants for expatriates. Besides recommending
non-racial salary scales, the Report also recommended
the abolition of racial housing zones. Houses were now
to be allocated according to grades and irrespective of
races. Kenya was to be transformed from a racially
segregated society into a non-racial, open society. On
the other hand, Lidbury marked a major step in the
creation of an African social elite.

LIVESTOCK PRODUCTS. Livestock industry in Kenya is
well-developed. In 1976, the total milk production was
estimated at about 1.2 million tons, of which 0.840 million tons came from smallholders, 0.153 million tons
from large-scale farmers and 0.193 million tons from
pastoral areas. It is estimated that between 1978 and
1983, the total milk production will grow by 5.1 percent
annually. In 1979, milk available for consumption per
head was about 47 kilogram. Beef production in 1975
was estimated at 141,000 tons, of which 13,000 tons
were exported. Beef production has, however, stagnated
since 1976 due largely to drought. Between 1978 and

1983, total output is planned to grow at 3.7 percent annually leading to a production of 164,000 tons by 1983.
Sheep and goat meat production was also affected by
drought in 1974-76.   The high rainfall in 1977 and 1978
resulted in substantial herd development.   Production in
1976 was about 65,000 tons and at an estimated annual
growth rate of 4.6 percent, the output in 1983 is expected to be 82,000 tons.   The large-scale pig production that used to produce bacon for the local and export
markets declined with changing price relations, farm
structure, and markets.   Smallholder pig production for
pork has developed gradually.   The annual output in
1976, for example, was 3,200 tons, and it has been increasing by 4.7 percent per annum.   In 1976, poultry
meat production was 28,100 tons and the total egg production was estimated at about 20,900 tons.   Egg production is expected to grow at the rate of 5.2 percent
per annum from 1979 to 1983.

LOME CONVENTION.   This is an economic arrangement
  establishing formal cooperation between the European
  Economic Community and the African, Caribbean, and
  Pacific (ACP) states which was signed in Lome, capital
  of Togo, on February 28, 1975.   Under the convention
  the ACP countries are entitled to certain trade prefer-
  ences and economic assistance while the EEC gets most
  favored nations treatment in its trade with the ACP
  states.   In Kenya the EEC supported projects have included the Upper Tana River Reservoir and Power station, the integrated District Development Programme in
  Machakos, the Bura Irrigation Scheme, Lower Tana River, Rural Industrial Development Programme and Mathare Valley Site, Service Scheme, Nairobi, Scholarship
  and training program.

LONDIANI.   One of the summits of the Mau Escarpment in
  the Rift Valley Province.   The word is a Swahili corruption of the Masai Oldoinyo Loltiyani, meaning "the
  mountain of the bamboos."

LONGONOT.   A prominent volcano, 9,111 feet high, situated
  in the Rift Valley about 45 miles from Nairobi.   The
  name is derived from Masai Oloonong'ot, meaning "mountain of many spurs or steep ridges."

LUGARD, FREDERICK GRUEBER (Later, Lord).   Born in
  Madras, India in 1858.   Educated at Rossall School in

England 1871-7, after which he entered Sandhurst in
1878.   After a few weeks he was commissioned in the
East Norfolk Regiment.   He volunteered for service in
India.   He fought in the Afghan War (1879-80); went
back to India (1880-1885); took part in the Suakin campaign (1885-1886); went back to Asia to take part in the
Second Burma War (1886-1887).   He first came to East
Africa in 1888 to recover from a broken love affair.
He sailed to Central Africa and was employed by the
Scottish missionaries in Nyasaland to fight against Arab
slave-traders (1888-1889).   In 1889 he arrived in Kenya
in the service of the Imperial British East Africa Company.   In the following year he led a caravan to Uganda;
surveyed Western Uganda in 1891; was involved in Civil
war in Uganda in 1892, before returning to England to
campaign there for the retention of Uganda.   In 1894-5,
he was employed by the Royal Niger Company and in
1896-7, he was in the service of the British West Char-
terland Company in Bechwanaland.   In 1897, he was appointed Commissioner for Nigerian hinterland and from
1900-1906 he was High Commissioner in Northern Nigeria, during which period he was created K.C.M.G.
(1901).   From 1907 to 1912, Lugard was Governor of
Hong Kong, where he founded the University of Hong
Kong in 1911.   In the same year he was created G.C.M.G.
He returned to Nigeria as Governor of Southern and
Northern Nigeria (1912-13), before becoming Governor-
General of Nigeria (1914-19).   He retired from the Colonial service in 1919, and in the following year he was
made a Privy Councillor.   In 1922, he published his
famous book, The Dual Mandate.   In 1923, he was appointed British member on the Permanent Mandates Commission of the League of Nations.   From 1926-45, Lugard was Chairman of the International Institute of African Languages and Cultures.   He was made a peer--
Baron Lugard of Abinger--in 1928 for his services to
the Empire.   In 1930, he was appointed a Member of
the Joint Select Committee on Closer Union in East Africa.   He died at Abinger in Surrey in 1945.

LUO.   The Luo represent the only group of River-Lake or
Western Nilotes in Kenya, the other representatives being the Acholi, Lang'o, Padhola, Palwo, Alur in Uganda
and the Shilluk, Nuer, Dinka, and Anuak in the Sudan.
After the Kikuyu, they are the second largest single
nationality in Kenya, numbering over two million.   They
migrated from their original homeland in the general

area of northern Uganda, southern Sudan and southwestern Ethiopia, in dribs and drabs, between about 1200 and 1800. The advanced party of the Luo, the Joka-Jok, reached Western Kenya during the first half of the 15th century. Today they are found mostly in the Nyanza Province of Kenya, where they constitute a majority in three out of the four Districts of the Province. They practice mixed farming, growing maize, millet, cotton, rice, sugarcane, groundnuts and keeping cattle, sheep and goats.

LUO UNION (EAST AFRICA). One of the oldest welfare societies in Kenya which started in Nairobi in 1925. Its aims included mutual help and welfare, social and economic development as well as the affirmation of cultural identity and integrity. From being a Nairobi-based organization, efforts were made from 1946 to extend its activities to cover the whole of East Africa. By April 1953, when the re-organized Luo Union was inaugurated with Oginga Odinga as its first Ker or President, it had 90 branches throughout East Africa, and its headquarters was transferred to Kisumu. Adala Otuko was Secretary General and Albert Awino from Nairobi its Treasurer. Following the murder of Ambrose Ofafa, a Nairobi City Councillor and Treasurer of Luo Union, Nairobi branch in 1954, the Ofafa Memorial Hall was built in Kisumu as the headquarters of the Union. When Oginga Odinga decided to join active politics, Pastor Joel Omer became President from 1956-1963. From 1964-66, Dr. William Ouko, a medical practitioner, was President, followed by Paul Mboya 1966-78 and Oselu Nyalick from 1978 to 1980.

LUO UNITED MOVEMENT (LUM). Between the formation of KANU in 1960 and the attainment of independence in December 1963, tension was caused within the party by presistent Kikuyu militancy. Fears were expressed by non-Kikuyu members of the party of Kikuyu domination in independent Kenya. One such expression was the formation of the Luo United Movement by urbanized Luo who already feared that they were being relegated to the role of minor partners by the Kikuyu. Founded in August 1962 in Nairobi, the movement was led by Z. Adholla, a militant who had been involved in the Kenya African Union and Mau Mau. He had been detained and he had been one of the few non-Kikuyu members of the Kenya Land Freedom Army. With KANU based at that time

on a Kikuyu-Luo-Kamba alliance, and with the formation
by Paul Ngei of the African People's Party (APP) in
November, 1962, it looked as if KANU was crumbling.
At the inaugural meeting in Nairobi, the leaders declared: "We will remain in KANU to give the Kikuyu
a chance to discipline themselves, put an end to oathing
and subversion and drop their ideas of dominating the
other tribes in Kenya." By the beginning of 1963, LUM
was dying largely because it was not supported by both
Oginga Odinga and Tom Mboya (prominent Luo and KANU
leaders at that time) and also because it never gained
a rural base.

LYTTELTON CONSTITUTION, THE (1954). Named after
the then British Colonial Secretary, Oliver Lyttleton
(later Lord Chandos). It introduced the principle of
multi-racialism into the affairs of government. It established a Council of Ministers, to whom were transferred most of the functions of the Executive Council.
The latter was retained, with greatly reduced powers.
All Ministers were members of the Executive Council
together with three additional nominated members--one
Arab and two Africans. The Council of Ministers was
not a Cabinet since the majority of its members were
still official. Nor did it diminish the powers of the
Governor. The racial composition of the Council of
Ministers was to be as follows: three Europeans from
whom a Minister without portfolio, Minister of Agriculture and Minister of Local Government and Housing
were to be appointed; two Asian Ministers, one without
portfolio and the second one in charge of Works. There
was to be only one African Minister who was to be in
charge of Community Development, an area regarded as
being largely African. This was the first time in the
history of colonial Kenya that Africans and Asians were
assigned executive responsibility. All the Ministers
now joined the official side, which meant that the Legislative Council had an official majority--a system which
continued until the establishment of self-government in
June 1963. The government was also to initiate by 1956,
an inquiry into the best methods of choosing African
members of the Council. The constitution was designed
to last until 1960. But as it turned out, the African
members of the Legislative Council that were elected on
the new franchise in 1957 made it unworkable. A new
constitution, the Lennox-Boyd Constitution, had to be introduced in 1958.

LYTTELTON, OLIVER (later, the Rt. Hon. Viscount Chandos
of Aldershot). Born in 1893. President of the Board
of Trade 1940-41; Minister of State and Member of War
Cabinet 1941-45; President of the Board of Trade and
Minister of Production 1945. Chairman of Associated
Electrical Industries Ltd. 1945-51, 1954-63. Secretary
of State for the Colonies from 1951 to 1954. Introduced
the Lyttelton Constitution of 1954 which introduced the
principle of multi-racialism.

- M -

MacDONALD, MALCOLM JOHN. Born in Lossiemouth,
Scotland, the son of Ramsay MacDonald. Educated at
City of London School, Bedales School, Petersfield and
University of Oxford. Member L.C.C. in 1927; elected
Labour M.P. for Bassetlaw in 1929; National Labour
M.P. for Bassetlaw 1931. He was appointed Secretary
of State for Dominions in 1935 and 1938; Secretary of
State for the Colonies in the same year; Minister of
Health 1940. In the following year he was appointed
High Commissioner to Canada; Governor-General Ma-
laya, Singapore and British Borneo 1946; Commissioner
General for United Kingdom in South East Asia 1948;
High Commissioner to India 1955. He was thus a sea-
soned politician and diplomat when he was appointed Gov-
ernor and then Governor-General of Kenya in 1963. When
Kenya became a Republic in 1964, he was surprisingly but
significantly appointed the first United Kingdom High Commissioner in Kenya. In 1965, he became British Special
Representative in East and Central Africa. He held the degrees of Doctor of Laws and Doctor of Letters of various
universities in North America and Asia. He was also Privy
Counsellor. Died in England on January 11, 1981.

MacGILLIVRAY, SIR DONALD CHARLES. Born in 1906,
Edinburgh. Educated at Sherborne school and Oxford
University. He was in the Colonial Civil Service from
1929 to 1957, serving in Tanganyika 1929-37, Palestine
1937-47, Jamaica 1947-52, Malaya 1952-57 as Deputy
and from 1954 as High Commissioner. He was appointed Chairman, Kenya Council of State 1958-63. He was
Chairman of Makerere University College Council, 1958-
61 and Deputy Chairman of Commission on the Constitution of the Federation of the Rhodesias and Nyasaland
in 1960. From 1961 to 1964, he was Chairman of the

University of East Africa Council and Chairman of the
Kenya Meat Commission Board 1962-64. Farmer and
Company Director.

MACHAKOS. A place of Masaku, a Mkamba leader in the
19th century. It was first established as a halting-place
and administrative post of the Imperial British East African Company in 1890. Mr. John Ainsworth, who had
been in charge of the Company's Transport Department
at Mombasa since 1889, was transferred to Machakos
in 1892 to administer the Province. He built the Machakos fort in 1893. Fruit farming and canning was introduced in the area by Reverend Stuart Watt. Today
Machakos is a thriving farming and administrative center, with fruit farming and canning concentrated in the
Mua Hills.

McKENZIE, BRUCE ROY (DSO, DFC). The only European
to have served as a full Minister in the government of
independent Kenya. Born at Richmond, Natal, in January 1919, he was educated at Hilton College, Natal,
and at an agricultural college there. At the outbreak
of the Second World War he joined the South African
Air Force, and was later seconded for service with the
Royal Air Force. He served in North Africa, the Med-
iterranean and Europe, and became a Colonel at the
age of 24--the youngest officer of that rank in the South
Africa Air Force.

   In 1946, he moved to Kenya and started farming
near Nakuru. His farm became famous for exports of
pedigree Friesian cattle. He first entered the Kenya
Legislative Council in 1957 as a nominated member, representing farming interests. In 1959 he was appointed
Minister for Agriculture, and in 1962 Minister for Settlement. In 1963 he was elected as a member of the
Kenya African National Union to the House of Representatives and was appointed Minister for Agriculture and
Animal Husbandry.

   Besides being Chairman of Cooper Motors Ltd.,
he was also a director of many firms and Corporations
including the East African Airways until its collapse in
1977 when he was appointed a director of the newly-
formed Kenya Airways. He died in air crash near Nairobi on the evening of May 24. He was in a light aircraft which exploded in mid-air while returning from a
visit to Uganda. The three other persons in the aircraft who died with him were Keith Savage, a Kenyan

businessman who had close business connections with
the Ugandan Government; Gavin Whitelaw, a visiting
British businessman; and Paul Lennox, the pilot.

MACKENZIE, SIR GEORGE SUTHERLAND.   Born in May
    1844.   He made a name for himself by exploring the
    Karun Valley in Persia.   He opened up direct commun-
    ication between Ispahan and Mahommerah, via Shuster.
    In 1888, he was appointed the first administrator of the
    Imperial British East Africa Company's territories, la-
    ter called Kenya.   On behalf of the Italian Government,
    he arranged treaties with the Somali on the Benadir
    Coast of East Africa.   For his work in East Africa and
    Persia, he was awarded the K.C.M.G. and C.B., as
    well as the Grand Cross of Crown in Italy, and Grand
    Cross of Brilliant Star (Zanzibar).   He was a Vice-
    President of the Royal Geographical Society and a mem-
    ber of the Council of the Royal Colonial Institute.

MACKINNON, WILLIAM.   Born in 1823 at the village of
    Campbeltown, Argyleshire, Scotland.   He had only el-
    ementary education.   In 1847, he went to India where
    he joined Robert Mackenzie, a former schoolmate, who
    was operating a small general store.   Under the name
    of Smith, Mackenzie and Company, the firm established
    its headquarters in Calcutta and soon became one of
    the leading mercantile companies in the Indian Ocean
    region.   In 1856, he founded the British Indian Steam-
    ship Navigation Company.   By the time of his death in
    1893, this company had a fleet of over one hundred
    vessels.   In 1878, he turned his attention to East Af-
    rica and leased a territory from Seyyid Barghash--a
    venture that yielded no results.   He then formed the
    Imperial British East Africa Company, which received
    a royal charter in 1888.   This is the company that es-
    tablished British administration in Kenya and Uganda.
    When it went bankrupt in 1895, it turned over its ter-
    ritories to the British government.

MACKINNON ROAD.   This road was begun by the Imperial
    British East Africa Company to connect the Kenya Coast
    with the Scottish Industrial Mission at Kibwezi.   Made
    largely at the personal expense of Sir William and Lady
    Mackinnon (who were among the founders of the mis-
    sion) and completed by his heirs as a memorial to him.
    The mission was established in April 1891 and in De-
    cember of that year the Company voted Rs. 5,000 to

begin the construction work. The road cost Rs. 60,000
to Kibwezi. The Company's attempt to recover some
of this cost by charging tolls on road users caused a
storm among the Mombasa businessmen. Mackinnon
died in June 1893 and in the end the road was bought
by the government and extended in 1896 to Mumias as
Scalater's Road.

MACLEOD, IAN. Born in 1913, Member of Parliament for
Enfield West from 1950. Minister of Health 1952-55;
Minister of Labour 1955-59. Secretary of State for the
Colonies 1959-61. Ended the State of Emergency in
Kenya in November 1959 and convened the First Lancaster House Conference in London in January 1960,
which lasted a month and which produced no agreement.
Macleod, however, imposed a constitution which gave
the Africans a majority in the Legislative Council for
the first time. Leader of the House of Commons from
1961.

McMILLAN, SIR NORTHRUP. A wealthy American sports-
man who came to Kenya on a shooting safari in 1904
and stayed to settle permanently. He started the Juja
Farm, which covered twenty thousand acres--partly
farming and partly a private game reserve--in 1905.
The farm was popular with distinguished game hunters.
He sponsored many scientific expeditions. He was
awarded the K.C.M.G. for his services during the 1914-
18 war. He died in 1925. His wife then lived at their
Nairobi home at Chiromo, which now houses the British
Institute in Eastern Africa. She founded the McMillan
Memorial Library in Nairobi in memory of her husband.

MADAN, CHUNILAL BHAGWANDAS. Born in Kenya in 1912
and educated at Government Indian School, Nairobi and
in London. Barrister-at-Law, Middle Temple 1936.
Appointed Q.C. in 1957. He was a Member of Nairobi
City Council (1937-48) and was Treasurer of the Law
Society of Kenya (1948-1953) and its President (1955-56)
and (1956-1960). Was several times President of Nairobi Indian Association. Represented the Central Area,
Nairobi, in the Legislative Council between 1948 and
1956. Became Specially Elected Member in 1957. Appointed Parliamentary Secretary to the Ministry of Commerce and Industry (1955-56) and then became the Asian
Minister Without Portfolio in 1956 on the retirement of
Hon. A.B. Patel. Retired from politics in March 1961
and became Kenya's first Asian judge.

MAENDELEO YA WANAWAKE (Progress of Women). The
leading women's organization in Kenya. Started in 1952,
it is country-wide and has clubs in rural areas involving
about 50,000 members. The main object of the movement is to raise the status of women, as well as to
teach the elements of child-care, nutrition, home economics, arts and crafts. The organization has produced
some dedicated women leaders such as Mrs. Jael Mbogo,
Mrs. Phoebe Asiyo and Mrs. Jane Kiano.

MAGADI, LAKE. At the bottom of the Rift Valley in the
Kajiado District, about 95 miles from Nairobi. It consists almost entirely of solid and semi-solid soda, which
is a valuable product and is extensively mined. Consequently, a mining town has sprung up on the shore of
the lake.

MAIZE. The staple food of the majority of Kenyans. It is
therefore grown almost everywhere in the country. Kenya is already a surplus maize producer, and efforts
are under way to set up manufacturing and processing
industries based on maize.

MAJIMBO see REGIONALISM

MAKASEMBO, DIXON ORUKO. Born in 1923 in Central
Nyanza. Educated at Kamagambo School 1938-40.
Worked in East African Medical Corps 1941-46; Kenya Tea Company 1947-49; Nandi Tea Company before
joining politics. He played a leading role in the post-
1952 Nyanza and Kenya politics, being largely responsible for organizing a power-base for Oginga Odinga in
Nyanza. He was Assistant Secretary African District
Association, Kisumu, 1954-56; KANU Chairman of Central Nyanza District 1960-63; elected Senator (KANU)
for Central Nyanza district, 1963. In Senate he was
appointed Chief Whip in 1963. He was killed in a car
accident on December 12, 1965.

MALINDI. A famous tourist resort on the Kenya coast. It
is one of the oldest towns in East Africa, having been
founded round about 470 A.D. By the time the Portuguese arrived in 1498, it was a thriving commercial
town, boasting of many mosques and important buildings.
The inhabitants of Malindi welcomed the Portuguese
whom they hoped to use against their great rival, Mombasa. When the Portuguese finally succeeded, with the
help of the Zimba, in defeating Mombasa in 1589, their

need for Malindi diminished. In 1593 the Portuguese and the Sultan of Malindi moved to Mombasa, with its better harbor, where they established their headquarters. Most of the trade shifted southwards thus effectively ending Malindi's commercial life. Malindi continued to decline until the latter part of the 19th century when it was re-established as a fishing village. In the 1930's it began to be visited as a holiday resort, and after the Second World War, the tourist business started to boom. Today Malindi is a major holiday resort patronized by tourists from all parts of the world.

MANUFACTURING. The manufacturing sector ranks second to agriculture in importance in the Kenya economy. It witnessed rapid growth during the post-independence period largely as a result of successful import substitution development. The rate of growth of this sector between 1972 and 1977, for example, was about 10.5 percent per annum. The sector provides employment for many wage-earners. In 1977, for instance, it employed 118,000 people, which was 13.1 percent of the total wage employment in the economy. The sector is also considerably diversified. The largest sub-sectors are food processing, basic metals, metal products, machinery and equipment, and chemical industries. The Manufacturing Sector's Gross Domestic Product rose from K. £45,559,000 in 1968 to K. £183,574,000 in 1976.

MARAKWET. A Kalenjin group living to the north of the Keyo, in the Elgeyo-Marakwet District in the Rift Valley, and numbering about 100,000. The altitude of their region rises from 3,500 feet in the Kerio Valley to 11,000 feet in the Cherangany Hills. Like the Keyo, they are cliff-dwellers. They practice mixed farming with irrigation.

MARINE TRANSPORT see COMMUNICATIONS AND TRANSPORT

MASAI. The largest group of the Maa-speakers (the others being the Samburu and the Njemps), who are a branch of the Plains Nilotes. They claim to have migrated into Kenya from an original home to the north of Lake Turkana, reaching the Rift Valley region of Kenya about five hundred years ago. They then expanded across Kenya and northern Tanzania. Today they are found largely in the two Masai Districts of Kajiado and Narok where they practice pastoralism and, increasingly, agriculture.

MASINDE, ELIJAH. Founder and leader of the Dini ya
Msambwa cult, which started in Western Kenya in 1942.
He was born in 1910. Attended several mission schools
including the Church of God at Kima, in Western Kenya.
A good football player, he was appointed a physical education instructor. From 1937 to 1942, he was employed as a Native Tribunal Court Process Server. He
started Dini ya Msambwa in 1942, a cult that was anti-
colonial and anti-European. He was sent to prison in
1945 for one year for causing disturbance. Deported to
Lamu in 1948, where he was detained until May 1961
when he was released. Since 1963, he has been imprisoned several times for defying authority and for
continuing to demand a complete reconstruction of the
Kenya society.

MATANO, ROBERT STANLEY. Born in 1924 at Mazeras
in the Coast Province and educated at the Meru Methodist School and Alliance High School, Kikuyu. He then
went to Makerere College, Kampala from 1946-48, where
he obtained a diploma in education. He taught at the
Ribe Boys School and Alliance High School, Kikuyu, before becoming an educational officer in Naivasha. He
went to Britain on a British Council bursary in 1956,
where he was attached to the Technical College, Cardiff.
In 1961, he was elected a Kenya African Democratic
Union (KADU) Member for Kwale to the Legislative
Council. He was one of the influential leaders of KADU.
He was appointed Parliamentary Secretary for Education
in 1961 and travelled extensively in the United States on
a leadership grant. During the 1963 General Election,
he was elected to the House of Representatives as a
KADU Member for Kwale West. He also became Vice-
President of the then Coast Regional Assembly. In the
Coalition Government of 1963 he was appointed Assistant
Minister for Education. With the dissolution of KADU
in 1964 and the merging of the Senate and House of Representatives in the same year, he was appointed, from
1965, to various positions: Assistant Minister for Foreign Affairs, (1965), Assistant Minister for Health (1966)
and Assistant Minister in the Office of the Vice-President (1966). On the death of Ronald Ngala in December
1972, Matano was appointed Minister for Information and
Broadcasting in 1973. Re-elected to Parliament as Member for Kwale West in 1974. In 1974 he moved to the
newly created Ministry of Co-operatives and in 1976 he
was appointed Minister for Local Government. He had
also taken over the mantle of political leadership of the

Coast Province following the death of Ngala.   In 1966,
he was appointed Assistant Secretary-General of the
ruling party, the Kenya African National Union (KANU).
Following the assassination of the Secretary-General,
Tom Mboya, in 1969, Matano became Acting Secretary-
General of the party, a position he held up to 1979.   He
was elected Secretary-General of the ruling party KANU
in 1979 and appointed Minister for Housing and Social
Services.

MATHU, ELIUD WAMBU.   Born at Riruta near Nairobi in
1910.   Educated at Riruta Primary School, Church of
Scotland Mission School at Kikuyu and at the Alliance
High School, Kikuyu.   He then went to Fort Hare University, South Africa, from where he went to Exeter
University, England and Balliol College, Oxford.   He obtained his B. A. and diploma in education.   On his return to Kenya, he became a teacher at the Alliance
High School, Kikuyu.   In 1943 he was appointed Principal of Dagoretti High School.   On October 5, 1944, he
was nominated as the first African member of the Legislative Council.   From that year until 1957, Mathu was
the Chief spokesman for the African masses in the Euro-
pean-dominated Legislature.   He displayed courage, in-
telligence, dedication and nationalism which, in effect,
laid a solid foundation for the more radical African politics that were ushered in by the first African elections
in 1957.   He supported the British Administration during
the Mau Mau war.   He was also a member of the Executive Council.   It was because of his collaborative
role during the Emergency that he lost election in 1957.
He was also a Kenya Representative in the East African
Legislative Assembly from 1948-60.   For four years,
1960-64, he worked as an official of the United Nations
Economic Commission for Africa.   From 1963-69, he
was the Chairman of the University of East Africa Council, a job he performed with great impartiality and ef-
ficiency.   From 1964 to 1977, he was Private Secretary
to the President of the Republic of Kenya and Comptrol-
ler of State House, Nairobi.   Was appointed Chairman
of the Kenya Airways Board of Directors in 1977.   He
retired in 1980.

MATI, FREDRICK MBITI.   Born in 1926 in Kitui and educated at the Alliance High School, Kikuyu 1942-45 and
Makerere College, Uganda 1946-47.   He then proceeded
to South Africa and was admitted to Fort Hare University 1948-50, where he developed strong interests in

African politics.   Among his contemporaries at Fort
Hare were Robert Sobukwe and Chief Gatsa Buthelezi of
South Africa and Herbert Chitepo of Zimbabwe.   He obtained a Bachelor of Arts degree.   On return to Kenya
in 1951, he found no suitable opening.   He therefore decided to join the Independence Schools movement in Ukambani, being appointed Supervisor of Independence Schools,
Ukambani, in 1952.   He was in charge of eight independent schools and he liaised with the independent schools
movement in Central Province.   With the declaration of
the State of Emergency in 1952, Fred Mati was picked
up and detained at Machakos for four months after which
he was restricted at his home in Kitui up to 1954.   From
1954 to 1956, he was a teacher at Kitui Government African School.   He applied for and secured a Government
bursary, for post-graduate work at Bristol University,
Britain to study education, 1956-57.   After teaching for
two years in Britain he returned home and was posted
to Machakos High School, as a Vice-Principal in 1960.
        In 1961, Mati was elected KANU member for
Kitui to the Legislative Council.   He was appointed Minister for Health and Housing in the Coalition Government
of 1962.   In the 1963 General Election he won the Kitui
North seat for KANU.   In 1965, the new Republican Parliament elected him Speaker, the first African to hold
this important post.   Since then he has presided with
dignity, fairness and firmness over the proceedings of
the Country's supreme legislative body.

MAU ESCARPMENT.   Forms part of the Western wall of
    the Rift Valley.   The name is derived from the Masai
    word "mao," meaning "a division."

MAU MAU.   A militant movement that advocated the em-
    ployment of organized violence in pursuit of its political
    and anti-colonial cause.   In terms of political objectives,
    there was little difference between Mau Mau leaders and
    leaders of the moderate Kenya African Union party.   The
    main difference was over political strategy.   Mau Mau
    leaders believed that political goals were attainable only
    through a violent struggle.   The movement probably
    started in the late 1940's, and the Declaration of a State
    of Emergency in October 1952 gave it added impetus.
    The result was a state of war between 1952 and Decem-
    ber 1956, during which at least 13,423 Africans were
    killed and thousands were wounded.   Several other Af-
    ricans were detained.   The Emergency cost £55.5 mil-

lion up to June 1959.   Some of the movement's prominent leaders were Dedan Kimathi, Waruhiu Itote, and
Stanley Mathenge.

MAULE, DONOVAN, O. B. E.   Born in Brighton, England
   and educated at King's College School, Wimbledon.   Being born of theatrical parents, he first appeared on the
   stage in 1909.   During the First World War, he served
   in the Army Service London Scottish (1914-18) and during the Second World War, he served as Supervisor of
   Productions, Central Pool of Artists (War Office) 1939-
   45.   During the inter-war period (1918-1939), he worked
   as Stage Director and actor in London, Paris, and New
   York.   In 1947, he came to Kenya with his wife Mollie,
   who is also an actress, and formed the Donovan Maule
   Theatre in 1948 in Nairobi, the first professional theatre
   in East Africa.   They managed this theatre until 1978,
   when they sold the company.

MAZRUI.   A clan of the Omani Arabs in the service of the
   Yarubi Imams who established an independent rule over
   Mombasa from 1746 to 1837, when Seyyid Said of the
   Busaidi dynasty conquered the town.   Under the Mazrui
   rule, the Swahili population of Mombasa became united,
   links were established with the Mijikenda people (most
   of whom were non-Muslim and non-urban), and a kind of
   overlordship was established over Pate, Vumba, and
   Tanga.

MAZRUI, ALI AL'AMIN.   A political scientist and writer,
   born on February 24, 1933, at Mombasa.   Educated at
   the Government Arab Boys' School Mombasa 1939-48,
   Huddersfield College of Technology 1955-57, University
   of Manchester 1957-60, Columbia University (New York),
   1960-61, and Nuffield College, Oxford 1961-63.   He
   started his working life as a Clerk in the Mombasa Institute of Muslim Education 1952-55.   From Oxford,
   where he obtained his D. Phil. degree, he was appointed
   Lecturer in Political Science at Makerere University
   College, Uganda 1963-65; Professor of Political Science
   1965-73; Dean of Social Science Faculty 1967-69.   He
   was also Associate Editor of the Transition magazine
   1964-73, which was originally based in Kampala, and
   Co-Editor of Mawazo Journal 1967-73.   He has also
   held the titles of Visiting Professor of University of
   Chicago, 1965; Research Associate, Harvard University,
   1965-66; Director, African Section, World Order Models

Project 1968-73; Visiting Professor Northwestern University, U. S. A. 1969; McGill and Denver Universities 1969; London and Manchester Universities 1971. In 1972, he was on a Dyason Lecture Tour of Australia. When he fell out with Amin, he went to America where he was appointed Professor of Political Science, University of Michigan, 1973. He has also been Senior Visiting Fellow, Hoover Institute of War, Peace and Revolution, Stanford University, 1973. He has been Vice-President of the International Political Science Association 1970-73; and of the International Congress of Africanists, 1967-73.

Mazrui is a prolific and controversial political commentator whose publications include the following: Towards a Pax Africana, 1967; On Heroes and Uhuru Worship, 1967; The Anglo-African Commonwealth, 1967; Violence and Thought, 1969; Co-Editor, Protest and Power in Black Africa, 1970; The Trial of Christopher Okigbo, 1971; Cultural Engineering and Nation Building in East Africa, 1972; Co-Editor Africa in World Affairs: The Next Thirty Years 1973; Africa's International Relations, 1978; Political Values and the Educated Class in Africa (1978); Africa's Political Realities: The 1979 Reith Lectures, 1979.

MAZRUI, MBARUK BIN RASHID AL. Son of the last independent ruler of Mombasa. His father had been defeated by the Busaidi dynasty in 1837. Had narrowly escaped being taken away, like many of his relatives, to die in prison. Went to Gasi to live with family members. From here he tried several times and unsuccessfully to fight against the forces of the Sultan of Zanzibar. He even tried to list the help of the Germans. In 1895, the British, who had declared a protectorate over the coast, prevented his nephew, Mbarak, who lived at Takaungu, from becoming Liwali. Mbarak decided to fight, and he was supported by his nephew Mbaruk. This led to the famous Mazrui uprising which covered the coast from Vanga to Malindi, and which was supported by other non-Swahili African groups such as the Giriama, Digo, and Duruma. The British brought in troops from India and Mbaruk and his army was defeated. He, however, refused to surrender. He and other leaders of the uprising sought shelter in Tanganyika, then ruled by the Germans. He was granted political asylum by Governor Von Wissmann. He thus became a pioneer political refugee. He retired to Dar-es-Salaam on a Ger-

man pension--an event that effectively marked the end
of the rule of the Mazrui dynasty in East Africa. He
was pardoned by the British in 1907, but declined to
return to Kenya. He died in Dar-es-Salaam in 1910.

MBATIANY. An eminent 19th-century Masai leader. Born
about 1820, possibly in the Arusha area of Tanzania, he
was the son of Supet who was a Masai oloiboni or ritual
leader, and who died in 1864, during the second lloikop
war. His childhood days were characterized by the con-
flicts between the pastoral Masai and the lloikop, popularly known as the Kwavi or agricultural Masai. The conflict was worsened by the decision of the Laikipiak--a
branch of the lloikop--to establish their own institution of
Oloibonis. Mbatiany succeeded his father in 1864. His immediate ambition was to unite all pastoral Masai. But the
struggle for the control of the Nakuru area--a strategic re-
gion--between the pastoral Masai and the Laikipiak, led to
the third lloikop war, popularly known as the war of Laikipia
between 1870 and 1875. Mbatiany was also bent on break-
ing the power of the Laikipiak Oloiboni. He defeated
them, and thus emerged as the undisputed Masai leader
and oloiboni, after over fifty years (1824-75) of internecine war. When he died in 1889, his sons, Senteu
and Olonana, quarrelled over succession, and this further
weakened Masai resistance to their enemies, which very
soon included the British.

MBEERE. The Mbeere live in the Embu district in the
Eastern Province, and number about 50,000. Their
earlier history is similar to that of the Embu except
that they had a prolonged period of conflict with the
Masai. Much of their land is not fertile and lacks adequate water. They therefore rely more on animal husbandry, especially cattle and goats, than on cultivation,
which is mainly practiced in well-watered areas. They
grow cotton, tobacco, maize, millet, cassava and bananas. They are also keen bee-keepers.

MBOYA, THOMAS JOSEPH. Born on a sisal estate at Kili-
ma Mbogo, Machakos District, on August 15, 1930. His
parents were from Rusinga Island in Nyanza Province.
He was educated at Kabaa in Machakos, St. Mary's
School, Yala in Nyanza, and the Holy Ghost College,
Mangu in Kiambu District, before training at the San-
itary Inspectors School at Kabete in Nairobi (1948-50).
Worked as Sanitary Inspector for the City of Nairobi

1951-53. It was during this time that he started his
public life. He founded the Kenya Local Government
Workers' Union in 1952, and was its national Secretary-
General from 1953 to 1957. In October 1952, he had
been appointed Director of Information and Acting Treasurer of the Kenya African Union. He soon assumed the
leadership of the Kenya Federation of Registered Trade
Unions, later renamed the Kenya Federation of Labour.
He was Secretary-General of K. F. L. from 1953 to 1963.
Thus at the age of 23, he took up the exacting and, at
that time, risky task of organizing Kenya workers to
fight for their rights. In the words of President Kenyatta, Mboya " ... adamantly, selflessly and courageous-
ly reinforcing the efforts of those who had started the
struggle for the emancipation of his people in Kenya as
well as brothers throughout the Continent of Africa. Had
it not been for his efforts and personal sacrifice Kenya's independence could have been hampered or serious-
ly comprised." Mboya was closely associated with workers' movements in East Africa and in the rest of Africa.
In 1955-56, he went to Ruskin College, on Sir William
Bowen Scholarship, to study Industrial Relations. Formed
the Nairobi People's Convention Party in 1957, of which
he became Chairman. Won election to the Legislative
Council in 1957, being one of the first eight African
elected members.
    Mboya's qualities as a debater and parliamen-
tarian were soon revealed. In many major issues, he
outwitted the colonial government. He became the Sec-
retary-Treasurer of the African Elected Members' Organization. In 1958, he was elected to the International
Confederation of Free Trade Unions (ICFTU) Executive
Board. In the same year, he was elected Chairman of
the First All-African Peoples' Conference in Ghana, and
henceforth he became increasingly involved in Pan-African affairs. In 1960, when the Kenya African National
Union was formed, Mboya became its Secretary-General,
a position he held until his death, after being re-elected
in 1966. In that position he proved to be a great organizer and tactician. For his contribution to the course
of African independence, Howard University awarded him
an Honorary Degree of Doctor of Laws in 1959. He organized the successful "air-lift" schemes to America,
and over 1,000 Kenyans owe their University education
to this personal crusade of Mboya which he scrupulous-
ly organized from his offices in Alvi House, Nairobi.
He was a Member of PAFMECA Council and its Chairman

in 1961. In the following year he was appointed Minister of Labour in the Coalition Government, 1962. In
this position he master-minded Kenya's Industrial Relations Charter. He was elected KANU Member for Nairobi Central to the House of Representatives in 1963
and in the same year appointed Minister of Justice and
Constitutional Affairs. In the latter capacity, he spear-
headed the drive to dismantle the complex apparatus
that constituted Regionalism. In 1964, he was appointed
Minister of Economic Planning and Development, a post
he held until his death. He wrote two books, Freedom
and After, and the Challenge of Nationhood. A staunch
nationalist, Mboya was assassinated on July 5, 1969.

MENENGAI. A large caldera situated north of Nakuru, which
occupies about thirty-five square miles. This crater is
one of the largest in Africa. Its name comes from a
Masai word meaning "place of the corpses," because,
according to Masai tradition, the llosekelai and Laikipiak sections of the Masai were defeated here in 1854
and driven over the sides to their deaths.

MERU. The Meru are a Central Bantu-speaking group numbering about 600,000 and comprising the Igembe, the
Igoji, the Imenti, the Mintini, the Tigania, the Mutham-
bi, the Mwimbi and the Chuka. With the exception of
the Chuka, all the other groups of the Meru claim to
have come from a place called Mbwa at the coast (probably Mbwara Matanga of Manda Island) at the beginning
of the eighteenth century. Their migration route was
via the Tana River and moved north-westwards until
they reached the region around Mount Kenya. By this
time they had adopted a collective name, Ngaa. The
community then fragmented to settle in different areas,
their common name eventually disappearing in the process. The name "Meru" was given to them by the Maa-
speakers, who called the forested parts of Tigania and
Imenti "Mieru," meaning "a quiet and still place." The
term also means "a people who do not understand the
Masai language." The origins of the Chuka still remain
unresolved. Today the Meru people practice mixed agriculture of cultivation and animal husbandry, growing coffee, wheat, maize and potatoes. They also keep bees.

MIJIKENDA. A group of coastal Bantu-speakers numbering
over a half a million people and consisting of nine groups:
the Giriama, the Kauma, the Chonyi, the Jibana, the

Kambe, the Ribe, the Rabai, the Digo and the Duruma.
Like "Kalenjin" and "Luhya," the name "Mijikenda,"
which means "nine villages" is a twentieth-century in-
vention which applies to all the nine groups who previously had no corporate names for themselves, but
who were called by others "Wanyika," meaning "bush-
people." When they first arrived in the present home-
lands from the mythical Shungwaya they established nine
villages called kaya. They should therefore have been
"Kayakenda," but they chose instead to adopt the Kiswahili word "miji" for "villages." In the nineteenth century, they expanded to occupy their present lands which
extend from north of the Galana River to the Tanzanian
border. They grew sorghum, millet, cassava, yams,
sweet potatoes, and later maize and coconut. Today
the economy of the Mijikenda is still basically agricultural, with a new cashcrop, cashew, added to the list.

MILLION ACRE SCHEME, THE. In 1962, it was generally
accepted that a permanent solution had to be found for
the problem of land hunger which had been a major cause
of political instability. As part of the political bargain
for independence, it was decided to launch the Million
Acre Scheme which aimed at settling about 34,000 African families on former European-owned land within
five years. A Ministry of Lands and Settlement was to
be created to implement the scheme on behalf of the
Land Development and Settlement Board.

MITCHELL, SIR PHILIP. Governor of Kenya from December 1944 to June 1952, three months before the outbreak
of Mau Mau uprising. He spent his early childhood in
Spain studying military history and classical Latin Literature. He later attended St. Paul's School and Trin-
ity College, Oxford. Posted to Nyasaland in 1912 as a
junior administrative officer; served in Central Africa
during the First World War; worked in Tanganyika from
1919 to 1935, first as a district officer, then as Assistant Secretary for Native Affairs 1926-28, Provincial
Commissioner and Secretary for Native Affairs 1928-34;
and finally as Chief Secretary 1934-35, working under
Governor Donald Cameron. From 1935 to 1940, he was
Governor of Uganda, where he was involved in elevating
Makerere College to a University Status. From 1940-
1944, he performed various jobs: he was Deputy Chairman of the Conference of East African Governors for
one year, coordinating the war effort of the three East

African territories; then he became Political Advisor to
General Wavell. Later he worked as British Plenipoten-
tiary in Ethiopia, and finally as Governor of Fiji and
High Commissioner for the West Pacific. He was in-
sensitive to African demands for political independence
in Kenya and believed in the protection of European
privileges. His rule led inevitably to the Mau Mau war.
He wrote African Afterthoughts in 1954.

MOGOGODO see YAAKU

MOI, DANIEL TOROTICH ARAP. Born in 1924 at Kurieng'wo
village, Baringo district in the Rift Valley. He was educated at Kabartonjo and Kapsabet African Inland Mission
Schools. He joined the Government African School Kapsabet, 1943-45, and then went to Kapsabet Teacher Training College in 1945-47. After teaching for some years
at Tambach Government African School, he became Headmaster of Kabarnet Intermediate School in 1948 and Vice
Principal of Tambach Teacher Training College, 1949-
54. In 1955, he left teaching after being nominated to
represent the Rift Valley Province in the Legislative
Council in place of Mr. J. K. Ole Tameno. He is thus
today the longest serving member of Kenya Parliament.
In 1957, he was returned to the Legislative Council as
one of the first eight African elected members of the
Legislative Council.
        On the formation of KADU in 1960, Moi was
elected its national Chairman. In the 1961 General
Election, he was returned to the Legislative Council as
a KADU member for Baringo. In the Coalition Government of 1962, he was appointed first Minister of Education and then Minister for Local Government. He was
re-elected to Parliament in 1963 as the KADU member
for Baringo North. He became the Shadow Minister for
Agriculture and First President of the Rift Valley Region, 1963. On the dissolution of KADU in 1964, Moi
joined the ruling Kenya African National Union (KANU)
and was appointed Minister for Home Affairs--a portfolio he retained until 1978. On the resignation of Mr.
Murumbi from the Government, Moi was appointed the
Country's third Vice-President in January 1967. He also became the Leader of Government Business in the
National Assembly, and hence a link was formed between the President and Members of Parliament. In
both capacities he worked hard to bring peace and development to Kenya. In the 1966 KANU elections, he

was elected the Party's Vice-President for the Rift Valley Province. He travelled all over the world, representing President Kenyatta at many high-level Conferences.

Moi succeeded Jomo Kenyatta as the Second President of the Republic of Kenya on August 22, 1978. On October 6, 1978, he was unanimously elected President of Kenya's ruling party KANU at a special delegates conference in Nairobi. On November 24, 1978, he was installed as Second Chancellor of the University of Nairobi and awarded an honorary doctorate. Re-elected unopposed to Parliament as Member for Baringo North and re-elected President in 1979. Besides politics, Moi is a keen farmer, Patron of the Boy Scout's Association of Kenya; Patron of the Kenya Historical Association and a leader of several social and welfare organizations.

MOMBASA. A port town also called Mvita, or "Island of War," which gives a clue to the long and bitter struggles that have characterized the history of Mombasa from its foundation about 900 A.D. By 1331 A.D., when Ibn Batuta visited the East Coast, Mombasa was a large town abounding with bananas, lemon citron and fish. Mombasa had a bloody history during the Portuguese Period, 1498-1698; the Omani Period, 1698-1724; the Mazrui Period, 1726-1837; and the al Busaid Period, 1837-1895. Today it is the second biggest town in Kenya, with the total population projected at 400,000. It is also the chief port of East Africa and a major tourist resort for both the local and overseas visitors. The "Island of War" has thus become an island of peace.

MORTIMER, SIR CHARLES EDWARD. Born in 1886, at Shipley in Yorkshire, England. Educated at Hartley College, Manchester 1907-10. Came to Kenya and worked in the Lands Department as a Clerk 1917-28. From 1928-38, he was Lands Secretary. Was a Member of the Legislative Council from 1938 to 1954, during which he held several official posts: Commissioner of Local Government, Lands and Settlement, 1938-1945; Member for Health and Lands and Local Government 1946-50 and 1952-54. He retired from public life in 1954. He was also a Knight of St. John and Chairman of its Council for Kenya.

MOYNE REPORT (Report by the Financial Commissioner [Lord Moyne] on Certain Questions in Kenya, Cmd.

4093 [1932]). When the Joint Select Committee of Parliament concluded its deliberations on closer Union in
East Africa in September 1931, it recommended that
certain major problems in Kenya should be investigated.
Mr. Roger Gibb was to investigate railway rates and
finance; the Carter Commission to investigate African
land claims; the Bushe Commission was to study judicial
organization; and Lord Moyne was to study racial taxation and expenditure in relation to the general budgetary
position of the Colony. In his Report, he recommended
the establishment of a Native Betterment Fund with a
statutory revenue; he concluded that the Africans were
over-taxed while the Europeans enjoyed "the amenities
of civilization in return for a relatively light scale of
contribution." He therefore recommended that the necessary increased revenue should be raised from non-
Africans. The best way to do this was through a system of income tax. The Report was strongly opposed
by the white settlers, especially the section recommending the introduction of an income tax. They demanded
financial control of Kenya's budget--a struggle that continued up to the late 1950's, when they finally lost it.

MUCHURA, JOHN MARK. Born in 1921 in Central Nyanza.
Educated at Maseno School and later trained as a Medical Training Instructor. From 1936 to 1958, he worked
in the Kenya Government as a Labour Inspector and Industrial Relations Officer. In fact, he was the first African to be appointed Labour Inspector. At one time he
was President of Kenya Civil Servants Union. He became a Specially Elected Member of the Legislative
Council, 1958-60. He has been Company Director and
Industrial Relations Consultant since 1960. In 1977, he
was appointed a member of the Kenya Industrial Court.
Thus since 1936, Mr. Muchura has been involved con-
tinuously in industrial relations problems, and his contribution in this field has been immense.

MULIRO, MASINDE. Born in 1921 at Matili village, in
Kimilili location, Bungoma district. Educated at Matili, Misikhu, Mwiri College, St. Mary's School, Yala
and Tororo College, Uganda. He then went to Cape
Town University, South Africa, where he read political
science, history and mathematics for his Bachelor's
degree. He also obtained a Bachelor of Education degree. He returned to Kenya in 1954 and was appointed
a teacher at Alliance Girls High School in 1955. In the

following year, he went to teach at Siriba College in
Nyanza. In 1957, he stood for elections for Nyanza
North Constituency, and was one of the first eight elected African members of the Legislative Council. He was
an M. P. from 1957 to 1979. He was appointed Minister for Commerce and Industry, Power and Communication from 1961 to May 1963. From 1963 to 1966 he
was the Chairman of Cotton Lint and Seed Marketing
Board, and Chairman of the Maize and Marketing Board.
He was re-elected to Parliament in 1969 and appointed
Minister for Co-operatives and Social Affairs. In 1974,
he was again elected to Parliament and was appointed
Minister of Works. He was, however, stripped of his
ministerial portfolio in 1975 for supporting a report of
the Parliamentary Select Committee appointed to probe
the murder of the M. P. for Nyandarua North, Mr. Josiah Mwangi Kariuki. He was the Vice-President of
the Kenya African Democratic Union from its inception
until it voluntarily dissolved itself in 1964. He is a
keen and successful farmer.

MULTI-RACIALISM. By 1952, when the Mau Mau war broke
out, it was evident that the system of parallel government that kept the different races separate had failed.
From 1954 to 1960, attempts were made through a series of legislation to introduce a multi-racial system that
aimed at involving all races in the affairs of government.
By recognizing the various communities as the basic units
of government, it was at variance with the principles of
democracy which recognize the rights of individuals. In
1960, the system was abandoned.

MUMIA, WA SHIUNDU. The last ruler of the Wanga Kingdom in Western Kenya. Born about 1851, he succeeded
his father Shiundu as Nabongo (King) in 1882. He was
visited by Joseph Thomson in 1883, and his village became a center for Swahili, Arab, and European traders,
adventurers, and missionaries travelling between Mombasa and Uganda. When the British Government declared a protectorate over the region and chose his village as headquarters, Mumia collaborated enthusiastical-
ly. Punitive expeditions against neighboring peoples
were organized from his village and he supported the
British conquest with his own troops. As a reward,
the British decided to create sub-imperialism of the
Wanga in 1907 by sending out his kinsmen to be headmen in non-Wanga areas. In 1909, he was made "Para-

mount Chief' of the new North Kavirondo district, in
effect demoting him from being an independent King to
a colonial Chief.   It was during the decade 1907-1917
that the Wanga influence in Western Kenya reached its
apogee.   After this, his influence waned, as the non-
Wanga people rejected the Wanga rule.   In 1920, the
British headquarters was transferred from Mumias to
Kakamega and to confirm the decline of his influence,
he was stripped of his powers as paramount chief in
1926--an act which he regarded as treacherous and un-
grateful.   He died in 1949.

MUMIAS.   A large village on the south bank of the River
Nzoia which was important as a staging post on the caravan route running north to Elgon and beyond, and later
on the caravan route to Uganda.   Thomson records arriving at the village in 1883.   It was then called Kwa
Sundu after Mumia's father who had recently died.   The
new young chief had continued his father's association
with the Swahili traders.   He now allied himself with
the European traders, adventurers and administrators.
Mumias became a government station in 1894 and was
the center from which Hobley, a British administrator,
carried out much of the work of bringing western Kenya under British administration.   In 1901, the provincial headquarters followed the railway to Kisumu, but
Mumias remained the administrative center for North
Nyanza until it was removed to the present station at
Kakamega as a result of several deaths from blackwater
fever.   Today Mumias has the largest sugar factory in
the country.

MUNGAI, NJOROGE.   Born at Dagoretti near Nairobi in
1927.   Educated at the Alliance High School, Kikuyu,
Nabumali High School, Uganda and Fort Hare University, South Africa, where he obtained a B. Sc. degree
in 1950.   He then went to Stanford University, California in the United States, where he gained his B. A.
in 1952 and M. D. in 1957.   He did post-graduate medical studies at Columbia University Presbyterian Medical Center, New York, 1958-59.   On his return to
Kenya, he practiced medicine at private clinics which
he set up: Thika Maternity Hospital, Riruta hospital,
Nairobi and Embu Clinics.   A founder member of KANU
and a member of its Executive Committee, he was
elected to the House of Representatives in the 1963 General Election as Member for Nairobi West.   He was

appointed Minister for Health and Housing 1963; in the following year he became the Minister for Internal Security and Defence. Following the 1969 General Election, he was appointed Minister for Foreign Affairs, a post which he retained until 1974 when he lost his seat in the General Election. He was nominated to Parliament in 1975. In 1977, he was elected Chairman of KANU in Nairobi. Dr. Mungai was the private physician to President Kenyatta from 1961-1978. He was elected to Parliament as Member for Dagoretti in 1979.

MURUMBI, JOSEPH. A politician, businessman and Africana collector, Murumbi was born on June 18, 1911, at Eldama Ravine. His parents were Peter Nicholas Zuzarte and Njambiak Ole Murumbi. He was educated at St. Pancras' European Boys School, Bellary, South India. Served in Burmah-Shell, Bellary South India, 1930-33; Clerk, Medical Department, Kenya Government, 1935-41; British Military Administration, Somalia--Chief Clerk, Somalia Gendarmerie, 1941-50; Assistant Controller of Imports and Exports, 1950-52. During the Mau Mau Emergency, he continued the fight for Independence abroad, working as Assistant Secretary of the Movement for Colonial Freedom 1952-57; Press and Tourist Officer, Moroccan Embassy, London 1957-62. He travelled extensively in Europe to champion the African cause. He came back to Kenya in 1962, and he was appointed Treasurer of the Kenya African National Union (KANU). He was elected to the House of Representatives in 1963 and appointed Minister of State in Prime Minister's Office, 1963-64; Minister of Foreign Affairs 1964-66; Vice-President of Kenya, December, 1966. Resigned from politics to devote his time to business and farming. Director of several Kenya companies. Built up one of the best Africana libraries, which has since been bought by the Government.

MWAMBICHI, JIMMY see TAITA HILLS ASSOCIATION

MWENDWA, ELIUD NGALA. A teacher and politician. Born in 1923 at Matinyani in Kitui. Educated at G.A.S. Kitui 1940-42, Alliance High School, Kikuyu, 1943-44; Kagumo Teacher Training College 1944-45. Teacher at the Government African School, Kitui 1947-52; Headmaster of Matinyani D.E.B. Intermediate School 1953-57. D.E.B. Schools Supervisor 1957-1958; teacher at Mutene Teacher Training College, 1959-61. He left teaching to join politics in 1961, being elected a Member of the Legislative Council for Kitui. He was appointed Minister for Health and Housing 1963; Minister for Labour and Social Services 1963-65; Minister for Commerce, Industry and Co-operative Development 1965-66; Minister for Power and Communications 1966-69; Minister of Labour 1969-74. He lost the election in 1974 and has since concentrated on business, although he is still the Branch Chairman of KANU in Kitui district.

- N -

NAIROBI. This city's name is derived from a Masai name "Enkare Nairobi," meaning "cold water." It is the capital city of Kenya, with a population of nearly a million. It is also the center of several regional and international organizations, including the United Nations UNEP and Habitat. It originated as a railway encampment in June 1899. By August of the same year, the railway headquarters (which had been in Mombasa) and the government administration of Ukamba Province (which was formerly at Machakos) had both been transferred to Nairobi. On April 16, 1900, the first Nairobi Municipal Regulations were published, by the newly created Municipal Committee, which remained in existence until 1919, when Nairobi became a municipality with a corporation. The boundary was extended to include residential areas such as Parklands. But it was not until 1928, following the recommendations of the Feetham Commission, that all the "autonomous" residential areas, such as Muthaiga, were absorbed. The boundaries of Nairobi as defined in 1928 were largely unchanged until 1963. It attained the city status in 1950.

NAIROBI STOCK EXCHANGE see STOCK EXCHANGE

NAIROBI TIMES, THE. Established on October 30, 1977, by Kenyan editor and publisher Mr. Hillary Ng'weno. It is a quality Sunday newspaper and owned by the Stellascope Limited, a local publishing company.

NAIVASHA, LAKE. Situated about eighty kilometers on the Nairobi/Nakuru road in the Rift Valley. It has more than 300 varieties of birds as well as good fishing for tilapia and bass.

NAKURU. A town whose name is derived from a Masai
     word meaning "the place where the cow does not eat"
     or "a place of dust." It originated as a railway sta-
     tion when the Uganda Railway reached the shores of
     Lake Nakuru in 1900. In 1908, the Provincial Head-
     quarters was moved from Naivasha to Nakuru, a move
     which accelerated development in the town. Indeed, by
     that time Nakuru was rapidly developing into the center
     of European settler activities in Kenya. The Settlers'
     Pastoralist Association was formed at Nakuru in the
     same year, and by the following year, the Association
     held the first Nakuru Agricultural Show. Rapidly, Na-
     kuru acquired the title of "Capital of the Highlands."
     It lies in the Rift Valley at an altitude of 6,071 feet
     and about 100 miles west of Nairobi. Its projected pop-
     ulation is about 67,000 persons.

NANDI. The Nandi Comprise the second largest group of
     Kalenjin people, numbering about 300,000 and occupying
     the highland region around Kapsabet in the Rift Valley
     Province. They put up a major resistance to British
     rule from 1895 to 1905. They practice mixed farming.
     For the early history, see the Kalenjin.

NATHOO, IBRAHIM ESMAIL. Born in Nairobi on July 5,
     1905. Educated at Government Indian School, Nairobi;
     Esplanade High School, Bombay; St. Xavier's College,
     Bombay; Trinity College, Cambridge (U.K.); and Owen's
     College, Manchester, was in public life in Kenya from
     1930 to 1961. First elected to the Legislative Council
     in 1946, and then re-elected unopposed to represent the
     Central area in 1948. With the partition of India into
     Pakistan and India, the Indian seats in Kenya were al-
     so split into Muslim and non-Muslim constituencies.
     Nathoo was elected unopposed as Member for the Mus-
     lim West Constituency in 1952 and again in 1956. He
     was Minister for Works from April 1954 to April 1961.
     Resigned from the Legislative Council in November,
     1961. He was active in welfare services and was Ed-
     ucational Administrator to H.H. the Aga Khan Central
     Council of Education for Kenya from 1945 to 1954. Be-
     fore that he had been Secretary of H.H. the Aga Khan
     Education Board in 1928 and its Chairman from 1937 to
     1942. He was Honorary Private Secretary to H.R.H.
     the Aga Khan from 1945 to 1957. In recognition of his
     services to his community, H.H. the Aga Khan con-
     ferred the title of "Vazier" in 1952 and "Count" in 1954
     upon him. He died in Karachi in 1963.

NATIONAL ANTHEM. The tune of Kenya's National Anthem
is that of a traditional Pokomo lullaby. It was prepared by a five-man commission headed by Kenya's
Music Advisor at the time, Mr. Graham Hyslop. The
other members of the Commission were Mr. G. W. Sen-
oga-Zake, Mr. Thomas Kalume, Mr. Washington Omon-
di and Mr. Peter Kibukosya. The music chosen was
to reflect the idiom of the traditional music of Kenya.
The tune had to be of the right length and of a stirring
quality, yet it had to possess the necessary dignity.
The tune also had to be one that could be sung by everybody, everywhere without difficulty. Regarding the words
of the anthem, the aim was that they should express the
deepest convictions and the highest aspirations of the
people of Kenya as a whole. The words had also to
stand the test of time.

NATIONAL BANK OF KENYA LTD. Incorporated in June
1968. The policy of the bank aimed at assisting African businessmen and African firms, with a view to
increasing their participation in the local industrial and
commercial sector. Branches of the bank were opened
in Mombasa (1970), Nakuru (1971), Kisumu and a branch
in Nairobi (1973).

NATIONAL CHRISTIAN COUNCIL OF KENYA. An organization of Protestant Churches that started in 1913. It
works through an Annual General Meeting to which the
Executive Committee and through it, the full-time officers of the General Secretariat, are responsible. They
sponsor national projects which include rural training
centers, village polytechnics, irrigation schemes, urban
community improvement, family life education, community relations, youth and social work, lay training, adult
literacy, scholarship program, communications, conference and holiday centers.

NATIONAL COUNCIL OF WOMEN OF KENYA, THE. The
umbrella organization which seeks to bring together all
non-political women's associations, societies, and clubs
in Kenya to discuss matters of common interest. It
was started in 1964, with Miss Margaret Kenyatta as
the first President 1964-66. The other Presidents of
the Council have been Mrs. Damaris Ayodo, 1967-68;
Miss Salome Nolega, 1969; Mrs. Phoebe Asiyo, 1970-
71; Miss Mary Gichuru, 1972-75; Mrs. Eda Gachukia,
1975-78; and Mrs. D. Ayodo, 1978-79. The Council is

affiliated with the International Council of Women, whose
headquarters is in Paris.

NATIONAL YOUTH SERVICE, THE. Established under the
Ministry of Labour in 1964 for boys and girls between
the ages of 16 and 30. The training, which lasts two
years, aims at turning the young persons into crafts-
men and farmers. Boys and girls are recruited from
all parts of the country and in this way the service contributes towards national unity. They build roads, plant
trees, clear bushes, construct dams and fences, build
houses, construct flood protection defenses, etc. The
Service operates several farms where trainees are in-
structed on practical and theoretical farming. There
is also a Vocational Training Unit which gives instruc-
tion in carpentry, masonry, motor mechanics, fitting
and turning, and electrical work.

NATIVE INDUSTRIAL TRAINING DEPOT (NITD), THE. A
school established at Kabete in 1924 as a result of white
settlers' demands for a more efficient training of African artisans whose services they needed on the farms
and in towns. The main emphasis was to train Africans
who could be employed in the European sector of the
economy. The school offered five-year courses in carpentry, joinery, masonry, bricklaying, blacksmithing,
painting, and tailoring. Students who were taking the
three-year technical courses at Missions schools had
to do two further years at NITD. The settlers' main
motive was economic: the African artisans were cheap-
er than the Asian artisans. By 1936, it was reported
that about 1,050 students had completed their courses
at NITD: 501 carpenters, 424 masons, 72 smiths, 38
painters, and 15 tailors.

NATIVE REGISTRATION ORDINANCE see "KIPANDE"
SYSTEM

NDEGWA, DUNCAN NDERITU. Born in 1925 at Nyeri. He
was educated at Kagumo, Alliance High School and Makerere University, where he obtained a teaching diploma.
He taught for five years in government schools before
going on to St. Andrews University in Scotland for an
honors degree in Economics and History. On his return, he was employed by the East African High Commission as a Statistician 1956-59. He was responsible
for Survey of African Consumption, Income and Expendi-

ture in Nairobi 1957-58. In 1959 he was seconded to
the Treasury as an Assistant Secretary. In 1960 he
was promoted to Senior Assistant Secretary and in 1962,
to Under Secretary. He was appointed Permanent Secretary, Ministry of Finance in June 1963 and at Independence in December of that year, he became Permanent Secretary in the Office of the President, Secretary
to the Cabinet and Head of the Civil Service. As head
of the Civil Service, he played a leading role in transforming the Civil Service from a colonial instrument
concerned largely with law and order into a national instrument of government concerned with development and
welfare. In 1967 he was appointed Governor of the Central Bank of Kenya and in that position he has had considerable influence on the monetary policies of Kenya.
In 1970, he was appointed by the President as Chairman
of a Commission of Enquiry into the structure of and
remuneration in the Kenya Civil Service. In May 1971,
he produced the famous "Ndegwa Report," which he described as "another milestone in the civil service."

NDISI, MESHAK AYAKO OKELO. Born in 1926 in Uyoma,
Central Nyanza. Educated at the C.M.S. School, Maseno and Alliance High School, Kikuyu. He was one of
the earliest trade unionists. He was the first General-
Secretary of Transport and Allied Workers' Union, 1948.
He assisted in drafting the constitution of Kenya Federation of Registered Trade Unions and became its Assistant Secretary-General. He attended a Labour Course
on a Trade Union Congress of Britain Scholarship at
Ruskin College, Oxford 1948-49. On his return, he resigned from his trade union and joined the Kenya Government. In 1950, he was appointed the first African
Assistant Industrial Relations Officer in the Labour Department. He was promoted Labour Officer in 1956;
Senior Labour Officer 1961; Assistant Labour Commissioner 1962; and Permanent Secretary in the Ministry
of Labour and Social Services in 1963. In 1967, he
resigned from the Kenya Government to join the International Labor Office, first as Eastern and Southern Africa Area Director, then as Regional Director for Africa in 1969, and finally as Assistant Director-General
in Geneva, a post he held until his retirement in 1978.

NEW AKAMBA UNION, THE. The first welfare organization of the Akamba was the Akamba Union, founded in
1948. The Union built the Akamba Hall in Starehe es-

tate in Nairobi as its headquarters. In May 1961, the
New Akamba Union was founded, "For Unity and Brotherhood of the Akamba People Throughout East Africa
and Overseas." The Union aimed at the improvement of
the economic, social, cultural, and welfare conditions
of all Akamba in all parts of Kenya and outside Kenya.
It had leadership problems until 1965, when the leaders, with Joseph Mulu Mutisya, who has also been
a Nominated Member of Parliament since 1974, as
Chairman took over. Dissolved in 1980 following
a government decision to abolish all ethnic organizations.

NEW KENYA GROUP, THE. Formed on April 2, 1959, by
the same liberal Europeans who had founded the defunct
United Country Party. It was led by Sir Michael Blundell, Sir Wilfred Havelock, R. S. Alexander, and Humphrey Slade. Two African members of the Group were
Musa Amalemba, a former member of the Nairobi City
Council and a Specially Elected Member of the Legislative Council, and C. W. Rubia. By September 1959,
the Group had developed into a political party--the New
Kenya Party--which aimed at integrating Africans into
the existing economic system heavily dominated by Europeans. It, for instance, advocated the lowering of land
barriers in the Highlands to qualified African farmers;
proposed the removal of racial barriers and the encouragement of foreign investment. Most of its original
membership and support was commercial and professional. It was strongly supported by British and Kenyan
commercial interests. Wealthy British-South African
interests contributed £10,000 to the Group. The Group
later co-operated very closely with the Kenya African
Democratic Union (KADU), especially over land issues
and the future constitution of an independent Kenya. It
was dissolved in 1961.

NGALA, RONALD GIDEON. Born in Kilifi in 1923. Educated at Alliance High School, and at Makerere University
College, Uganda, where he qualified as a teacher. He
taught at Kaloleni School in 1946, became Headmaster of
Maynard School, Mbale, Taita-Taveta district and from
1952 to 1955 was headmaster of Buxton School in Mombasa. He was then sent on an educational course to
Redland College, Bristol, and on his return was appointed
Supervisor of Schools in the Mombasa area 1957-58. He

became a member of the Mombasa African Advisory
Council in 1953, and in the following year, he became
a Member of the Mombasa Municipal Board. In March
1957, he was elected to the Legislative Council as Member for Coast Rural Constituency under the Lyttleton
Constitution, which for the first time allowed direct African elections to the Kenya Legislative Council. He
soon gained much respect for his integrity and nationalism. Appointed Minister for Labour, Social Security
and Adult Education in 1960. Re-elected as Member
for Kilifi in 1961 and appointed Leader of Government
Business and Minister of Education. In 1962, he became Minister of State for Constitutional Affairs. He
was the President of the Kenya African Democratic Union
(KADU) from its formation in 1960 until its voluntary
dissolution at the end of 1964. He was re-elected to
the House of Representatives as Member for Kilifi in
1963, where he was Leader of the Opposition. Under
Regional Government, he was the first President of the
Coast Regional Assembly. On the dissolution of KADU,
he joined the Kenya African National Union (KANU) and became Chairman of its coast branch. In 1966, he was appointed Chairman of the Maize Marketing Board. On May
4, 1966, he joined Cabinet as Minister for Co-operatives
and Social Services. He was re-elected to Parliament
in 1969 and appointed Minister for Power and Communications. Author of Nchi na Desturi Za Wagiriama,
1949. Ngala died in a Nairobi hospital, following a
road accident, on December 25, 1972.

NGEI, PAUL JOSEPH. Born in 1923 at Kangundo in Machakos. A grandson of the famous paramount chief Masaku,
whose political homestead the Europeans used to refer to
as Masaku's or, later, as Machakos. He was educated
at Alliance High School, Kikuyu and Makerere College,
Uganda, 1948-50. He went to Makerere after war service (1941-45). When he left Makerere, he joined the
East African Standard (now the Standard) as a reporter,
during which time (1950-51) he also took part in the
film Where No Vultures Fly. Between 1951 and 1952
he was Secretary of the Machakos branch of the Kenya
African Union (KAU). On October 20, 1952, he was
one of the KAU leaders arrested and later charged with
managing Mau Mau. Together with Kenyatta, Ngei was
imprisoned for seven years, followed by a further two-
year period of restriction at Lodwar. On May 25, 1961,
he was allowed to return to Kangundo, where he re-

mained under "area arrest" till July 14, 1961, when he
was set free.

Contrary to his expectation, Ngei had to fight
hard to re-enter the political limelight in Kenya.   He
expected to be given a post in the Machakos KANU
branch.   This did not happen, and he had to fight for
recognition.   He resigned from KANU and formed the
African People's Party in 1962.   In the General Elections of 1963, the APP won a convincing victory in
Ukambani and Ngei was elected APP Member of Machakos North.   In the same year, he dissolved his party
and rejoined KANU.   He was appointed Chairman of the
Maize Marketing Board, 1963-65.   In April 1965, he
was appointed Minister for Co-operatives and Marketing.
In February 1966, he was moved to the Ministry of
Housing and Social Services.

On February 23, 1966, Kenyatta suspended Ngei
from the Cabinet in order to facilitate an inquiry into
the maize shortage of 1965.   The Commissioners "found
no evidence of corruption in a legal sense, but several
instances of unfairness by businessmen and politicians
taking advantage of their positions."   Ngei was rein-
stated in his Ministry in July 1966.   In 1969 elections,
he retained his seat and his Ministry.   But after the
1974 elections, he was switched to the Ministry of Local
Government.   Mr. Raphael Samson Mbondo successfully
filed a petition in the Kenya High Court against Ngei
in July-Nov. 1975.   The High Court also found Ngei
guilty of an election offense and was barred from con-
testing an election for five years.   It looked like the
end of the road for Ngei.   Parliament was, however,
requested to pass a Bill--in one day--to amend the Kenya Constitution to empower the President to alter or set
aside the judgment of the High Court in respect of election offenses arising out of election petitions.   The act
was to take effect from January 1, 1975, and thus re-
troactively to cover all cases involving election offenses
arising out of petitions heard by the High Court since
1974 General Election.   The Constitution of Kenya Amendment Bill No. 25 of 1975 was passed.   On January 12,
1976, a by-election was held at Kangundo, and Ngei was
returned to Parliament with a big majority.   He was
then appointed Minister of Co-operatives.   Re-elected
to Parliament in 1979 and appointed Minister for Works.

NGUGI, WA THIONG'O.   A novelist, Ngugi was born in
1936 at Limuru, Kenya.   Educated at Alliance High

School, Kikuyu, Makerere University College, Uganda
and Leeds University, England. Chairman of the Department of Literature, University of Nairobi, until
January 12, 1978, when he was detained under the Public Security Act. Released from detention on 12 December, 1978. Has written several works dealing largely with the Emergency period in Kenya, including The
Hermit (play) 1962; Weep Not Child (novel) 1964; The
River Between (novel) 1965; A Grain of Wheat (1967);
Homecoming (essays) 1972; Secret Lives (short stories)
1974; The Trial of Dedan Kimathi (a play, with Micere
Mugo), 1976; Petals of Blood (novel), 1977.

NJEMPS. The Njemps are also known as the Il Tiamus.
They are a Maa-speaking group which either split off
from the Samburu or from the Laikipiak Masai. They
live in the area to the south and east of Lake Baringo.
They provided most of the food (using irrigation methods) to the 19th-century caravans that stopped for re-
stocking at Baringo en route to Uganda and Zaire. They
are also keen fishermen and they keep cattle, sheep,
and goats. In demographic terms, they are the smallest group of Plains Nilotes, although they represent the
largest group of Maa-speaking cultivators in Kenya.

NJONJO, CHARLES. Born in 1920 in Kiambu; son of ex-
Senior Chief Josiah Njonjo. He was educated at Alliance High School, Kikuyu, Kings College Budo, Uganda,
Fort Hare University College, South Africa, Exeter University College, England, and London School of Economics. In 1954, he became a Barrister-at-Law at
Gray's Inn, London. In the following year, he was appointed to Government Service. In 1961, he acted as
Senior Crown Counsel, and in the following year he was
appointed Deputy Public Prosecutor. He was Kenya's
Attorney-General from 1963 to April 25, 1980. In that
capacity he was a member of Parliament and a Cabinet
Minister. He has played a leading role in the constitutional changes that have taken place since Kenya attained independence, beginning with the First Amendment Act (Act 28 of 1964) which established Kenya as
a republic with an executive President. He has also
been a staunch believer in the rule of law, a position
which has encouraged the Kenya judiciary to function in-
dependently of any direct political interference.

NJORO. A small town to the Northwest of Nakuru in the

Rift Valley. It was originally planned to be the administrative headquarters of British East African federation which was to include Uganda and the British East
African Protectorate, as Kenya was then called. Two
thousand acres of land were reserved for this purpose.
The plan never materialized and Kenya and Uganda
evolved separately. The area is also important for the
history of agriculture in Kenya. This is where Lord
Delamere established his famous Equator Ranch in 1904.
He experimented with wheat production between 1904 and
1908, when he succeeded in producing rust-resistant
wheat which is still grown in Kenya. The area also
pioneered mixed farming by growing wheat, barley, oats,
maize, and potatoes and by importing grade cattle,
sheep, and horses. One of these early settlers, Lord
Egerton of Tatton, made a gift of 800 acres of land to
establish a Farm School in the late 1920's. This was
the beginning of the now famous Egerton Agricultural
College.

NOMINATED MEMBERS OF PARLIAMENT. Introduced into the House in 1968 to replace the former Specially
Elected Members. The Act No. 45 of 1968 provides
that there shall be twelve Nominated Members appointed
by the President. There are no guidelines or rules
laid down for their nomination. They are full-mem-
bers of Parliament and can be appointed to Ministerial
posts with the exception of that of the Vice-President
which is reserved for elected members only.

NOMIYA LUO MISSION. The first independent Church in
Kenya was founded by John Owalo in 1910. He declared
himself a Prophet and denied the divinity of Christ, who
was regarded simply as another Prophet. The Church
still has a large following in Western Kenya.

NORTH KAVIRONDO CENTRAL ASSOCIATION, THE. One
of the most active district political organizations in
Western Kenya during the inter-war period. Founded
in 1932 in order to organize the people to resist any
moves to alienate more land to the Europeans. The
fear was generated by the discovery of gold in the Kakamega area in 1931, which led to widespread prospect-
ing by European miners. With Andrea Jumba as Chairman and Erasto Ligabala as Secretary, the association
initially concentrated in the southern locations of Tiriki,
Maragoli, Idakho, and Isukha. Most of the members

belonged to the Friends African Mission and their leaders were young men with no officials of the government. In 1933 it had 50 members; by 1936 it claimed a membership of 300; and by 1938 it had 800 members.

Both the government and the missions were hostile to the association. They sent many petitions both to Central government and to London, especially on land issues. It was their defense of the African land that won them much support from the public. The association also played a leading role in forging a Luyia identity. The initial name of the association was, in fact, the "Abaluyia United of North Kavirondo." In 1935, they published a pamphlet called "Abaluyia" affirming their identity. It was largely through the association's efforts that the name came to be adopted. Thirdly, they campaigned ceaselessly, though unsuccessfully, for a Paramount Chief of the Abaluyia. The association had connections with the Kikuyu Central Association, and it even sent students after 1938, to Githunguri. It also worked closely with the Luo section of the Kavirondo Taxpayers and Welfare Association, especially under the leadership of Zablon Aduwo Nyandonje and John Paul Olola, both of whom were traders and who had founded the Kisumu Native Chamber of Commerce in the late twenties. Olola and Aduwo assisted some members of the NKCA from Maragoli and Tiriki to found the North Kavirondo Chamber of Commerce. In 1941, the association accepted the government request to dissolve voluntarily because of the war, but they were allowed to hold annual feast days. When the Kenya African Union was started in the district after the war, the NKCA was absorbed into it.

NYAGA, JEREMIA. Born in 1920 at Kigare in Embu District, Eastern Province. He was educated at Kangaru C.M.S. School; Kagumo Government School (1934-36); Alliance High School, Kikuyu (1936-40); and Makerere University College (1940-43). Joined Kahuhia Teacher Training Centre in Murang'a in 1943, and from 1944-47 was Headmaster of Intermediate School, Kahuhia. From 1947-52, Headmaster of Embu Government African School. He went to Oxford University, England to take a teachers' diploma (1953-54). On his return, Nyaga went to Kangaru Teachers' Training Department (1954-55) before he was promoted to be Assistant Education Officer in Kiambu (1956-58). He left teaching to join politics in 1958: elected Member for Embu in the Legislative Coun-

cil in 1958; elected Deputy Speaker of the Legislative
Council, 1960; re-elected to Parliament in 1963 as
Member for Embu South, and appointed Parliamentary
Secretary in the Ministry of Works, Communications
and Power.   In 1964, he became Assistant Minister of
Lands and Settlement and then Assistant Minister for
Home Affairs 1964-1966.   Appointed Minister of Educa-
tion 1966 and Minister for Natural Resources 1968-69.
Became Minister for Information and Broadcasting in
1969.   Re-elected to Parliament as Member for Embu
South in 1969 and appointed Minister for Agriculture.
Re-elected to Parliament in the same constituency and
appointed Minister for Agriculture 1974-79.   In the General Election of 1979, re-elected to Parliament and appointed Minister for Livestock Development.   Awarded
Elder of the Golden Heart.   He is Chief Commissioner
of Scouts, Kenya.

NYAMWEYA, JAMES.   A lawyer and politician.   Born on
December 28, 1927, at Kisii.   Educated at Nyanchwa
Mission School, Kamagambo Training School, Kings
College, London University 1954-58, where he obtained
an LL.B. (Honors) degree.   He then got his Barrister-
at-Law qualification at Lincoln's Inn, London.   Before
going abroad for further education, he had worked for
a short time as a teacher 1949-54.   On his return, he
was appointed Legal Assistant in the Ministry of Legal
Affairs, Kenya, 1958-59.   He then resigned to go into
private practice, 1959-63.   He was elected a KANU Member of the House of Representatives representing Nyari-
bari in 1963.   He had been a Founder Member and a
Member of the Central Executive Committee of KANU
from its inception, as well as being KANU Chairman of
the Kisii Branch 1962-64.   He was appointed Parliamentary Secretary to the Ministry of Justice and Constitutional Affairs in 1963 to assist the late Tom Mboya; and
in the office of the Prime Minister 1964-65.   He was
then appointed Minister of State, Provincial Administration and Civil Service in the Office of the President,
1965-66; Leader of Government Business in the House
of Representatives, May-December 1966; Minister of
State, Foreign Affairs, Office of the President, and
Leader of Government Business in the National Assembly, January 1967; Minister of Power and Communications until December 1969; Minister of Works, 1969-74;
Minister of Labour, November 1974 to 1979.   He holds
an honorary LL.D. (U.S.A.).

- O -

ODEDE, FANUEL WALTER.   An educator and veteran politician.   Born in 1912 in Uyoma, Central Nyanza District.   Educated at Maseno Secondary School and at Alliance High School in 1931.   Appointed an Instructor at
   the Veterinary Training Centre at Maseno, from where
   he was sent to Makerere College, Uganda, for further
   training in Veterinary Science.   He returned to Kenya
   in 1941 and was appointed an Assistant Veterinary Officer at Maseno.   In 1945, during the temporary ab-
   sence of Bishop Beecher, he was nominated to take his
   place as the African Representative Member in the Legislative Council.   He went to Britain for advanced study
   in Veterinary Science and was appointed Lecturer in the
   subject at Makerere University College on his return.
   He came back to Kenya in 1952 to become Director of
   the Associated Press of East Africa Ltd., which purchased the Nairobi Tribune Press.   The paper was soon
   proscribed by the Government.   He became the President of the Kenya African Union (KAU) following the
   arrest of Kenyatta in 1952.   In the following year, on
   March 10, he was also arrested and charged with being
   connected with the Mau Mau movement and supporting
   the use of violence.   He was detained at Kwale Detention Camp at the coast, and from 1957, was employed
   in detention as Assistant Veterinary Officer.   He was
   released from detention and restriction in October 1960.
   He was elected to the Legislative Council as a National
   Member in 1961.   From 1969 to 1974, he was the
   Chairman of Siaya District branch of KANU.   He was
   nominated to Parliament on October 31, 1974.   Odede
   died on December 24, 1974.

ODERO-JOWI, JOSEPH GORDON.   Born in 1929 in South
   Nyanza and was educated at the Government African
   School, Kisii, Maseno Secondary School 1946-49, and
   Kagumo Teacher Training College.   He then went to
   the University of Calcutta where he obtained his B.A.
   (Hons).   Before he returned to Kenya, he took a one-
   year post-graduate course in economics at the University of Delhi 1957-58.   In 1958, he was appointed Lecturer in Economics at the African Labour College, Kampala.   Between 1960 and 1961, he worked with the United
   Nations Economic Commission for Africa in Ethiopia and
   America before returning to the African Labour College
   as Principal.   He won the 1963 elections, and was re-

turned to the House of Representatives as the KANU
Member for Lambwe. He was appointed Parliamentary
Secretary, Ministry of Labour and Social Services and
Chairman of the National Wages Policy Advisory Committee, 1963. When Kenya became a Republic in December 1964, he was appointed Assistant Minister for
Labour. In the same year, he had become the Chairman of KANU in South Nyanza. In the following year,
he was appointed Assistant Minister for Finance. On
the establishment of the East African Community in December 1967, Odero-Jowi became the first East African Minister for Finance and Administration. He contributed substantially towards the development of this
regional grouping. With the assassination of Tom Mboya
in August 1969, Odero-Jowi was appointed Minister for
Economic Planning and Development. He lost his seat
in the 1969 General Election and was appointed Kenya's
Permanent Representative to the United Nations in 1970.
Between 1970 and 1974, he effectively championed various Third World causes and emerged as an acute ob-
server of international politics. He also presided, for
a brief period, over the proceedings of the Security
Council. He was largely responsible, at the UNO level,
in having Nairobi chosen as the Headquarters of the
United Nations Environment Programme. He fought
and won the Ndhiwa seat in the 1974 General Election.
In 1976, he resigned from his seat, to take up a job
with the United Nations in Canada.

ODHIAMBO, THOMAS RISLEY. Born February 4, 1931,
    and educated at Kisumu, Ng'iya and Maseno Junior
    Primary School, C. M. S. Maseno School 1943-1949;
    Makerere University College (1950-53) and University
    of Cambridge (1959-65), obtaining an M. A. in Natural
    Science and a Ph. D. in Insect Physiology. One of the
    most distinguished Kenya Scientists and one of the lead-
    ing authorities in the world on tropical insects. He was
    employed as a Technical Assistant in the Agricultural
    Division at the Tea Research Institute of East Africa,
    Kericho 1954-1955; Assistant Agricultural Officer, Ser-
    ere Experimental Station (Entomology Division), Uganda
    1955-1956; Curator of Insect Collections, Kawanda Re-
    search Station, Uganda 1956-1959; Entomologist in the
    Ministry of Agriculture and Cooperatives, Uganda,
    (1962); Lecturer in Zoology, University College Nairobi,
    1965-1967; Senior Lecturer and Reader in 1967, 1969
    respectively; appointed first Professor and Head of the

new Department of Entomology, University of Nairobi,
in 1970; Dean of the new Faculty of Agriculture 1970-
1971; First Director of the International Centre of Insect Physiology and Ecology (ICIPE) in Nairobi since
1970. Under his able leadership, the Centre has
achieved world acclaim, as a center of excellence; has
been involved in numerous public activities as a Consultant or expert, and has attended many international
conferences in all parts of the world; a Fellow of at
least fourteen Scientific Societies including Royal En-
tomological Society of London since 1959, New York
Academy since 1962, Indian National Science Academy
from January 1977, Royal Society of Tropical Medicine
and Hygiene, London, since January, 1978. In March
1979, he became the first African to be inducted by the
Italian National Academy of Science to an academic
Chair and also elected a member of the academy. He
has published more than 85 papers and monographs in
scientific periodicals and six children's scientific books.

ODINGA, AJUMA OGINGA. Born in October 1911 in Sakwa
Location, Central Nyanza. One of the most controversial politicians in Kenya, who has been a rebel all his
life. He was educated at Maseno School (1930-34), the
Alliance High School, Kikuyu (1934-36), Makerere College, Uganda (1937-1940) gaining a diploma in teaching.
He taught at Maseno School 1940-42, was headmaster
of Maseno Veterinary School 1943-46. One of the founders of Luo Thrift and Trading Corporation and its Managing Director from 1947 to 1962. From 1947 to 1949,
Odinga was a Member of the Central Nyanza African
District Council.

In an attempt to organize the Luo community into a united force, he played a leading role in the reor-
ganization of Luo Union from being a Nairobi-based
welfare body into an East African organization with its
headquarters in Kisumu. He was the president of Luo
Union (E.A.) from 1952 to 1957, when he resigned to
contest the first African elections to the Legislative
Council. He won the election and became one of the
eight first African elected members of the Legislative
Council--T. J. Mboya, R. Ngala, B. Mate, L. G.
Oguda, Masinde Muliro, Daniel arap Moi, Muimi and
Oginga Odinga. He became Chairman of the African
Elected Members Organization with Mboya as Secretary.
In the General Election of 1961, he was returned to the
Legislative Council as one of the two members for Cen-

tral Nyanza. He was elected to the House of Representatives as Member for Bondo in the 1963 General Election and was appointed Minister for Home Affairs. When
Kenya became a Republic in 1964, he was appointed
Vice-President and Minister without portfolio. He was
also Vice-President of KANU from June 1960 (when
KANU was formed) to 1966 (when the post was abolished).
He resigned as Vice-President of Kenya and from KANU
in 1966 to lead an Opposition Party, the Kenya People's
Union (KPU), which he and Bildad Kaggia formed in
that year. In 1969, he was arrested and detained and
his party proscribed. He was released towards the
end of 1971, after which he re-joined KANU. He was
appointed Chairman of Cotton, Seed and Marketing Board
in November 1979. He is the author of Not Yet Uhuru
(1967).

OGOT, BETHWELL ALLAN,   Born August 3, 1929, at Luanda, Central Nyanza.   Educated at Luanda Primary
School (1938-42), Ambira School (1943-45), Maseno
Secondary School (1946-49), Makerere University College (1950-52), St. Andrews University, Scotland (1955-
59) and School of Oriental and African Studies, London
University (1960-61).   Mathematics Master, Alliance
High School, Kikuyu (1953-55), Lecturer in History,
Makerere University College (1959-64); Senior Lecturer
in History, Nairobi University College, (1964-65); Reader in History 1966-67; Professor and Head of History
Department 1967-77.   First Director of Institute of African Studies, University of Nairobi 1965-75; Dean, Faculty of Arts, University College Nairobi 1967-69; Deputy
Vice-Chancellor, University of Nairobi 1970-72.   Outside the University, Ogot was Secretary-General of the
East African Institute of Social and Cultural Affairs
1964-69; founder and Chairman of Board of Directors
of the East African Publishing House 1964-74; Secretary-General of Jomo Kenyatta Foundation 1968-69.   He
has served in various organizations, for example, Member of East African Examination Council 1967-74; Member of the National Commission for UNESCO since 1968;
Trustee of the National Museums of Kenya 1969-1977;
Member of the Executive Committee of the Association
of African Universities 1972-1978; Member of the Executive Council of the British Institute in Eastern Africa
1969-1978; Member of the East African Legislative Council 1974-77; Founder Member and Past Vice-President
of the East African Academy; Founder Member of the

Historical Association of Kenya and its Chairman since
its inception in 1966; Member of the International Scientific Committee for the Preparation of UNESCO General History of Africa, a Member of its Bureau and
President of the Committee since 1977; Member of the
Executive Council of the International African Institute,
London, since 1978; President of the Pan-African Association for Prehistory and Related Studies since 1977;
Director of the International Louis Leakey Memorial Institute for African Prehistory, Nairobi, 1977-80. He
has published fifteen books and over eighty papers in
learned journals. Editor of East Africa Journal 1964-
74; and Transafrican Journal of History 1971-1979.

OGOT, GRACE EMILY AKINYI. A trained nurse and mid-
wife, journalist broadcaster, author, and business woman. She was born in 1930 in Central Nyanza. Educated
at Maseno Junior School, Ng'iya Girls' School, Butere
Girls' High School, Mengo Nursing Training Hospital
1949-53; St. Thomas Hospital, London and British Hospital for Mothers and Babies, London (1955-58) where
she obtained her S.R.N. and S.C.M. Returned to Kenya and worked as Nursing Sister and Midwifery Tutor
at Maseno Hospital in Western Kenya. Married in 1959
and returned to England in the same year. Worked with
the British Broadcasting Corporation, Africa Division,
as Script Writer and Announcer for about two years.
Returned to Kenya in 1961 to take up a new appointment
as District Community Development Officer, and Head-
mistress of Kisumu Homecraft Training Centre. She
was the first African woman to be nominated Councillor
of Kisumu Municipality. From 1963-64, she was the
Nursing Sister in charge of Students Health Service at
Makerere University College. In 1965, she was appointed Public Relations Manager for an international
airline in Nairobi. She has been Chairman of Kenya
Writers Association since its inception. Was a Member
of the Kenya Delegation to United Nations General Assembly, New York, in 1975; and a Member of the Kenya Delegation to the 19th General Conference of UNESCO
in 1976. She is a former Member of the Rent Tribunal
and is a Member of the Teacher's Tribunal. She has
been the Managing Director of Lindy's Limited since
1968. Regularly contributes feature articles on womens'
affairs to newspapers and magazines since 1960. Has
published several works: The Promised Land, Novel,
1966; Land Without Thunder, Short Stories, 1967; The

Other Woman, Short Stories, 1975; Short Stories from
Kenya, published in Sweden 1976; The Graduate (novel),
1980; Island of Tears (short stories), 1980; plus several short stories in magazines and book anthologies all
over the world. A co-author of A Glossary in English,
Kiswahili, Kikuyu and Dholuo (1957).

OHANGA, BENAIAH APOLO. Born in 1913 in Gem, Central
Nyanza. Educated at Maseno School and Alliance High
School, Kikuyu. Trained as a teacher. In 1949, he
went to Britain for Primary Education and Local Government Courses. In 1961, he went for a course in
Public Administration in West Germany. He was a
teacher from 1933 to 1945. He became a Member of
Central Nyanza District Education Board from 1943 to
1948. A good linguist, he became Secretary of the Luo
Language Committee and a Member of the Kenya Language Board in 1945. In that capacity he visited Sudan
and Zaire to try to evolve a common orthography for
Nilotic languages. From 1947 to 1957, he served as
the second African Member of the Legislative Council,
working with Eliud Wambu Mathu who had been appointed
in 1944 as the first African Member. In 1954, he was
appointed the first African Minister, being given the
portfolio of Community Development and Rehabilitation.
Like his colleague Mathu, he was defeated in the first
African General Election of 1957. He was then appointed Education Officer in the City of Nairobi in 1958.
In 1962, he became District Education Officer. In the
following year, he was appointed Secretary/Executive
Officer, Kenya Overseas Scholarship Advisory Committee.
He was also a Member of Nairobi City Council from
1961-63. From 1963, he became Inspector of Children
in the Ministry of Home Affairs and Administrative Officer in charge of Young Persons Act, 1963. In 1966,
he was appointed First Vice-President, Central Organization of Trade Unions (Kenya). He has now retired
from public service.

OIL PIPELINE. The Government-owned Kenya Pipeline
Company started operating the 449-kilometer, Mombasa-
to-Nairobi oil pipeline in February 1978. It cost £42.5
million and is designed for transporting up to 5,200 million liters of oil per annum.

OJAL, JOEL MESHAK. A distinguished educationist. Born

on January 26, 1918, at Ramba Asembo in Siaya District. He was educated at Ramba School 1924-31; Maseno School 1932-34; Alliance High School, Kikuyu 1935-
36; Makerere College 1937-1939, obtaining a Teacher's
Diploma; London Institute of Education 1947-48, where
he obtained another Teacher's Diploma; Hull University
College 1948-1952, where he studied Geography, Geology and Botany for his B. Sc.   Taught at Government
African School Kisii 1940; Alliance High School (1941-
1946); Maseno High School (1947 and 1952-1959); St.
John Teacher Training College, Ng'iya and Acting Principal for six months, (1960-1961); Government of Kenya
Civil Service 1962-1972, where he worked as Assistant
Secretary in the Ministry of Education 1962-63; Assistant Secretary in the Provincial Administration, Kisumu
1963; Permanent Secretary, Ministry of Local Government 1963-1964; Permanent Secretary in the Office of
the Vice-President 1964-66; Permanent Secretary, Ministry of Natural Resources 1966-1972.   Since March
1972, he has been in charge of general administration
at the International Centre of Insect Physiology and Ecology (ICIPE) in Nairobi. Has attended many conferences as
member of the Kenya delegation.   He is a Member of
the Association for the Advancement of Agricultural Sciences in Africa, African Association of Insect Scientists,
and Kenya Bible Society; was Vice-Chairman of East African Natural Resources Research Council (EANRRC)
from 1976-1977, and Chairman of all its Coordinating
Committees.

OJIAMBO, JULIA AUMA.   Born in Samia Location, Busia
District, Western Province.   Educated at Sigalame Primary School, Butere Girls School and Alliance Girls
High School, Kikuyu.   She then joined the Royal Technical College, Nairobi, where she studied Education and
Home Economics.   Went back in 1956 to teach at her
former school, Butere Girls School.   Married Dr. Hilary Ojiambo, who was then the Registrar of Mulago Hospital and a Lecturer at the Makerere Medical School.
Worked with Professor Jelliffe of Makerere University
on problems of nutrition, while also working as Assistant Warden at the Y. W. C. A. of Uganda.   She then became the manageress of Makerere University Guest
House.   When her husband returned to Kenya, Julia
came back with him, and joined the Kenya Y. W. C. A.
She then took a job with the East African Railway Welfare Section, which put her in charge of women's activi-

ties in the East African region.   She obtained a Fellowship from FAO/UNICEF for a course in Community Nutrition and Public Health and to complete her undergrad-
uate course in Nutrition Science at Queen's College, London University.   On her return to Kenya she became the
first African woman Lecturer at the then Royal College,
now University of Nairobi, where she taught for ten
years.   Completed her M. Sc. degree at Harvard University, U. S. A. in Public Health and registered for a
Ph. D. at McGill University, Canada.   She completed
her doctorate at the University of Nairobi in 1973 and
continued to teach at the Kenyatta University College,
University of Nairobi, until 1974, when she resigned to
join politics.   She was elected M. P. for Busia Central,
and appointed Assistant Minister for Housing and Social
Services, the first woman in Kenya to be so honored.
In 1979, she retained her seat in the General Election
and was appointed Assistant Minister for Basic Education.   Has been awarded the Ceres Medal by the Food
and Agricultural Organization (FAO) for her services
in promoting health services for mother and child in
the community.   She is the author of The Trees of
Kenya (1978).

OKERO, ISAAC OMOLO.   Born in 1929 at Ulumbi in Gem,
    Central Nyanza.   Educated at Ambira (1943-45); Ma-
    seno Secondary School (1946-47); Alliance High School
    (1948-49).   He joined Makerere University College in
    1950, but was sent down as a ringleader of a students'
    strike.   He obtained a scholarship to Bombay Universi-
    ty to study law in 1953, graduating with an LL. B. in
    1955.   In 1956, at the 6th International Students Con-
    ference in Ceylon, he was elected Secretary of this or-
    ganization.   For the next three years, he ran this body
    from its headquarters in Leiden, Holland, during which
    period he travelled extensively in Europe, Asia, Latin
    America, Africa, and North America.   He then pro-
    ceeded to London to study law, qualifying as a Barrister
    in 1961.   On his return to Kenya, he worked as a State
    Counsel in the Attorney-General's Chambers, rising
    three years later to the post of Deputy Public Prosecutor
    (Supernumerary).   In 1965, he resigned from this to be-
    come the East African Commissioner of Customs and
    Excise.   In 1969, he resigned from the Commissioner's
    job to establish the Omolo Okero Advocates firm in Nai-
    robi.   Following the death of C. M. G. Argwings-Kodhek
    in a car accident in 1968, and the detention of Wasonga

Sijeyo in 1969, Omolo Okero won the Gem seat in the 1969 General Election. He was appointed Minister for Health. In early 1974, he was appointed Minister for Power and Communications, a portfolio he retained after the 1974 General Election. In 1976, he was elected Chairman of KANU for Siaya district in Nyanza. In 1978, he was appointed Minister of Broadcasting and Information, and following the death of Kenyatta, he was transferred back to the Ministry of Power and Communications.

OKIEK, THE. A group of hunters and gatherers who are Kalenjin-speakers and who live in forest regions adjacent to Kalenjin areas. The word "Okiek" is a Kalenjin word which seems to mean the same thing as "Il-Torobo" in Masai. The Okiek and the Dorobo are therefore likely to be of the same derivation. See also DOROBO.

OKULLU, JOHN HENRY. Journalist, author, and prominent church leader. Born in Asembo, Central Nyanza, in 1930. Educated at Bishop Tucker Theological College, Mukono 1956-57. Obtained a scholarship to Virginia Theological Seminary, U.S.A., where he attained a B.D. degree (1963-65). Before his conversion, he worked as a clerk for Military Construction Unit, 1948-51; and then as a Clerk for the East African Railways and Harbours, in Kampala, Uganda from 1952-56. Was Ordained in 1958. On his return to Uganda from U.S.A., he became the Publicity Secretary of the Church of Uganda, Rwanda and Burundi and the first African editor of New Day, a Church of Uganda publication. He was also the Executive Officer for the joint Protestant-Catholic Council of Uganda. He returned to Kenya in 1967 and became assistant editor of Target and Lengo, the National Christian Council of Kenya publications, and in 1968 he became the first African editor of both publications. Until 1971, when he became the Provost of All Saints Cathedral in Nairobi, Okullu turned what were formerly religious publications into major national weekly newspapers that dealt with a wide variety of issues, religious and secular, in a provocative and analytical style. As Provost of All Saints Cathedral, he soon transformed the church into a major national forum, from which he interpreted the Christian message into secular terms. In February 1974, he was consecrated bishop of Maseno South, where he has succeeded in

organizing a comprehensive program aimed at improving the spiritual and social and economic welfare of
his flock. In 1973, he was awarded an Honorary Doctor of Divinity degree by Virginia Theological Seminary,
his old Seminary. He serves on numerous local and
international bodies, including the Central Committee of
the World Council of Churches and since 1977, he has
been the Chairman of the Council's Communications department. He is the author of Church and Politics in
East Africa (1975), which is a best-seller, and Church
and Marriage in East Africa (1976).

OLANG', MOST REVEREND FESTO HABAKKUK. A Kenyan
ecclesiastic born on November 14, 1914, at Maseno.
Educated at Alliance High School, Kikuyu, St. Paul's
Theological College, Limuru, and Wycliffe Hall, Oxford.
He worked as a teacher at Maseno Secondary School
1936-39 and at Butere Girls School 1940-45. He was
Ordained Deacon in 1945 and consecrated Bishop in
1955. From 1961 to 1970, he was Bishop of Maseno
and in 1970 he was appointed Archbishop of the Anglican Church in Kenya. He retired in 1979, having rendered stirling service to the Church.

OLOITIPTIP, STANLEY SHAPSHINA OLE. Born at Loito-
kitok and educated at Loitokitok Government School and
Narok Government School. He joined the army soon
after leaving school 1943-46, rising to the rank of Ser-
geant major. On leaving the army, he was elected
Moran leader by the Masai elders 1946-48. He then
joined the medical services, working in the Tanganyika
Medical Service, Masailand 1948-50; Special Graded
Dresser for Kajiado District, 1950-60. When the Masai
United Front was formed, he was elected its district
Chairman in 1956. He joined KADU 1960-62, before
changing to join the ruling party KANU in 1963. He
also became the district Chairman of KANU in the same
year. In 1964, he was appointed an Assistant Minister
of Commerce and Industry; and after the 1969 General
Election, he became Assistant Minister for Health. In
1974, following a General Election, Mr. Oloitiptip became the Minister for Natural Resources. In 1976, he
was re-elected KANU Chairman for Kajiado District.
Appointed Minister for Home Affairs in 1978. Re-
elected to Parliament in 1979 and re-appointed Minister
for Home Affairs. In 1980 he became the Minister for
Local Government. A fiery politician and a spokesman
for the Masai, Mr. Oloitiptip is a wealthy farmer.

OLONANA see LENANA

OLORGESAILLE. A famous prehistoric site in the Kajiado
District on the way to Lake Magadi, about 45 miles
from Nairobi. It has an abundance of stone tools. The
stone-dwellers of the area lived on large animals that
became extinct about 50,000 years ago.

OMAMO, WILLIAM ODONGO. Born in 1928 in Sakwa location, Central Nyanza. Educated at Maranda and Maseno Secondary School, 1946-49. Then he won the Government of India's cultural scholarship to study agriculture, obtaining a B.Sc. (agriculture) in 1955. On
his return to Kenya, he was employed as a lecturer at
Siriba College in Nyanza. He next went to Pakistan to
do post-graduate work, obtaining an M.Sc. in Agricultural Economics in 1959. In the following year, he
went to the University of Oregon in the United States
where he studied agricultural economics and extention
methods, obtaining another M.Sc. in Agriculture in
1961. Fully trained, Omamo returned to Kenya to
work in various capacities in the Ministry of Agriculture before joining politics. He carried out an agricultural economics survey of Central Province between
1961 and 1963. In March 1963, he was appointed the
first African District Agricultural Officer in South Nyanza. He was promoted in the same year to be the
first Nyanza Regional Agricultural Officer. In the following year, he was transferred to the headquarters of
the ministry as an Assistant Director of Agriculture in
charge of economic planning. Within a year, he was
promoted to become the principal of Egerton College,
Njoro. In 1969, he resigned from his post to contest
the Bondo Parliamentary seat which had become vacant
following the detention of Oginga Odinga. He won the
election and was appointed Minister of Natural Resources
in 1969. He was an effective minister and a great pro-
moter of harambee projects in his constituency. He
lost his seat in the 1974 General Election and was appointed Executive Chairman of the Mumias Sugar Company.
In 1975, he was nominated to Parliament, following the
death of Walter Odede. He also became Chairman of the
Kenya Sugar Manufacturers Association. He is one of the
most successful large-scale farmers in Kenya today. He
resigned from all these posts in 1979 to contest election,
which he lost. Appointed Chairman of Agriculture Finance
Corporation, 1980. In the same year he was appointed Chairman of the University of Nairobi Council.

OMARI, DUNSTAN ALFRED.   A Kenyan by naturalization
in 1972, a business executive and administrator.   Born
in 1922 at Newala, Tanzania.   Educated at St. Joseph
Secondary School, Chidya, St. Andrews Secondary School,
Minaki, Makerere University College and University of
Wales (Aberystwyth), where he obtained a B.A. degree.
Worked as Education Officer (Broadcasting Duties) 1953-
54; District Officer 1955-58; District Commissioner
1958-61.   In 1961-62, he was the Tanganyika High Commissioner in the United Kingdom.   He was then appointed Permanent Secretary, Prime Minister's Office
and Secretary to the Cabinet, Tanganyika, 1962; Permanent Secretary, President's Office and Secretary to
Cabinet, Tanganyika 1962-63; Secretary-General, East
African Common Services Organization 1964-67; 67-68
(now called East African Community) being the first
East African to hold the post.   He then became the
Chairman, East African Currency Board 1964-72; Member, Presidential Commission of Inquiry into the Structure and Remuneration of Public Service in Kenya 1971-
72; Chairman E.A. Railways Salaries Review Commission 1971-72.   He is at the moment Chairman, Kenya
Board of Standard Bank Ltd. and a director of several
companies.   He published Talks on Citizenship in 1954.

O'MEARA, REV. FATHER JOHN JOSEPH.   A prominent
educationist.   He was born in 1907 in Ireland.   Educated at Christian Brother and Blackrock College Dublin, University College Dublin and Kimmage Manor,
Dublin.   Ordained in 1935 in Ireland.   Came to Kenya
in 1937 as Junior Master at Kabaa (1937-40).   Became
Assistant Headmaster at the Holy Ghost College, Mangu
1940-42 and Headmaster at the same college 1942-48.
He was Diocesan Education Secretary in 1949-50 and
Educational Secretary General 1951-65.   Became General Secretary of the Kenya Episcopal Conference, 1961-
65.

OMINDE, SIMEON HONGO.   One of the pioneer University
dons in East Africa.   Born in 1924 at Nyahera in Kisumu district, he was educated at the Alliance High
School (1943-44), Makerere University College, (1945-
48), before he went to teach at Maseno Secondary School,
1949-50.   From 1950 to 1954, he studied at Aberdeen
University, during which time he won the Silver Medal
of the Royal Scottish Geographical Society.   He then
moved on to Edinburgh University to take a diploma in

education, 1954-55.   In 1955 he was appointed Lecturer
in Geography at Makerere College rising to Senior Lecturer before he left Makerere College in 1963 to become the Head and Professor of Geography at the University of Nairobi.   In 1963, he obtained his Ph.D.
from the University of London.   In 1964, he was appointed Chairman of the Kenya Education Commission
and in the same year he became Chairman of Kenya
Central Scholarship Board, an important honorary post
which he continues to hold with distinction.   Since 1964
he has been on the board of the International Labour Institute.   In 1966, he was Chairman of the International
Hydrological decade.   Professor Ominde has made a
substantial contribution in the field of population studies
in Africa.   He was appointed Director of the new Institute of Research in Population Studies at the University
of Nairobi in 1977.   His professional publications are
numerous and include Land and Population in Western
Kenya, Land and Population Movements in Kenya, The
Population of Kenya, Tanzania and Uganda, East African Atlas 1967-68 (joint editor), Studies in East African
Geography and Development (editor), and Population
Growth and Economic Development in Africa (joint editor).

OMOTIK (also, O-LAAMOOT-L, plural LAAMOOT).   The
Omotik live in the Narok District of the Rift Valley.
According to their tradition, they originally lived on
Mount Ngulot to the South of River Amala (Mara) at the
Southern fringes of the Mau Forest.   Like the Yaaku,
they were originally hunter-gatherers.   During the co-
lonial period they began to mix with the neighboring
Masai, adopting their pastoral economy, culture, and
language.   Today there are less than one hundred Omo-
tik speakers left.

ONEKO, ACHIENG' RAMOGI.   Born in 1920 at Kabudha in
Uyoma, in the present Siaya district.   He has spent
sixteen years in restriction, detention and imprisonment for political reasons.   He was educated at Maseno High School and privately.   He was employed as
a meteorological observer/clerk in Nairobi from 1941
to 1945.   In 1945, Oneko left his job to start and edit
a Luo-language weekly called Ramogi.   In 1949 he was
nominated to Nairobi Municipal Council--the first Luo
member of the Council, which at that time had only two
African members--and remained on the Council for ten

months.   In 1949, Oneko moved to Kisumu, ostensibly
to help Odinga to organize the Luo Thrift and Trading
Company, but in reality to organize Luo support for the
Kenya African Union, which he had joined in 1946.   He
first met Kenyatta when covering his meetings as a
newspaperman.   In 1950, he became Chairman of the
Nyanza branch of KAU.   At the end of 1951 Achieng',
with Mbiyu Koinange, went to London as the KAU delegation to discuss the land question and independence,
but they were cold-shouldered.   Both in Britain and in
Paris, where they went to approach the United Nations,
Achieng' and Koinange held many press conferences in
which they explained the African views about the future
of Kenya.

Early in 1952 Achieng' returned to Kenya while
Mbiyu Koinange stayed on in Britain.   He was elected
general Secretary of KAU towards the middle of 1952.
In October 1952, he was arrested with Kenyatta and
other prominent KAU members.   A few months later
he was brought to trial at Kapenguria with Kenyatta,
Kungu Karumba, Fred Kubai, Paul Ngei, and Bildad
M. Kaggia.   Achieng' was acquitted on appeal on January 15, 1954, but detained under Emergency regulations on Manda Island until the middle of 1959, when
he was moved to Marsabit then later to Kapsabet.   Finally, in May 1961, he was allowed to return to his
home in Nyanza.   This was four days before Kenyatta
was released.   He was appointed Private and Personal
Secretary of Kenyatta.   In the 1963 General Election,
he was elected KANU Member for Nakuru and appointed
Minister for Information, Broadcasting and Tourism.
It was through this Ministry that KANU hoped to educate
the masses about the meaning of independence.

In 1966, Achieng' Oneko resigned from both KANU
and the Government to join the Kenya People's Union.
He fought the "Little General Election" on the KPU ticket and lost.   Towards the end of 1969, the Government
proscribed the KPU and arrested and detained all its
leaders, including Odinga and Oneko.   He was not released until October 1975.   He rejoined KANU in 1976.
Appointed Chairman of the Kenya Films Corporation in
1980.

ONYANGO, GRACE MONICA AKECH.   Teacher and pioneer
woman politician.   Born in Sakwa, Central Nyanza.   Educated at Gobeyi and Ramba primary schools and thence
to Ng'iya Girls School in 1942-47.   From Ng'iya she

went to Vihiga Training Centre for teacher training,
1948-49. Taught in several schools in Kisumu District
from 1950. Elected Councillor in Kisumu Municipality
in 1963 and in 1965 she became the first woman mayor
in Kenya, when she was elected Mayor of Kisumu. She
went to East Germany for a Local Government Seminar
and to Bulgaria for a Public Health Seminar. She was
also elected to serve in various organizations: she
was Secretary of Kisumu branch of Luo Union; Assistant Girl Guides Commissioner, Kisumu District; Chairman, Kisumu branch of Child Welfare Society; Visiting
Justice, Nyanza Women's Prison, and a member of the
Y.W.C.A. In 1969, she became the first woman in
Kenya to be elected to Parliament as Member for Kisumu town. She was Secretary General of Luo Union
1968-78 and re-elected to Parliament for the same constituency in 1974 and 1979.

ONYONKA, ZAKARIAH. Born in 1941 in Kisii. Educated
at Mosocho school, Nyabururu (1952-54), St. Mary's
School, Yala (1955-58). He went for further studies to
America, gaining B.A. degree at the Inter-American
University, Puerto Rico (1960-62) and his M.A. and
Ph.D. in Economics at Syracuse University, New York
(1963-68). On his return he was appointed Research
Fellow, University College Nairobi. In the same year,
he resigned from the University to contest the General
Elections of 1969. Elected Member of Parliament for
Kitutu West and appointed Minister for Economic Plan-
ning and Development; Minister for Information and
Broadcasting 1970-73; and then Minister for Health 1973-
74. Re-elected to Parliament in 1974 as Member for
Kitutu West and appointed Minister for Education, 1974-
76. From 1976 to 1979, Minister for Housing and Social Services. Re-elected to Parliament in 1979, and
appointed Minister for Economic Planning and Development.

ORGANISATION OF AFRICAN TRADE UNION UNITY. A
Continental trade union movement founded in Addis-
Ababa in April 1973 under the auspices of the Organisa-
tion of African Unity with Mr. James Dennis Akumu of
Kenya as the first Secretary General. Its Permanent
Secretariat is based at Accra, Ghana.

ORGANISATION OF AFRICAN UNITY (OAU). Founded in
Addis-Ababa on May 26, 1963, to promote unity and

solidarity among African States. Its main aims are to
intensify and coordinate efforts to improve living standards in Africa, to eradicate all forms of colonialism
from Africa, to defend sovereignty, territorial integrity
and independence of African States, and to promote international cooperation, in accordance with the charter
of the United Nations. An Assembly of Heads of State
meets at least once a year to coordinate policies. Its
permanent secretariat was established at Addis-Ababa,
Ethiopia in July 1964, with Diallo Telli of Guinea as
the first Secretary General.

ORKOIYOT (plural, ORKOIK). A ritual leader of the Kipsigis and the Nandi. The institution appears to have
emerged in the 19th century. Barsabotwo, for example,
is said to have been the first Nandi orkoiyot, and he
was probably of Masai origin. Kipchomber arap Koi-
legei, brother of the most famous of the Nandi orkoik,
Koitelel arap Samoei, was the first Kipsigis orkoiyot.

ORMSBY-GORE COMMISSION (1924). The question of
closer union for British territories in East and Central
Africa was a major preoccupation of British and colon-
ial governments in the region between 1920 and 1960.
Several commissions were appointed to inquire into the
desirability of either all of the six territories involved--
Kenya, Uganda, Tanganyika, Zanzibar, Nyasaland, Northern Rhodesia--coming together to form such a federation
or confederation and some of them doing so. The first
Commission to be so appointed was the Ormsby-Gore
Commission which was composed of the Honorable W.
Ormsby-Gore (Chairman), Major A. G. Church and Mr.
F. C. Linfield. It was appointed in July 1924, with
terms of reference that included a study of measures
to accelerate the general economic development of British Dependencies and the means of securing closer co-
ordination of policy on such important matters as transportation, immigration, taxation etc. It left England
in August 1924, and returned in December of the same
year. The Commission reported that there was a need
for greater co-operation and understanding, not only between the six administrations, but between unofficial residents as well. But it found no support in Africa for
the idea of a federation. It concluded that a union of
services would therefore be inadvisable without political
union. They concluded (on p. 9), "We are satisfied that
any further development in the direction of Federation,
whether it be unification of particular services or ul-

timately Political Federation, will come, if it comes
at all, as a result of local discussion of local needs
and common problems.   Federation cannot be imposed
from without.''   But it recommended that co-operation
could be fostered by regular, periodic, rotating conferences of the Governors and of responsible officials
of the various Government Departments.   This was the
origin of the East African Governors' Conferences, which
evolved into meetings of the East African Authority consisting of the Presidents of Kenya, Uganda, and Tanzania.   (Cmd. 2387, 1925).

OROMA.   These people are erroneously called "Galla,"
which is the Arabic name for them.   The Oroma of
Kenya live along the Tana River where they are called
the Wardaa by the Borana.   They are, along with the
Borana, part of a large number of Oroma-speaking peoples, most of whom live in Ethiopia where they make
up almost half of the total population.   The Oroma language is related to Beja and Somali and, more distantly,
to Ancient Egyptian.

OSOGO, JAMES CHARLES NAKHWANGA.   Teacher and poli-
tician.   Born November 10, 1932, at Bukani in Bunyala,
Busia.   Educated at Port Victoria Primary School, St.
Mary's High School, Yala, Railway Training School,
Nairobi (1950-52), Kagumo Teacher Training College,
(1953-54).   He taught at Sigalame School in 1955, Withur
School 1956, Barding School 1957, Ndenga School 1958,
and Port Victoria School 1959.   He was then appointed
Headmaster of Kibasanga School in 1960 and of Nangina
School 1961-62.   He became Vice-Chairman of the Ken-
ya National Union of Teachers, Central Nyanza 1958-62;
Member Central Nyanza African District Council, 1956-
58; and Vice-Chairman, Kenya Social Guild, 1961-63.
He was then elected a KANU Member for Ruwamba to
the House of Representatives in 1963.   He was appointed
Assistant Minister, Ministry of Agriculture, 1963-66;
Minister for Information and Broadcasting 1966-69; Min-
ister for Commerce and Industry 1969-73; Minister for
Local Government 1973-74.   Re-elected to Parliament
and appointed Minister for Health 1974.   Re-elected to
Parliament 1979 and appointed Minister of Agriculture.
He was Chairman of Kenya Youth Hostels Association
1964-70, Patron, 1970.   He was made Elder, Order of
the Golden Heart (Kenya), Order of the Star of Africa
(Liberia), Grand Cordon of the Star of Ethiopia, and
Grand Cross of the Yugoslav Flag.

OTIENDE, JOSEPH DANIEL. Teacher and politician. Born
in 1917 in Maragoli and educated at Maseno School, Alliance High School 1930-32, and Makerere College 1933-
36. He was a school teacher from 1937 to 1948. Joined
Local Government and worked for Kakamega African
District Council from 1949 to 1950. From 1955-62, he
was Assistant Clerk to the A.D.C. A founder Member
and General Secretary of the Kenya African Union 1950-
52. Elected KANU Member for Vihiga constituency to
the House of Representatives in 1963. Appointed Minister of Education 1963-64 and Minister for Health 1964-
69. Housing and Social Services were added to the Portfolio in 1966. He is the author of Abaluhya People of
North Nyanza.

OTUNGA, H. E. CARDINAL MAURICE. A Kenyan ecclesi-
astic born in January 1923 at Chebukwa. Educated at
Holy Ghost College Mangu, St. Peter's Seminary Kaka-
mega, St. Mary's Seminary Ggaba; studied Theology at
Pontifical College "de Propaganda Fide," Rome, Italy.
He was ordained a priest in 1950; consecrated titular Bish-
op of Tacape 1957; appointed Bishop of Kisii 1960; titu-
lar Archbishop of Bomarzo in 1969 and Archbishop of
Nairobi in 1971. He was created Cardinal by Pope Paul
VI in 1973.

OUKO, ROBERT JOHN. Teacher, administrator, and politician. Born on March 31, 1932, at Kisumu. He was
educated at Ogada School, Kisumu; Nyang'ori School,
Kakamega, Siriba College, Nyanza, Haile Sellassie I
University (1958-62), where he obtained a B.A. degree
(with distinction) in public administration, political science and economics. In 1962, he was one of the first
Kenyans to be selected for Foreign Service training
and he was sent to Makerere University College where
he took a course in International Relations and Diplomacy in 1962. In the following year, he went for Foreign Service training to Rome and London. Before going to Addis-Ababa, he had worked as a teacher 1952-
55 and as a District Revenue Assistant 1955-58. He
was appointed Assistant Secretary in the Department of
Foreign Affairs, in the Office of the Prime Minister
1962-63. Senior Assistant Secretary in 1963; Permanent
Secretary, Ministry of Foreign Affairs 1963-64; Ministry of Works 65-69. He was then appointed East African Minister for Finance and Administration 1969-70,
and for Common Market and Economic Affairs, 1970-77.
During this period he played a crucial role in the devel-

opment of the now defunct East African Community, not
only as a Minister, but also as a Member of East African Legislative Council where his analytical mind and
his oratory skills were greatly felt.

With the demise of the East African Community
on June 30, 1977, he was nominated to the Kenya Parliament and appointed Minister for Community Affairs,
charged with responsibility for integrating the former
East African Community services into the Kenya Civil
Service.   Elected to Parliament in 1979 as Member for
Kisumu Rural and appointed Minister for Foreign Affairs.   He was President of African Association for Public Administration and Management (1971-74); Fellow of
the Kenya Institute of Management, and in 1971, he was
awarded an Hon. LL. D. by the Pacific Lutheran University.

OWEN, THE VENERABLE ARCHDEACON WALTER EDWIN
(1878-1945).   Educated at St. Enoch's School, Belfast
and Islington Theological College.   Ordained in 1904;
Rural Dean, Buddu, Uganda, 1915; Chaplain to British
East Africa Forces, 1916; Archdeacon of Nyanza 1918-
1945.   He is well remembered in Nyanza for his human-
itarian, legal, and missionary work.   A memorial erect-
ed in his honor at Kisumu reads, "He devoted his life
fearlessly to the fight for justice for all and to the care
of the sick and the needy."   He was also a very active
amateur archaeologist and palaeontologist who made several discoveries of significance in Western Kenya in the
late 1930's and early 1940's.

- P -

PAN-AFRICAN FREEDOM MOVEMENT OF EAST AND CEN-
TRAL AFRICA (PAFMECA).   Founded in September
1958 at Mwanza, Tanzania, with Mr. Francis Khamisi
of Kenya as its first Chairman.   It was a regional organization of the All African Peoples' Conference.   Members of PAFMECA were African nationalist and trade
union organizations of Zaire, Kenya (only the Kenya African National Union was a member and not the Kenya
African Democratic Union), Malaŵi, Zambia, Rhodesia,
Ruanda, Burundi, Tanganyika, Uganda and Zanzibar.
The organization met annually; its aims were the coor-
dination and promotion of independence movements throughout East and Central Africa.

PANAFRICAN PAPER MILLS. A modern integrated pulp and paper mill (one of the largest of its kind in Africa) established in 1970. The construction of the Mills at Webuye in Western Province started in 1972 and was completed in late 1974. It is an example of cooperation between the developing countries: Kenya and India (through Paper Mills Ltd., which is part of the Birla group of industries). Besides exporting paper, the PPM already satisfies more than 80 percent of the country's domestic paper requirement.

PARLIAMENT. The supreme law-making body. Its other function is that of financial control. No taxation or revenue can be levied without parliamentary authority. Also, no public money can be expended without parliamentary authority. Parliament also has ultimate power of control over the Government, in that if it passes a vote of no confidence, it can be dissolved or the Government has to resign. Hence, a government can only stay in power so long as it enjoys the confidence of Parliament.

PINTO, PIO GAMA. Born in Nairobi on March 31, 1927. In 1935, he was sent to India for his education and he remained there for nine years. He joined the Indian Air Force in 1944 for a short while. At the age of 17 he started agitating for the liberation of Goa. He was a founder member of the Goa National Congress whose aim was to liberate Goa from Portuguese rule. In order to avoid arrest by the Portuguese authorities, he left India and came back to Kenya in 1949. He immediately plunged himself into the nationalist struggle. He worked with the Colonial Times and the Daily Chronicle --two radical Indian-owned newspapers. He also worked closely with the Kenya African Union leaders as well as trade Union leaders. When the Emergency was declared in 1952, he was working with the East African Indian National Congress. He sent money and arms to forest fighters. In 1954, he was arrested in the notorious Operation Anvil and spent the next four years in detention on Manda Island on the East Coast with the so-called "hard-core" Mau Mau. Between 1958 and October 1959, he was restricted at Kabarnet. On his release, he rejoined the struggle for Kenya's independence. In 1960, he founded the Kenya African National Union (KANU) newspaper, Sauti ya Kanu. With funds obtained from Pandit Nehru, Pinto founded the Pan African Press

Ltd. which published Sauti ya Mwafrika, Pan Africa
and the Nyanza Times. He himself edited Pan Africa,
besides working as Director and Secretary of the Pan
African Press Ltd.

In 1963, Pinto was elected a Member of the East
African Central Legislative Assembly and in July of the
following year a Specially Elected Member of the Kenya
Parliament.

In 1964, he was one of the founders of the Lu-
mumba Institute established just outside Nairobi to train
KANU party officials. He continued to be involved in
the liberation of Portugal's colonies, working closely
with FRELIMO and the Committee of Nine of the OAU.
On Wednesday, February 24, 1965, Pinto was assassinated in Nairobi--independent Kenya's first political assassination.

PINY OWACHO see YOUNG KAVIRONDO ASSOCIATION

PIRBHAI, SIR EBOO. Born in 1905. Educated at Duke of
Gloucester School, Nairobi. Member of Nairobi Municipal Council 1938-46; Member of Legislative Council,
1952-60. Director of Companies. Representative of
H.H. The Aga Khan in Africa; President, Aga Khan Supreme Council for Africa. Awarded Brilliant Star of
Zanzibar 1956; O.B.E. 1946; Knighted 1952.

POKOMO. The Pokomo live on the banks of the Tana River.
They are divided into four main groups who occupy dif-
ferent areas and speak different dialects which are mu-
tually intelligible. The four areas are the Lower Pokomo, from Kipini to Bubesa in Salama location; the
Upper Pokomo from Matanama to Roka; the Welwan (or
Malakote) from Roka to Garissa; and the Munyo Yaya
(or Northern Pokomo or Korokoro), stretching from
Garissa through Mbalambala. In the Upper and Lower
Pokomo, Bantu languages related to the Mijikenda languages and Kiswahili are spoken. The Munyo Yaya speak
Oroma and the Welwan speak their own language. The
languages spoken reflect the diverse origins of the Po-
komo--Bantu from the legendary Shungwaya, Boran, Kamba, Oroma, and Waata. The exodus from Shungwaya
is said to have taken place sometime at the beginning
of the seventeenth century. The Boran and Oroma elements are said to have arrived in the area about five
to six generations ago. Today they number about 50,000
and are predominantly an agricultural people growing
plantains, sugar cane, rice, and maize.

POKOT. The Pokot are the most northerly of all the Kalenjin. They practiced agriculture on the northern section of the Cherang'any Hills (employing irrigation systems), and kept cattle, sheep, goats, donkeys, and oc-
casionally camels in the plains. For the early history,
see the Kalenjin.

PRESIDENT. Both the Head of State and the Head of Government, and the Executive authority is vested in the
President. He appoints and dismisses the Vice-President, Ministers, and Assistant Ministers. He also al-
locates to them responsibilities. In relation to Parliament, the President has powers to dissolve it and,
since 1968, to nominate twelve Members of Parliament.
With regard to the Civil Service, the President appoints
the Attorney-General, the Controller and Auditor-Gen-
erals, the Commissioner of Police, the Permanent Sec-
retaries, the Solicitor-General, the Director of Person-
ell, and Senior diplomatic envoys. The President also
has powers in relation to the judiciary. He appoints
the Chief Justice, the puisne judges and the Judges of
Appeal and members of the Judicial Service Commission.

PRIVATE OWNER FREEHOLD LAND. Comprises former
Crown land in respect of which freehold interest was
granted by the Crown in the early years before the
1920's, or else was converted into freehold in 1961 under the "Conversion of Leases Regulations, 1961." It
also includes 1) agricultural trust land in respect of
which individual claims have been fully adjudicated under
the Land Adjudication Act and the freehold interest in
the land registered under the Land Act and 2) the land
in the coastal strip in respect of which individual claims
have been adjudicated by a Recorder of Titles under the
Land Titles Act. It also includes land in certain areas
of the former Crown land that have been purchased by
the Settlement Fund Trustees and subsequently allocated
to settlers under a loan repayment system on completion of the repayment of their loans.

PYRETHRUM. This type of chrysanthemum is used for non-
toxic insecticides. Kenya produces 80 percent of the
world's supply of this product.

- R -

RAILWAYS <u>see</u> COMMUNICATIONS AND TRANSPORT

REGIONALISM.   Also known by its Swahili name of majim-
    bo, regionalism was an essential aspect of the Indepen-
    dent Constitution of Kenya which aimed at protecting the
    minorities from abuses of political power.   The sys-
    tem was also intended to provide for effective sharing
    of political power.   Seven Regions were established,
    each with a Regional Assembly and elected members.
    The boundaries of the Regions could not be altered uni-
    laterally by the Central Government.   Each Region had
    its own establishment, headed by a Civil Secretary.   In
    practice, power was never devolved on the Regions as
    had been envisaged because the KANU Government was
    opposed to the system.   The first Amendment Act of
    1964 stripped the Regions of most of their substantive
    powers and the Amendment Act of 1965 changed the
    names of the Regions and their Assemblies to Provinces
    and Councils.   Hence, in practice, Regionalism was
    dead by 1965, although it was not until 1968 that the
    system was legally abolished, and Kenya reverted to a
    unitary system of government.

RENDILLE.   The Rendille are Eastern Cushitic-speakers
    who are linguistically related to the Somali and the Soni.
    They live in northern Kenya between Lake Turkana and
    Mount Marsabit, and they number about 20,000.   Like
    the Somali culture, the Rendille culture is a camel cul-
    ture, and they are pastoral nomads.   Unlike the Somali,
    the Rendille are not traders.

RENISON, SIR PATRICK.   Governor and Commander in
    Chief British Honduras 1952-53; Governor and Com-
    mander in Chief of British Guyana 1955-59; and Gov-
    ernor and Commander in Chief of Kenya from 1959 to
    1962, when he was in charge of the post-Emergency
    arrangements and negotiations which paved the way for
    political independence in Kenya in 1963.

RIBEIRO, ROZENDO AYRES.   Born in Goa on February
    17, 1870.   He came to Kenya in December 1898 living
    in Mombasa for a year before moving to Nairobi.   He
    was the first private medical practitioner in Nairobi
    and used to ride a Zebra on his visiting rounds.   He
    was the first to record plague epidemic in Nairobi in
    1900 and manufactured Dr. Ribeiro's Anti-malarial Pills.
    He was appointed Portuguese Vice-Consul in Nairobi
    from 1914 to 1922.   He donated to the Goan Community
    the Dr. Ribeiro Goan School in Nairobi, besides sup-

porting many other Goan social institutions.   He died
on February 2, 1957.

ROMAN CATHOLIC MISSION OF THE CONSOLATA.   Established at Turin, Italy, where its headquarters is situated.   The first missionaries arrived in East Africa in
1902, and the Vicariate Apostolic of Kenya was established in 1905 and covered Central and Eastern Kenya.
In 1926, the Vicariate was subdivided into the Vicariate
Apostolic of Nyeri which embraced Nyeri and Murang'a
districts and part of Kiambu district, and the Prefecture Apostolic of Meru, which covered the Meru and
Embu districts.

ROMAN CATHOLIC MISSION OF THE HOLY GHOST.   The
Roman Catholic Missionary Society of the Holy Ghost,
a French Order, was established in Paris in 1703.   It
organized Provinces in other countries.   The Mission
at Zanzibar was opened on December 25, 1860, by Mon-
seigneur Tava, afterwards Bishop of Grenoble in France.
In 1862, the Mission was entrusted to the Fathers of
the Society of the Holy Ghost.   The Mission at Mombasa was begun in 1892.   In the same year, the Mission opened a station at Bura in Taita.   It opened St.
Austin's Mission in Nairobi in 1899.   The Fathers of
St. Austin's were the pioneer coffee planters in the
country.   By 1930 the Mission had established eighteen
stations, the principal ones being Zanzibar, which was
the see of the Bishop, Bomba, Mombasa, Mwabaya,
Nyondo, Bura, Kilungu, Nairobi, St. Austin's Kiambu,
and Mangu.

ROSS, WILLIAM McGREGOR.   A pioneer colonial civil servant, who served for twenty-three years (1900-1923).
He was educated at Southport Grammar School, Liver-
pool University, and Royal University of Ireland, obtaining a B.A., and M.Sc. and a B.E.   For the first
five years in East Africa (1900-1905), he was Assistant
Engineer on the Uganda Railway.   From 1905 until his
retirement in 1923, he was Director of Public Works.
From 1916 to 1922, he was a member of the Legislative Council.   He and Norman Leys were the first serious and knowledgeable critics of the colonial policies
and administration in Kenya.   His book, Kenya from
Within, was published in 1927 and is a fearless attack
on colonial policies on land, labor and race relations.

ROYAL AGRICULTURAL SOCIETY OF KENYA   see   AGRI-
   CULTURAL SOCIETY OF KENYA

- S -

SABAOT.   A collective name for four groups of Kalenjin
   people: the Kony, the Sapei (or Sebei), the Pok, and
   the Bungomek, who live on the Mt. Elgon region on the
   Kenya-Uganda border.   One of the groups--the Kony--
   used to live in caves on the southern slopes of the mountain.   Like the other Kalenjin people (usually called Highland or Southern Nilotes), they practice highland agriculture, although originally they were largely pastoralists and hunter-gatherers.

SADLER, LIEUT.-COLONEL SIR JAMES HAYES.   Son of
   Colonel Sir J. Hayes Sadler, K.C.M.G.   He received
   his commission in 1870 and served with the 61st Foot
   and 33rd Bengal Native Infantry, and eventually received his lieutenant-colonelcy, Indian Staff Corps.   He
   joined the Political Department in India in 1877, and
   was Assistant Agent to the Governor-General, Baroda,
   in 1881.   After a number of years of varied service,
   he became Acting Consul at Muscat in 1892 and Consul
   in 1897.   In 1898, he became Consul-General in British Somaliland.   From 1901 to 1905, he was Commissioner to Uganda Protectorate.   In December 1905, he
   was appointed Commissioner and Commander-in-Chief,
   East African Protectorate, and was officially announced
   to be Governor--the first person to have the title in
   Kenya--in April 1907.   From 1909 to 1914, he was Governor of Windward Islands.   He received the Coronation
   medal in 1902, and made a C.B. in the same year.   He
   had been awarded the K.C.M.G. in 1897.

SAID, SEYYID (SEYYID SAID IBN SULTAN).   Born in Oman
   in 1791.   He came to power in 1806 as a member of
   the Busaidi dynasty.   In that position he ruled Oman
   and controlled trade in the Western Indian Ocean.   With
   the defeat of the French by the British during the Na-
   poleonic wars, Said felt free to turn his attention to
   East Africa.   He was determined to bring the Swahili
   Coast under his sway.   In 1827, he paid his first visit
   to East Africa when he went to Mombasa to demand that
   the rulers of Mombasa reaffirm their old allegiance to
   Oman.   In 1837, he eventually succeeded in ending the

Mazrui dynasty rule in Mombasa. He signed commer-
cial treaties with the United States, Britain, and France.
He encouraged the development of a clove industry in
Zanzibar. In 1840, he moved his headquarters from
Oman to Zanzibar, and promoted Arab and Swahili car-
avan trade with the interior of Kenya and Tanzania. He
also wielded political influence over the coastal region.
He died in 1856.

SAINT JOSEPH'S FOREIGN MISSION. Usually known as the
Mill Hill Mission. It was a branch of the St. Joseph's
Society for Foreign Missions, a congregation of secular
priests established to propagate the Gospel to non-Euro-
pean societies by his Eminence Cardinal Vaughan at
Mill Hill in London in 1866. It entered Kenya from the
north, where the Vicariate Apostolic of the Upper Nile
(which embraced part of Buganda), the East Province
of Uganda, and Western Kenya (up to the Kikuyu Escarpment) was entrusted to St. Joseph's Society in 1894 by
His Holiness Pope Leo XIII. Bishop Hanlon, who was
appointed its first Bishop, arrived at Mengo on September 6, 1895. In 1926, the Kenya section of the Vicariate was cut off and made into a separate Prefecture
Apostolic, its first Superior being the Right Rev. Mgr.
G. Brandsma, who resided at Kisumu. The territory
assigned to the Mill Hill Fathers in Kenya was called
the "Prefecture Apostolic of Kavirondo," which was
somewhat misleading, since the area covered stretched
from the Uganda border to the Laikipia Escarpment; and
the southern boundary embraced the area from Lake Magadi, along the Tanganyika border, to Lake Victoria.
By 1930, mission stations in Kenya included Kibuye in
Kisumu town, Aluor, Rang'ala, Asumbi, Kakamega, Mumias, Nangina, and Kisii.

SAKUYE. A small group of Galla-speakers who live in Moy-
ale around Dabel in North-eastern Kenya. They number about 5,000 and culturally they resemble the Gabbra.
Their pastoral economy is based on camel and goat industry. During this century they have gradually been
converted to Islam and there is a real possibility of
the group being absorbed by the Somali.

SALVATION ARMY. Commenced operations in Kenya in
1921. Its Territorial Headquarters, situated on Moi
Avenue, Nairobi, was opened on April 10, 1929. By
1930, it had established stations at Nairobi, Thika Mc-

Millan Estates in Ukambani, Maragua, Saba Saba, and
Makindi--all in Murang'a District; Malakisi, Ndakaru
and Kisumu in Western Kenya; Nakuru and Mombasa.
It published a monthly paper, The War Cry or Sauti ya
Vita, in English and Kiswahili.

SAMBURU. The most northerly group of the Maa-speakers.
They inhabit the Samburu District, which lies to the
south and southeast of Lake Turkana. They moved into Kenya together with the Masai. The name "Samburu" means "butterfly," and was given to them by their
neighbors. They refer to themselves as Loikop. They
practice pastoralism, keeping cattle, goats, sheep, and
more recently, camels.

SAMOEI, KOITALEL ARAP. The most famous of the Nandi
orkoik. Leader of the Nandi Resistance against British
imperialism, 1890-1906. He died fighting.

SANYE. The Sanye originally lived on the southern Taru
Desert as hunters and gatherers, hunting particularly
the elephant. When much of their land was turned into the Tsavo National Park, their way of life as hunters was severely undermined. Today they are scattered from the mouth of the Tana River to the Tanzania
border. Many of them have been absorbed by their neighbors such as the Orma or the Giriama whom they are
supposed to have taught how to manufacture iron arrow-
heads. They are known by various names: Ariangulu,
Liangulu, Langulo, Laa, Waat, Waatha, Wasi, Asi.

SCALATER'S ROAD. In order to improve communication
between Mombasa and Kampala, it was decided to extend the Mackinnon Road from Kibwezi to Lake Victoria
so that Uganda could be supplied regularly by wagon
carts with the goods it needed. Captain Scalater, R.E.,
who had constructed a similar road in Malaŵi (then Nyasaland), was entrusted with the job. He and his staff,
Lt. Smith and four engineer N.C.Os., began work in
August 1895. The road more or less followed the old
caravan track but by-passed Machakos and took a new
route over Mau and through Nandi to Mumias. It was
a narrow tract road and unpaved. It took about 18
months to complete and cost about £17,000. On completion of the road, Scalater was made head of the Uganda transport service. Before he could begin this work,
he died of blackwater fever at Zanzibar in July 1897.

This road was soon superseded by the Uganda Railway
from Mombasa to Kisumu.

SCOTT, LORD FRANCIS.   Born in 1879, the sixth son of
the sixth Duke of Buccleuch.   Educated at Eton and Oxford.   He married the daughter of the fourth Earl of
Minto.   Served in the British Army in 1899; was appointed A.D.C. to the Viceroy of India in 1905; and
served in the South African War and the First World
War before immigrating to Kenya in 1919, where he
settled at Rongai as a farmer.   He soon emerged as
an outspoken leader of the white settlers who represented their interests at various times up to 1948 in
both the Legislative Council as well as in the country's
Executive Council.   With the death of Lord Delamere
in 1931, settler leadership passed into his hands and
he used both his royal connections (through the Duke of
Buccleuch, he was related to the Royal Family) as well
as his many connections in the British upper classes to
further European interests.   He died in 1952.

SENATE.   Included in the Independent Constitution with the
hope that it will safeguard regionalism.   Members of
the Senate were elected directly from the forty districts
and the Nairobi area.   It was a continuous body, with
one third of its members resigning every two years,
and the maximum length of a member's tenure being
six years.   The Senate could delay financial Bills for
about two months and other Bills for a year.   Approval
of Senate was needed for amendment of the constitution
and declaration of an emergency.   In practice, the Senate failed to safeguard regionalism and other constitutional rights.   In December 1966, legislation was introduced that led to the merger of the Senate and the House
of Representatives.   Members of both houses were declared members of the new National Assembly.   Thus a
unicameral legislature was established to replace the
former bi-cameral one.

SERONEY, JEAN MARIE.   An eminent parliamentarian.
Born at Kapsabet in 1925 and educated at Government
African School Kapsabet 1938-40, Alliance High School
1941-44, Makerere University College, 1945-46, Alla-
habad University, India, 1947-51, Inner Temple, London, 1952-55, where he was called to the Bar.   In 1956,
he returned to Kenya and joined the Registrar General's office as a legal assistant 1956-58, after which he

left to start his own practice (1959-61). He was elected to the Legislative Council in 1961, and appointed
Parliamentary Secretary in the Ministry of Defence in
1963. In the same year he was elected Member of Parliament for Nandi North and member of the Regional
Assembly for Nandi south on a KADU ticket. He was
charged with sedition in 1969 for publishing the Nandi
Declaration, a document in which he attacked the sale
of Nandi land to non-Kalenjin settlers. He was convicted and fined. In the same year he was re-elected
to Parliament as Member for Tinderet, a seat he retained with a bigger majority in the 1974 elections.
The quality of his contribution in Parliament was recognized by his colleagues in 1975 by electing him Deputy
Speaker of Parliament. It was in the course of per-
forming his duty as Deputy Speaker that he made state-
ments about the ruling party KANU that led to his detention in October 1975. He was released from detention in December 1978. In December 1980, he was appointed Chairman of the Industrial Development Bank of Kenya.

SHIKUKU, JOSEPH MARTIN. Born in 1933 at Magadi. Educated at Magadi Soda Primary School, Mumias Secondary School and St. Peter's Seminary at Kakamega. He
wanted to train for the priesthood. He, however, left
the Seminary, went back to Magadi to work for the Magadi Soda Company, before joining the East African Railways and Harbours as a train guard, 1952-56. His next
job was with the Caltex Oil Ltd. as a clerk, 1956-58.
When the colonial government allowed Africans to form
political parties, Shikuku joined the Nairobi People's
Convention Party, then led by Tom Mboya, and rose to
become its general secretary in 1959. In 1960, when
KANU was formed, Shikuku parted company with most
of his colleagues in the Nairobi People's Convention
Party and joined the newly formed Kenya African Democratic Union (KADU) as its National Youth Wing Leader, and the following year became its secretary-general. In the "Kenyatta Election" of 1961, he stood against
Mboya for the Nairobi East seat and lost heavily. In
the 1963 General Election, he stood in his home area
of Butere and was returned to Parliament as a KADU
Member. In Parliament he regarded himself as the
"President of the Poor."
        In 1964, he joined KANU together with other
KADU members, after disbanding their party. Shikuku
continued to play the role of the Opposition in Parliament. After the 1969 General Election, in an attempt

to contain Backbench dissidents, Shikuku was appointed
an Assistant Minister in the Office of the Vice-President and the party's Chief Whip.   Shikuku, however,
continued to play the role of the Opposition, attacking
all aspects of Government policy. After the 1974 Election, Shikuku was not appointed Assistant Minister. He
continued to harass the government as a Backbencher.
In October 1975, Shikuku maintained, during a motion
in Parliament recommending action against a Nominated
Member, Philip Njoka, who had called a Parliamentary
Select Committee "a bunch of rogues," that KANU was
dead. He was arrested from Parliament building and
detained. He was released from detention on December
12, 1978. Re-elected to Parliament as Member for Butere in 1979 and appointed Assistant Minister for Livestock Development.

SINGH, CHANAN. A prominent lawyer, journalist, politician,
and historian. Born at Iholaha village in Punjab, India
in 1908 and left school before matriculating. He came
to Kenya in 1923 and took employment as a locomotive fitter
and later as a clerk in the Kenya and Uganda Railways
and Harbours. Studied privately passing matriculation
in 1931 and obtaining a B.Sc. (Econ) in 1940. He was
called to the Bar in 1944 and resigned from the Railway to set up private practice in Nairobi. In the Railway, he edited the Railwayasian, the Railway Asian
Union's Journal. He served as Secretary and President
of the Nairobi Indian Association, a Member of the Central Executive Committee of the Kenya Indian Congress
and was the first President of the Indian Youth League.
For about fourteen years, he wrote the editorials and
editorial notes of the Colonial Times of Nairobi, a radical paper that supported the nationalist cause. In 1952,
he was elected to the Legislative Council as member of
the Central Area, Nairobi (1952-56). In February 1960,
he founded and became President of the Kenya Freedom
Party, which grouped together the Asian radicals, both
Muslim and non-Muslim, and demanded independence,
individual citizen rights (irrespective of race), and social integration. Re-elected in 1962. Appointed Parliamentary Secretary, Minister of State for Constitutional Affairs, 1962-63; President Law Society of Kenya,
1958. In 1963, he was Specially Elected Member (KANU)
in Parliament and appointed Parliamentary Secretary,
Prime Minister's Office, 1963. In 1964, he was appointed Puisne Judge. He died on July 2, 1977 from a heart
attack.

SINGH, JOGINDER. Top Kenya rally-driver. Born on February 9, 1932, at Kericho, where his father worked for the Kenya Tea Company. He attended schools in Kericho, from which he went to the Indian High School (now Jamhuri High School) in Nairobi in 1946. He graduated from Jamhuri High School in 1951 and in the following year joined his father, who had opened a garage in Nairobi in 1952. In 1955, he left his hot-tempered father to join D.T. Dobie and later Overseas Motor Transport Ltd. In 1958, he became the first patrolman of the Automobile Association of Kenya. In the same year he started rallying in local competitions, and in 1959 he competed in the East African Safari Rally for the first time, driving an old Volkswagen, which he had prepared himself. He finished in the ninth position overall. Since then he has competed in all the nineteen safari rallies, winning three times--in 1965, 1974, and 1976. He started his own business in 1966, combining motor car sales with a workshop. He married in 1956 and has one son, Jatinder. He has also competed in motor rallies in Ivory Coast, Australia, Austria, Greece, and Ethiopia.

SINGH, MAKHAN. A pioneer trade unionist. Born in 1913 in India he came to Kenya in 1927. Educated at the Government Indian High School, Nairobi. From 1935 to 1950, he was involved in championing, sometimes single-handedly, the cause of trade unionism. He transformed the Indian Trade Union founded in 1934 into the Labour Trade Union of Kenya in 1935, with himself as Secretary. He hoped to turn it into a multiracial trade union. He organized a successful two-month strike in Nairobi in 1937 that demanded wage increases. In 1939, his union changed its name to the Labour Trade Union of East Africa, with a view to extending trade union activities to cover the whole of East Africa. In 1940, Makhan Singh was interned in India for the duration of the war. He returned from India on August 22, 1947. The authorities tried, unsuccessfully, to declare him a prohibited immigrant. In 1948, he worked for the Indian Congress. In the following year, he took over the African Workers Federation, which had been founded by Chege Kibachia, Livington Kienze, and M. K. William in Mombasa. All these trade union leaders had been arrested and restricted or imprisoned. Singh renamed it the East Africa Workers' Federation and declared himself the Secretary. On May Day, 1949, a new work-

ers' organization called the East African Trade Union
Congress was launched in Nairobi with Fred Kubai as
President and Makhan Singh as Secretary. It soon became a ginger group within the Kenya African Union.
In 1950, he successfully organized the boycott of visit
of the Duke of Gloucester who was to present the Charter conferring city status on Nairobi. On May 15, 1950,
Fred Kubai and Makhan Singh were arrested. The latter was tried and deported to Maralal where he was restricted for eleven years. He was released in October
1961 and he attempted unsuccessfully to re-enter the
trade union movement in Kenya. He retired from public life and devoted the rest of his life to writing a history of trade unionism in Kenya. Volume I of this
study was published in 1969 and entitled History of Kenya's Trade Union Movement to 1952; and the second volume was published posthumously in 1980. He died in
1976.

SIRIKWA. The Sirikwa were probably a Maa-speaking group
who originated in the area east of Mt. Elgon, from
where they occupied the Uasin Gishu Plateau. Later
they were dispersed to different parts of the Rift Valley by other Masai groups. They are supposed to have
occupied different parts of the Rift Valley between the
8th and 16th centuries. The people are associated with
the so-called "Sirikwa holes" at such places as Lanet
and Moiben on the eastern Uasin Gishu plateau. Other
related elements of this culture are stone-walled structures surrounding the circular hollows, terraces and irrigation works, deep wells and often large earth dams;
draught or "bao" boards carved into rock outcrops;
stone engravings and petroglyphs; stone cairns and "burial" mounds.

SLADE, HUMPHREY. Born in London in 1905. Educated
at Eton and Oxford University, where he read classics
and philosophy, and at Lincoln's Inn, where he was
called to the Bar. He came to Kenya in 1930 as an
Advocate with Hamilton, Harrison, and Mathews. He
became a member of the Kenya Regiment and Deputy
Judge Advocate General for East Africa 1939-41. From
1950 to 1963, he was a farmer in the North Kinangop
area, where he was elected to the Legislative Council
in 1952 and in 1956 by the European voters. He was
one of the white "diehards." In 1958, he stood for one
of the twelve new seats of "specially elected" members

who had no specific constituency but who were elected
by other MPs to represent national interests. In 1960
he was nominated by the Governor, Sir Patrick Renison,
to become Speaker of the Legislative Council. In 1963,
he was elected Speaker of the National Assembly. He
retired from Parliament in 1970 and went back to his
legal firm. He was President of the Law Society of
Kenya in 1947 and 1948; first President of the Child
Welfare Society of Kenya in 1956, 1957 and 1958; a Director of several companies. He is author of The Parliament of Kenya.

SOCCER. The most popular spectator sport in Kenya.
Crowds of up to 20,000 gather in the Nairobi City Stadium or the Mombasa Stadium for the big matches. The
top clubs have been, for some time now, Gor Mahia,
Abaluhya, Luo Union, and the Kenya Breweries.

SOMALI. The Somali are a Cushitic-speaking people living
in Northeastern Kenya who number about 300,000 people
and who, like the other Sam-speakers, originated in the
area east of River Omo, south of Lake Zwai, and northeast of Lake Turkana. The Somali probably split from
the Rendille and the Soni in the area around the present
Marsabit, sometime between 300 B.C. and 200 A.D.
The group that was later to emerge as the Somali then
moved in a southeasterly direction towards the coast.
Thus the Somali did not originate in Arabia or descend
from the Prophet Mohamed as some of the nationalist
historians claim. Their region is semi-arid; hence,
the Somali practice pastoralism, relying mainly on the
camel. Traditionally the Somali ate neither fish, poultry, nor eggs.

SOMALIA-KENYA RELATIONS. When the frontier between
Kenya and Ethiopia was established in 1907, a small
Somali population was included in the Northern Frontier
District (NFD) of Kenya. This population was subsequently increased by migration. In 1924, as part of an
Anglo-Italian accord, Jubaland Province (whose population was largely Somali) was transferred by Britain from
Kenya to Italian Somaliland. This was later to be regarded by the Somali as marking the first step in the
creation of Greater Somalia. In July 1960, British Somaliland and Italian Somalia united and became independent as the Northern and Southern Regions of the Somali
Republic. The same month saw the formation of North-

ern Province People's Progressive Party (NPPPP), a
secessionist Somali Party in Kenya's NFD. In the 1961
Elections, the NPPPP candidate was returned unopposed,
and the differences between the two major political par-
ties--the Kenya African Democratic Union (KADU) and
the Kenya African National Union (KANU)--made any
compromise on the Somali issue difficult.

In October 1961, the Somali leaders (led by President Aden Abdullah Osman) visited Ghana and with Dr.
Nkrumah signed a communiqué defending the redrawing
of colonial boundaries. It recognized, "The imperative
need to restore ethnic, cultural and economic links, ar-
bitrarily destroyed through the partitioning of Africa by
the colonialists." During the same month Jomo Kenyatta was released and he immediately decided to pay a
visit to Ethiopia. Jomo Kenyatta as leader of KANU
and Ronald Ngala as leader of KADU visited Somalia
in July and August of the following year to discuss the
issue. Kenyatta, in a speech at Mogadishu airport on
July 30, 1962, referred to the NFD question as a "very
touchy question." He made it clear that the NFD was
"part of Kenya" and the question was "a domestic affair of Kenya." Mr. Ngala, in a speech on August 16,
1962, in Mogadishu, explained that in the proposed Majimbo constitution, each region of Kenya would be protected from unnecessary interference from the center,
and hence, the Somali in Kenya need have no fear.

In October 1962, the British Government appointed a Commission "to ascertain and report on public opinion in the NFD." The Commission's Report, which was
published in December 1962, revealed that five out of
the six Northern Frontier Districts favored secession
and union with the Somali Republic. In March 1963,
Britain announced that the NFD, would become the sev-
enth region of Kenya. The Somali Government reacted
sharply and broke off diplomatic relations with Britain.
In the same year in July, the Ethiopia/Kenya agreement on "cooperation and mutual defence assistance"
was signed. Both KANU and KADU committed themselves to not giving up "a single inch of Kenya's land."
When Kenya became independent, a State of Emergency
was declared in the NFD, now renamed the North Eastern Province (NEP) on December 26, 1963, "in view of
the continued raids by Shifta (bandits) on military and
police posts in Kenya." At the OAU Conference of
Heads of State held in Cairo from July 17 to 21, 1964,
it was solemnly declared that "all Member States pledge

themselves to respect the borders existing on their
achievement of national independence." But the vision
of a "Greater Somalia" continued to be the goal of the
Somali Government, which now made no territorial
claims on Kenya, but demanded self-determination for
the people of Northeast Kenya.

On the initiative of President Nyerere, abortive
talks at ministerial level were held between Kenya and
the Somali Republic from December 10 to 14, 1965, at
Arusha aimed at ending the long-standing Kenya/Somali
border dispute. The relations between the two countries rapidly deteriorated during the first half of 1966.
Kenya severed all relations with Somalia, and a virtual
state of war existed between the two states. Somali re-
iterated their stand that they "will never give up their
struggle for reunification." In August 1966, President
Nyerere visited Somalia and Kenya with a view to re-
conciling the opposing sides. The position of the Kenya Government was stated in a white paper published
in April 1967. It was ready to participate in negotiations leading to conclusion of a peaceful settlement provided that the Somali Government renounced all territorial claims to Northeastern Kenya, halted the supply
of arms and ammunition to shifta gangs, and accepted
the OAU resolution stating that the boundaries of states
at the time of independence must be accepted and held
inviolable by all OAU members.

A new situation was created in Somalia by the
Presidential elections. On June 10, Dr. Abdirashid
Ali Sharmarke replaced President Aden Abdullah Osman as President of the Somali Republic, and on July
15, a new Government was formed with Mr. Mohammed Haji Ibrahim Egal as Prime Minister and Minister of Foreign Affairs. The Prime Minister announced
that the Somali Republic "makes no claims on the territory of any of our neighbours." At the OAU Heads
of State meeting held in Kinshasa from September 11-
14, 1967, President Kaunda played a major conciliatory
role which made it possible for the Kenya delegation
(led by the then Vice-President, Daniel arap Moi) and
the Somali delegation (led by Mr. Egal) to enter into
an agreement. The two governments expressed their
desire to respect each other's sovereignty and territorial integrity; to resolve any outstanding differences
between them in the spirit of Paragraph 4 of Article
III of the OAU Charter; to ensure maintenance of peace
and security on both sides of the border; and to refrain

from conducting hostile propaganda through mass media against each other.

The two governments accepted the invitation of President Kaunda to meet in Lusaka in October 1967 in order to improve, intensify, and consolidate all forms of co-operation. The talks were eventually held at Arusha at the request of President Kenyatta and were presided over by President Kaunda. Both President Nyerere and President Obote attended as observers. A Memorandum of Agreement was signed by the President of Kenya and the Prime Minister of Somalia on October 28, 1967, normalizing the relations between the two countries. In January 1968, Kenya and Somalia formally resumed diplomatic relations; and in July of the same year, President Sharmarke made a state visit to Kenya. For the next twelve years, a state of co-existence has prevailed between the two states, with the dream of "Greater Somalia" surfacing every now and then. But it has not led to armed conflict.

SOVIET UNION-KENYA RELATIONS. On November 20, 1964, the U.S.S.R. and Kenya signed an Agreement on Technical and Economic Co-operation. A delegation led by Oginga Odinga and Joseph Murumbi visited Moscow as a preliminary to the conclusion and signing of the Agreement. The U.S.S.R. thus became the first foreign country with which Kenya signed an agreement for economic co-operation. In practice, however, this agreement has never worked satisfactorily. The 1964 Agreement provided for two gift projects and seven loan credit projects. The two gift projects were a two hundred bed hospital to be built in Kisumu (which later materialized) and a 1,000 student technical college. The seven loan credit agreements were clearing of bushes in the inshore region of Lake Victoria, a sugar factory, a cotton textile mill, a fish cannery, fruit and vegetable processing factories, a 50 kw. radio transmitter, and Kano Irrigation Scheme. The local costs for these projects were to be financed by the extension by the Soviet Union to Kenya of commodity credit. In other words, the projects were to be financed through the sale of Soviet goods in Kenya to generate enough local currency which would in turn be given to the Kenya Government as a loan to cover local costs of the projects. The Kenya Government later was unable to accept this arrangement.

In January 1966, a delegation led by the Minister

for Economic Planning and Development and including
the Minister for Agriculture, Animal Husbandry and
Marketing and the Minister for Commerce, Industry and
Co-operative Development visited Moscow to take part
in discussions aimed at the revision of the Agreement.
Only the gift projects were now acceptable to the Kenya
Government. However, instead of building one 1,000-
student technical college, there were to be established
two technical secondary schools of 500 students each in
Western and Central Provinces. Even these were never built. No agreement was reached on any of the sev-
en loan credit projects. Since then, no new economic
projects have been initiated as part of the U.S.S.R.-
Kenya economic co-operation. Diplomatic relations
were established between Kenya and the U.S.S.R. a
day after independence was proclaimed and have, on
the whole, remained cordial. In the field of high-level manpower, more than 800 Kenyans have received
higher education in the Soviet Union. Graduates from
Soviet higher educational establishments are now working successfully in medical, agricultural, industrial
and research institutions. Cultural exchange programs
between the two countries have also been encouraged.
Soviet variety shows, orchestras and other companies
have performed in Kenya, and the Bomas of Kenya
national dance and song ensemble was a great hit in
the Soviet Union. The works of such Kenyan writers
as Ngugi wa Thiong'o, Grace Ogot, and Meja Mwangi
have been translated into Russian and published in the
U.S.S.R. in mass editions.

SPEAKER. Presides at meetings of Parliament. He is
elected by the Assembly from among elected members,
excluding Ministers and Assistant Ministers, or from
persons who are qualified to be elected as such. He
has a casting but not an original vote.

SPECIALLY ELECTED MEMBERS. First introduced into
the Legislative Council in 1958. Their number was
in the proportion of one for every ten elected members. The system was incorporated into the independent constitution, and in 1966 their number was fixed
at twelve. They were chosen by the elected members
acting as an electoral college. They were introduced
with a view to bringing into the Legislative Council
people who as professionals or businessmen would not
look at issues entirely in communal terms as had been

the case since 1907 when the Council was established. They were replaced by Nominated Members in 1968.

SQUATTER. A term used extensively during the colonial period to refer to a labor tenant. He provided part-time labor in return for the right to cultivate a piece of land and grazing rights for his livestock. Most of the squatters were found on the European settlers' farms, especially in the Rift Valley Province.

STANDARD, THE. This newspaper was started by A. M. Jeevanjee in Mombasa in 1902 as The African Standard, which was then bought by C. B. Anderson and R. M. Mayer in 1910. Moved to Nairobi where it incorporated The Nairobi Advertiser, and was renamed The East African Standard. Continued to publish a sister paper, Mombasa Times, in Mombasa. In 1923, it absorbed a Nairobi weekly, The Leader of British East Africa, which had hitherto provided it with stiff competition. In 1965, it amalgamated with The Mombasa Times, and it adopted its present name in 1974. It is today owned by the Lonrho Group. It is thus the newspaper with the longest history in East Africa.

STAREHE BOYS' CENTRE. Founded in 1959 by Geoffrey Griffin, a former officer of the King's African Rifles, and later Colony Youth Organizer. Started as a private venture aimed at helping homeless boys and drawing public attention to the enormous social problem of juvenile vagrancy in Nairobi. The largest local supporters of the center are the Shell/BP Oil Company and the Sheikh Trust, set up by a local businessman, Gabby Sheikh. The Save the Children Fund, of which Griffin is the representative in Kenya, is the principal overseas supporter. Today the Centre caters to 1,300 boys, of which 800 are boarders. About 60 percent of the boys are helpless and pay no fees; 30 percent contribute a proportion; and the remaining 10 percent of the pupils pay the full fees. The school has primary and secondary sections. Mr. Griffin remains a Voluntary Director of the Centre, for he is the full-time director of Kenya's National Youth Service.

STEWART, CAPTAIN SIR DONALD. The first Commissioner and Commander-in-Chief of the East Africa Protectorate appointed solely to the mainland in 1904. A separate consular appointment was made for Zanzibar. Hence, Kenya ceased to be administered through a dip-

lomat attached to the Court at Zanzibar. Before coming to Kenya, he had taken part in the Afghan war (1879-
80), had fought in several other places. (Trasvaal in
1881 and Sudan in 1884-8), and was Political Officer in
the Ashanti Expedition in 1896. From 1896 to 1904,
when he came to East Africa, he was Resident at Ku-
masi in Ghana. During his tenure, the East Africa
Protectorate was transferred from the Foreign Office
to the Colonial Office on April 1, 1905. Died in 1905.

STIRLING, DAVID. Born in 1915 in Scotland. A staunch
Roman Catholic, he was educated at Ampleforth and at
Magdalene College, Cambridge. Commissioned in 1939
into a Scots Commando brigade, he was allowed while
in Egypt in 1940 to form his brigade, The Special Air
Services (SAS), which was highly successful in conducting raids on Axis airbases behind the formal battle-
front. He was the founder and First President of the
Capricorn Africa Society, which initially aimed at establishing a British Dominion in Africa covering the
area between the Equator and the Tropic of Capricorn
based on civilized standards. The Society was founded
in Southern Rhodesia with a group of white businessmen
in 1949, but was soon expanded to cover East and Central Africa, including Kenya. Also at this time, Stirling was a member of the Migration Council, a British
body designed to press for the emigration and settlement of 20 million people from the United Kingdom in
the Commonwealth. His society did much to prepare
the white settlers and businessmen for political independence. In 1958, he resigned as President of the
Society and was succeeded by the Chairman of the Kenya Branch of the Society, Michael Wood. Stirling continued to promote European business and settlement in
East and Central Africa. His elder brother, William,
had already established the construction firm of Stirling-
Astaldi in East and Central Africa. He himself established a television and film network trading between African States and Western producers. In 1967, he established the "Watchguard," a political security agency
that offered a counter-coup service to Heads of State
for a fee.

STOCK EXCHANGE. The Nairobi Stock Exchange was inaugurated in 1954. It controls the transaction of business conducted by brokers, who must be accredited members and through whom an investor buys or sells shares

in a free market. Of greatest importance to the country is the constant opportunity the Exchange affords to
the Government to float its loans to the public. Before independence, Africans were not allowed to participate in the buying and selling of stocks and shares.

SUNDAY NATION. A newspaper launched in October 1960
    by the East Africa Newspapers (Nation series) Limit-
    ed as The Nation. When its sister paper, The Daily
    Nation, was founded in March 1961, it was renamed
    Sunday Nation.

SUSWA. A prominent volcano about 15 miles west of the
    escarpment on the Nairobi-Nakuru road. The word in
    Masai means "place of the dusty plain," although in
    Dorobo "susua" means "grass," which is probably a
    reference to the good grazing in the outer crater.

SWAHILI. The Swahili are found along the East Coast of
    Africa and the offshore islands and number about 12,000
    people in Kenya. The name "Swahili" is derived from
    the Arabic word "sawahil," the plural of "sahel," mean-
    ing "the coast." The Swahili culture is, however, Af-
    rican and their language, Kiswahili, is one of the most
    widely-spoken African languages. It is largely an ur-
    ban culture and most of them are followers of the Is-
    lamic faith. The emergence of the Swahili as a distinct
    group extends from about the eighth century A.D. to
    the nineteenth century.

SWYNNERTON PLAN FOR AFRICAN AGRICULTURE, THE.
    In 1945, under the first post-war development program,
    an African Land Development Organization was estab-
    lished with a £3 million allocation for the reconditioning
    ing of African areas and for African settlement. In
    1954, at the height of the Mau Mau Emergency, the
    whole position of Kenya agriculture was reviewed with
    special reference to the development of African agri-
    culture, and a plan for the next five years was accepted
    by the Kenya Government. This was known as the Swyn-
    nerton Plan (named after Mr. R. J. M. Swynnerton,
    formerly Director of Agriculture in Kenya, upon whose
    report it was based) and it aimed at the expenditure of
    some £10.5 million on the intensification of African
    agricultural development. The Swynnerton Plan em-
    braced various measures to raise output in the African
    areas of high potential, including the consolidation of

holdings, farm planning, the expansion of cash crops,
and the provision of water supplies. It also included
settlement and reclamation schemes in areas that at
that time were little used.

- T -

TAIFA LEO. In the late fifties, Mr. Charles Hayes started
this Swahili weekly newspaper. In 1960, it was bought
by the Nation Group and turned into the first Swahili
daily newspaper in East Africa, with Mr. John Abuoga
as its first editor.

TAITA. The Taita, who number about 120,000 people and
who live on the three Taita Hills (Dabida, Sagalla, and
Kasigau) in the Coast Province, belong to the Northeast
Coastal Bantu. Their origin is a complex question,
some of them claiming to have come from the mythical
Shungwaya, others from the Pare and Kilimanjaro regions, and still others from the aboriginal inhabitants
of the area. They practiced an agricultural economy,
using complicated irrigation systems, and growing millet, sugar cane, bananas, beans and later maize, cassava, and tobacco. They also keep cattle, sheep and
goats.

TAITA HILLS ASSOCIATION. Formed in 1939 mainly to
fight for the return of Taita lands that had been alienated to European settlers. Other grievances that led
to the formation of the Association included forced labor and high taxation. It was led by Jimmy Mwambichi of Msau (born in 1908, educated at Mbale Mission
and Kaloleni Mission School in Kilifi District, taught
for a year in 1934, worked for the Mwatate Sisal Estate as a clerk for one and a half years before he went
to work in Moshi) and Mengo Woresha Kalondi (born in
1915, educated at Mlalenyi Shelemba Mission School,
worked in Mombasa as a cook for the P.C., joined Buxton School, worked for the Kenya Bus Services in Mombasa, before he moved to Nairobi, where he came in
contact with Kikuyu politics). The former served as
Secretary of the Association while the latter was the
Chairman. The Association worked closely with the
Ukamba Members Association and the Kikuyu Central
Association. It organized the Voi strike of February
1940, which lasted for four days and which protested the

arrest of some of the Association's leaders. On May
28 and 29, 1940, the leaders of the Association, together with those of UMA and KCA (23 leaders in all),
were arrested by the British Government. Under the
Defence Act, the leaders of the three associations were
detained at Kapenguria. On June 6, 1940, the three
associations were declared to be dangerous societies
to the good government of the Colony and therefore unlawful societies. By then the THA had about 4,000
paid-up members. The pressure applied by the Association had forced the Government to extend the boundaries of the Taita Reserve at Mwatunge and in the Wun-
danyi area. The plan to move the Taita from the hills
to the lowlands, which was one of the grievances that
had sparked the movement, was abandoned.

TAVETA. The Taveta are a small group of the Northeast
Coastal Bantu who number about 7,000 people and who
live in the Taita/Taveta District of the Coast Province.
They do not claim a Shungwaya origin, and hence do
not claim any relation with the Pokomo, Mijikenda, or
Taita. It would appear, however, that the proto-Ta-
veta consisted of heterogenous elements that gradually
coalesced into a distinct people by the eighteenth century. They practice a mixed economy.

TEA. Kenya is the largest producer of tea in Africa. For
a long time the tea industry was dominated by multi-
national companies such as Brooke Bond and Company
Ltd. or the African Highlands Produce Company Ltd.
The situation has rapidly changed since the establishment of the Kenya Tea Development Authority in 1964
to develop the smallholder tea industry. The industry
is therefore fast becoming smallholder, with over 70,000
farmers presently growing tea.

TELECOMMUNICATIONS SERVICES see COMMUNICATION
AND TRANSPORT

THARAKA. These Central Bantu-speakers number about
53,000 and live in Tharaka country in Meru District
in the Eastern Province. Their earlier history links
them with the earlier migrants from Igembe and Tigania who included some Gikuyu and Embu groups. In
their low country near the Tana Valley, they keep cattle and goats and practice some agriculture.

THOMSON, JOSEPH. Born in 1858 in Scotland. He studied

geology at the University of Edinburgh and in 1878 he
joined an expedition to Lakes Nyasa and Tanganyika.
He became the leader of the expedition when the original leader died of dysentery. Despite his youth, the
expedition successfully completed its original program
of exploration in Tanzania, Zambia, and Zaire, eventually returning to London in 1880. In the following
year, he returned to Africa to look for minerals in
Mozambique on behalf of Sultan Barghash of Zanzibar.
He found none. In 1882, he was sent to East Africa
by the Royal Geographical Society to scientifically ex-
plore the "snowy range of Eastern Equatorial Africa."
He covered about 3,000 miles "through Masailand" in
ten months. He confirmed the existence of the snow-
covered mountains of Kilimanjaro and Kenya, studied
the Rift Valley and Lake Baringo and proved that the
route between Mombasa and Buganda was passable and
that the Masai were not as wild as had been made out.
By early June 1884, he was back in Mombasa. He
was awarded the Royal Geographical Society Founder's
Medal in 1885--the youngest person ever to receive
the medal. In the same year, he published his book
of travel and exploration, Through Masai Land. His
other book, To the Central African Lakes and Back
(London 1881), contains the account of his first journey.
He was elected a Fellow of the Royal Geographical Society.

THUKU, HARRY. A pioneer nationalist. Born in 1895.
From 1907 to 1911, he attended the Gospel Missionary
Society school at Kambui. He left Kambui for Nairobi
in 1911 to look for work. He enrolled as a compos-
itor and machine-minder on the European settler newspaper, Leader of British East Africa. He learned much
from what he read about settler politics.
        Thuku left the Leader in 1917 and was employed
as a telephone operator and dispatch clerk at the Treasury in 1918. In May 1921, when attempts were made
to reduce African wages, the Nairobi Africans felt the
need to organize themselves under a non-ethnic label.
On July 1, 1921, the East African Association was founded, with Harry Thuku as its President. He developed
a working relationship with the Young Baganda Association and corresponded with Marcus Garvey, the leader
of the Universal Negro Improvement Association. By
February 1922, Thuku was advocating civil disobedience
as a political weapon. He was arrested for threatening

peace and good order, his arrest leading to riots and
deaths. He was detained for nine years, first at Kismayu from 1922 to 1925, when Jubaland was ceded to
Italy. Here he ran a small school for Indian and Somali children. He was detained for brief periods at
Lamu, Witu, and finally at Marsabit. He was released
in December 1930. He was elected President of Kikuyu Central Association in August 1932 and presented a
memorandum to the Carter Commission in February
1933 on behalf of the KCA. His position as President
was being challenged by Jesse Kariuki and Joseph Kang'-
ethe, who disapproved of his moderate approach to politics. Between 1933 and 1935, when Thuku broke away
to form the Kikuyu Provincial Association, there were
two KCAs. From now on, he became a loyalist. When
the Second World War broke out in 1939, he joined the
chiefs in sending Kikuyu loyalty to the government. Thuku opposed the Mau Mau fighters. From then on, he
concentrated on farming until his death on June 14, 1970.

TINDERET. One of the summits of the Mau Escarpment in
the Rift Valley Province of Kenya. It is about 8,663
feet high. Its name is derived from the Kalenjin word
"tindir" meaning "excessive noise or thunder." According to a Kipsigis belief, a rainy season always
starts at Tinderet. Indeed, lightning over the mountain
signals the beginning of a rainy season.

TIPIS, JUSTUS KENDET OLE. Born in 1923 at Narosora.
Educated at Narok Masai School and Veterinary School.
Appointed Veterinary Assistant 1939-41. Was in the
Army Service 1942-46 and attained the rank of Warrant
Officer Grade II. After war, he was District Clerk
in Olonguruone 1947-48, before becoming Assistant
Farm Manager in Cole Estates Ltd. 1949-57. He
joined politics and was elected Member for Central
Rift to the Legislative Council in 1958. He was re-
elected Member for Narok in 1961. He was appointed
Parliamentary Secretary to the Ministry of Agriculture
and later to the Ministry of Defence. In the Coalition
Government of 1962, he was appointed Minister for Social Services. In 1963, he was KADU Member for Narok East to the House of Representatives. He joined
KANU in 1964 and became Chairman of the Rift Valley
Provincial Council. Elected National Treasurer of KANU
in 1966 and re-elected to the same post in 1979. Although he lost the Narok North seat to Mr. Moses Tinga

Maria in 1969, he recaptured it in 1974 election. Appointed Assistant Minister in the Ministry of Home Affairs 1974-78, when he was transferred to the President's Office. Re-elected as Member for Narok North to Parliament in 1979 and appointed Assistant Minister in the President's Office.

TOURISM. Next to coffee, tourism is the biggest foreign exchange earner. Between 360,600 and 383,100 visitors arrived in Kenya in 1978 and 1979. The total number of vacationing visitors in any one year has averaged about 73 percent, with business and transit visitors sharing equally the balance of 27 percent. The total number of tourists rose, for example, from 268,400 in 1978 to 278,600 in 1979. Of this total, 66 percent came from Europe, 11 percent from North America, 15 percent from Africa, and 6 percent from Asia. The five leading countries from which tourists came to Kenya in 1979 were West Germany, 59,000; United Kingdom, 39,800; U.S.A., 25,600; Switzerland, 23,600; and Italy, 16,300. Estimated receipts from expenditures incurred by tourists in Kenya rose from K. £60.0 million in 1978 to K. £62.0 million in 1979.

TOWEETT, TAAITTA ARAP. Born in May 1925 at Tebesoonik near Litein in Kisyaara Location, Kericho District. Educated at Chebwagan Primary School, African Government School Kabianga (1939-43), Alliance High School, Kikuyu (1944-47), and Makerere University College (1948-49), where he studied sociology, English literature and history. He decided to become a social worker, and therefore joined Jeans School, now Kenya Institute of Administration, Kabete, where he trained for social welfare work. Appointed Welfare Officer in Kericho, 1950. Awarded a scholarship by the Kipsigis County Council in 1955 to the South Devon Technical College, Torquay, to study for a diploma in public and social administration. Studied privately and obtained a B.A. (1956) and B.A. (hons) 1959, from the University of South Africa. On his return from Britain in 1957, he was appointed Community Development Officer for Nandi District, the first African CDO to be recruited locally in Kenya. Elected to the Legislative Council in 1958 as the member for the Southern Area, a constituency comprising mainly Kipsigis and Masai districts. Appointed Assistant Minister for Agriculture (1960); re-elected to the Legislative Council 1961; appointed Minis-

ter of Labour and Housing 1961, Minister of Lands, Surveys and Town Planning 1962. Elected KADU Member
for Buret in 1963. Joined KANU and resigned from
Parliament. In 1969, he was returned to Parliament
as Member for Buret and appointed Minister for Education. Re-elected to Parliament in the 1974 General
Election and was appointed Minister for Housing and Social Services. Obtained his M.A. in linguistics from
the University of Nairobi for which he had registered
in 1973. Became Minister for Education in 1976, and
in 1977, he successfully defended his Ph.D. thesis on
"A Study of Kalenjin Linguistics." In 1976, he was
elected President of the 19th General Assembly of UNESCO,
but lost the election in 1979. He is the author of A
Study of Kalenjin Linguistics (1979), English-Kiswahili-
Kalenjin Dictionary (1979), and Oral Traditional History
of the Kipsigis (1980).

TRANSPORTATION see COMMUNICATIONS AND TRANS-
    PORT

TRUST LAND. Comprises all the land that, prior to De-
    cember 12, 1963 (when Kenya attained independence),
    was known as special areas together with certain areas
    formerly known as special reserves, settlement areas
    and the former Northern Province. It also includes all
    the urban land within municipalities, townships, and
    trading centers within the special areas formerly known
    as Native Land Units. Trust land is vested in the Coun-
    ty Council within whose areas of jurisdiction the land
    is situated. With the exception of the urban land all
    the other trust land is held in trust for the benefit of
    the people occupying the land under customary laws.

TSAVO. The biggest game park in East Africa, covering
    an area of 20,000 square kilometers. It has the larg-
    est number of elephants in the world, estimated at over
    20,000. It is located on the Nairobi/Mombasa road.

TUGEN. The Tugen are the third largest group among the
    Kalenjin with a population of about 150,000. They oc-
    cupy the lowland region to the east of the Kerio River
    and a range of hills above the Kerio River Valley, with
    Kabarnet as the administrative center. They practice
    mixed-farming. President Daniel arap Moi is a Tugen.

TURKANA. The Turkana are a Plains (or Eastern) Nilotic-speaking group, who are said to have moved into Kenya from Koten, in northeastern Uganda, where they probably separated from the other members of the group-- the Karamajong and the Jie from about 1700. They entered Kenya from the Dodoth escarpment between 1700 and 1750, proceeded to the Tarach River Valley and thence to the present Turkana District. Today they number about 300,000, and comprise the second largest group of pastoralists in Kenya, after the Somali.

- U -

UGANDA RAILWAY. In 1895, the British Parliament approved the construction of a railway line (the "lunatic line") from the port of Mombasa across the East Africa Protectorate to Lake Victoria. It reached Lake Victoria at Kisumu, then called Port Florence, in January 1902. A fleet of steamers connected ports in Uganda with Kisumu. In 1924, a direct railroad to Uganda was constructed from Nakuru via Eldoret. On February 3, 1926, the Kenya and Uganda (Transport) Order in Council was published changing the name of the railroad to the Kenya and Uganda Railways and Harbours. The control of the railway, harbor, and steamship services was henceforth to be vested in the High Commissioner for Transport, who ex officio, was the Governor of Kenya.

UKAMBA MEMBERS ASSOCIATION, THE. Started in 1938 in the Ngelani sub-location in the Iveti location as a movement against compulsory destocking which the Governor Brooke-Popham had ordered in order to provide the Liebigs, who had constructed a meat factory at Athi River, with the cattle they needed. The Ngelani people refused to reclaim the 2,500 cattle that had been taken away in order to have them branded. Instead they demanded to see the Governor. The movement was led by Samuel Muindi, popularly known as Muindi Mbingu, who was President; Elija Kavulu, Isaac Mwalonzi, and Simon Kioko, who were wealthy stock-owners. They organized a march on Nairobi with about 2,000 men, women, and children from Ngelani to force the Governor to see them. They remained in Nairobi for six weeks until the Governor promised to see them in Ukambani, where he made several concessions. The resistance then spread to other parts of Ukambani. On Oc-

tober 4, Muindu Mbingu was arrested and deported to
Lamu. The Government was, however, forced to abandon its destocking campaigns. With the main grievance
thus removed, most branches of the association ceased
to function. However, the Ngelani group continued to
campaign for the release of Muindu Mbingu, for better
educational facilities, and for the return of their stolen
land in the Mua Hills. They had links with the Kikuyu
Central Association. It was proscribed together with
the Kikuyu Central Association in 1940, and the lead-
ers--Kavulu, Mwalonzi and Kioko--were detained.

UNITED COUNTRY PARTY, THE. When the Lyttleton Constitution embodying the multi-racial principle was introduced in 1954, a major split occurred among the Europeans. One group led by Michael Blundell--the liberal
Europeans--formed the United Country Party (for Europeans only) in July 1954 to support the Lyttleton Constitution. In practice, however, it operated as a European pressure group committed to the sanctity of the
"White Highlands," to the encouragement of European
immigration and the restriction of Asian immigration,
to segregated education, and to communal electoral rolls.
The other European party formed in the same month
was the Federal Independence Party (FIP), which advocated "provincial autonomy" for Kenya, and was opposed
to multi-racialism. The United Country Party believed
in working closely with the government. It was accused
by its opponents of introducing divisive politics among
the Europeans. In the general election of October 1956,
it won six seats to FIP's eight. The two European parties agreed to work together in the new government
where Blundell and Wilfred Havelock represented the
UCP and Briggs represented the FIP. The United Country Party was formally dissolved in January 1957.

UNITED METHODIST CHURCH. Of British origin, the United Methodist Church was established in East Africa in
1862. Its work was concentrated largely among the Mijikenda people, the Wapokomo and the Wakamba. Later it expanded its work into Meru, in Eastern Kenya.

UNITED STATES-KENYA RELATIONS. Since Kenya attained
her political independence, a complex network of economic, cultural, and political ties has grown up between
Kenya and the United States. Between 1951 and 1979,
for example, Kenya has received from the United States

through the technical cooperation program, financial assistance amounting to $204.4 million, of which $103.9
million was in grants and $100.5 million in loans. Most
of this aid has been provided since independence. In
the 1960's, the aid concentrated on the goal of increasing rates of economic growth without concern as to how
the benefits of such growth would be distributed. During the 1970's, the program's emphasis was on equity
in development and now in the 1980's aid is aimed at
benefitting the poorer majority of the population, especially in the rural areas. Since independence, American investments in Kenya have grown considerably and
by March 1980, stood at $210 million, representing 125
firms (including such multinationals as General Motors,
Firestone, and IBM) divided into manufacturing and distribution: 49 percent are in distribution, 6 percent in
insurance and finance, 3 percent in petroleum and mining, and 20 percent in other categories.

In the field of education, Kenyans have been going to the U.S.A. in large numbers for higher education since the 1960's. By June 1980, there were at
least 3,000 Kenyans studying in higher education institutions in the U.S.A. The U.S. Peace Corps, which
began in 1961 under the late President John F. Kennedy,
sent its first volunteers to Kenya in 1965. In the first
half of 1980, for instance, there were about 270 volunteers, spread throughout the country, working in health,
education, rural and urban development.

Politically, the relations between the two countries have been cordial. During the visit of Kenya's
President, Mr. Daniel arap Moi, to the U.S.A. at the
beginning of 1980, an agreement was reached whereby
Kenya would allow the U.S.A. to use Mombasa port facilities for defense purposes, without turning it into a
military base.

UNIVERSITY OF NAIROBI. Started in 1956 as the Royal
Technical College of East Africa, incorporating the Gan-
dhi Memorial Academy. In 1961, it was renamed Royal
College and became the second University College of
East Africa, after Makerere University College in Uganda. With the inauguration of the University of East Africa in 1963, it changed its name to University College
in the following year, and became one of the three con-
stituent colleges of the University. It continued in special relationship with the University of London until 1966.
When the University of East Africa was dissolved in 1970,

the University of Nairobi was created by an Act of Parliament, with Kenyatta University College as a consti-
tuent college. It has nine faculties and five institutes.

- V -

VASEY, ERNEST ALBERT. A financial consultant. Born
on August 27, 1901. Received his earlier education
only up to the age of twelve, his last school being Brom-
ley. He went to neither a secondary school nor to a
university, his earlier years being spent largely in
struggling against poverty and circumstances. He started his political career in 1929 through the medium of
A. J. Gibbs, conservative agent in Anthony Eden's division, Warwick and Leamington. His ability was quick-
ly manifest. He served on the executive committee of
the National Conservative Association, the West Midlands Unionist Association and the Junior Imperial League.
He soon earned the reputation of being one of the most
forceful orators in the Midlands area.
          He came to Kenya in 1936, and in the following
year adopted Kenya as his permanent home. In 1938,
he was elected to represent Nairobi Westland Ward and
he remained a Member of the Nairobi Municipal Council
up to 1950. He was Mayor of Nairobi in 1941-42 and
again from 1944-46. He entered the Legislative Council in 1945 to represent the Nairobi North Constituency.
During the same year his public services were recognized by the award of the C.M.G. He later became
Chairman of the European Elected Members' Organization and of the Unofficial Members' Organization. When
he crossed the floor of the House in 1950 to become
Member for Health and Local Government, it was a
great loss to the Elected Members' Organization. At
this time, he was regarded as a Liberal in the context
of European politics in Kenya. He was appointed Member for Education, Health and Local Government 1951-
52; Minister for Finance and Development 1952-59. In
1960, he was invited to Tanganyika where he became
Minister for Finance 1960-62. He then became Financial and Economic Adviser World Bank Development Service 1962-66; Resident Representative of IBRD in Pakistan 1962-66. He was awarded second class Brilliant
Star of Zanzibar and Hilal-i-Quaid-i-Azam of Pakistan
in 1966. Besides politics and finance, theatre also
played a significant role in Vasey's life. He was in

fact a professional actor by the age of fifteen, and he continued to be active in theatre circles in Kenya. His publications include Report on African Housing (1950) and Economic and Political Trends in Kenya (1956).

VISRAM, ALLIDINA SETH. Played a leading role in the early history of East Africa, especially in laying firm foundations of trade in Uganda and of several agricultural industries such as cotton, sugar, rubber, and tea, as well as of shipping across Lake Victoria. Born at Kaira in Cutch in 1851, he came to East Africa at the age of twelve. Between 1885 and 1888, he joined Seth Nasser Virjee and had a chain of stores between Bagamoyo and Ujiji. But as the Uganda Railway project matured, Visram diverted his attention to Kenya and opened a chain of stores along the railway line, always being one station ahead of the Uganda Railway Construction camp.

By 1904, Visram was working everywhere in East Africa with the colonial governments to expand business and to develop agriculture. He had by this time over 170 branches in Kenya and Uganda and a few plantations employing thousands of Indians and Africans. He also had several dhows and a small steamer on Lake Victoria and a well-organized transport service from Mombasa to Uganda. Extensive experiments were carried out on his plantations to determine which types of sugar cane, cotton, tea, rubber, wheat, and rice were suitable for local conditions. He also owned several ginneries, the first of which he opened in Entebbe in 1910. He died at Kampala on June 30, 1916. His son, the late Abdulrasul Allidina Visram, built, furnished, and gave to the Government of Kenya the well-known Allidina Visram High School in Mombasa to commemorate the name of his illustrious father.

VIVA MAGAZINE. Established in 1974 and published monthly. It is the only serious and full-color women's magazine in Kenya.

VOICE OF KENYA, THE. Radio broadcasting in Kenya is one of the oldest in Africa, having been started in 1928. Kenya was indeed the first British Colony to have a regular public wireless broadcasting service. The Cable and Wireless organization was given a 25-year license to operate the services in English and Hindustani. In 1953, the BBC was invited by the Kenya Government

to send a Commission of Inquiry to advise on the future
of radio broadcasting. The Commission submitted its
Report in 1954, which formed the basis of broadcasting
in Kenya until independence. In 1958, the Government
decided that broadcasting in Kenya should be controlled
by a single independent public corporation and that part
of revenue should come from advertising. In 1959, the
Kenya Broadcasting Service was established as a department of the Chief Secretary's Office. But on July 1,
1962, it became an independent public service corporation controlling the radio and television services of Kenya. The Kenya Broadcasting Corporation was to provide independent and impartial broadcasting services of
information, education and entertainment. Soon after
independence, the Corporation was nationalized and its
name changed to the Voice of Kenya. It has three services: the General Service which broadcasts in English,
the National Service which broadcasts in Kiswahili, and
the Vernacular Service which caters to 16 African languages.

- W -

WAIYAKI, MUNYUA. A descendant of the famous Waiyaki
    wa Hinga. Born in 1932 at Kikuyu. Educated at Al-
    liance High School, Kikuyu; Adams College, Natal (1946-
    47); Fort Hare University College, South Africa (1947-
    51), where he obtained a B.Sc. degree; University of
    St. Andrews, Scotland (1952-57), where he read medicine
    and obtained M.B. and Ch.B. Worked in Sweden and
    Scotland, before returning to Kenya in 1958. From
    1958 to 1959, he was a Medical Officer in the Kenya
    Medical Department. Resigned in 1959 to join private
    practice. Became interested in politics and was Chair-
    man of the Nairobi branch of the Kenya African National
    Union (1960-68). Elected Member of Parliament for
    Nairobi North East and appointed Parliamentary Secre-
    tary, Ministry of Defence. From 1964-66, he was As-
    sistant Minister for Health and Housing, but soon re-
    signed from Government over differences with the Gov-
    ernment on party policies. Re-elected to Parliament
    in 1969 as Member for Mathare, Nairobi. Elected Dep-
    uty Speaker of Parliament, 1969-74. Re-elected Mem-
    ber for Mathare in 1974 and appointed Minister for For-
    eign Affairs 1974-79. Re-elected Member for Mathare
    in 1979 and appointed Minister for the new ministry of
    Energy.

WAIYAKI WA HINGA.   A Kikuyu leader who died defending
his land against British imperialism.   He lived at Dagoretti in Kiambu district.   He was originally a Masai
from Laikipia who migrated to Dagoretti area, where
he became assimilated into Kikuyu society and changed
his name from Ole Koyaki to Waiyaki, a reflection of
a major social transformation.   He entered into "blood
brotherhood" with Captain Lugard in 1890 according to
which harmonious relations were to be promoted and
maintained by the Kikuyu and the Europeans.   Unfortunately, other European employees of the Imperial British East Africa Company, accompanied by their Swahili
and Sudanese soldiers, never respected the treaty of
friendship.   They raided Kikuyu villages for food and
showed no respect to Waiyaki.   The latter ordered his
men to destroy Dagoretti Fort and to drive the British
caravan back to Machakos Fort.   The British sent Mr.
Smith to build a new fort, which was named Fort Smith,
and left a Mr. Purkiss in charge.   Waiyaki objected to
any fort being built in his area without his sanction.
When he went to the fort to protest, a fight ensued in
which Waiyaki's skull was fractured.   He was taken as
a prisoner to Kibwezi, where he died soon after arrival
in 1892.   He was thus the first imperialist martyr in
Kenya.

WAMAE, MATU.   Born in 1938 in Nyeri.   Educated at Kagumo High School before joining ESSO Oil Company.
He won a scholarship to India to study Economics
at the University of Delhi, from which he graduated
in 1962.   He joined the Treasury as an Auditor and
moved to the Central Bank of Kenya in 1965.   Within three years, he rose to be the Bank's General
Manager.   In 1969, he became the Executive Director
of the Industrial and Commercial Development Corporation, a post he held until 1979.
          To a large extent, Wamae was responsible for
the success of the ICDC, which has developed into a
widely diversified commercial and industrial conglom-
erate involved in over thirty subsidiary companies, including wholly-owned subsidiaries such as the Kenya National Trading Corporation (KNTC) and the Kenya Film
Corporation.

WAR COUNCIL, THE.   Set up administratively at the request
of the European settlers to superintend the conduct of the
Emergency.   It consisted of the Governor, Deputy Gov-

ernor, the Commander-in-Chief, and an unofficial Minister nominated by the Governor. Sir Michael Blundell
served in that unofficial capacity.

WARIITHI, HENRY CLEMENT. Born on December 16, 1931,
in Mukurueni, Nyeri District. He was educated at Tumutumu Primary School and the Alliance High School,
Kikuyu (1946-49). He worked with the Ministry of Works
for a short time in 1951, before proceeding to India to
study for a Bachelors degree in economics and political
science at Wilson College, Bombay 1951-55. With a
Government of India scholarship, he went to study law
at the Government Law College, Bombay 1955-57. With
James Nyamweya and C.M.G. Argwings-Kodhek, they
drew up the Constitution of KANU. Also with Argwings-
Kodhek, they acted as legal advisers to KANU during
the Constitutional wrangles of 1960-1963. In 1963, he
was elected as KANU Member for the Othaya South Tetu Constituency, Nyeri. He became Chairman of the
Backbenchers and in that capacity played a leading role
in efforts to merge the Senate and the House of Representatives in 1964. He continued as Chairman of Backbenchers in Parliament even after the merger. He was
also appointed first Chairman of the Business Premises
Rent Tribunal, a position he held until 1974. In 1968,
he was appointed Chairman of the Teachers' Remuneration Committee, and his Report was adopted by the Government. He lost his seat in the 1969 General Election,
but won it back in 1974. He was appointed Assistant
Minister in the office of the President. Re-elected to
Parliament in 1979 and appointed Assistant Minister for
Industry.

WASAWO, DAVID PETER SIMON. A distinguished academic born in Gem, Central Nyanza. Educated at Maseno
School, Alliance High School, 1942-43, Makerere University College, Oxford University where he obtained an
M.A. (Hons), and London University where he completed his Ph.D. Appointed Assistant Lecturer in Zoology,
Makerere University College, 1953-54; Lecturer, 1954-
60; Senior Lecturer, 1960-63; Reader in Zoology and
Vice-Principal, Makerere University College, 1964-65.
Appointed Deputy Principal, University College, Nairobi, 1965-68; Professor of Zoology, University of Nairobi, 1968-73. Dean Faculty of Science, 1970-72.
        Wasawo was UNESCO consultant to the Govern-
ment of Tanzania on the setting up of a Science Council.

He served on several specialist committees: Executive
Committee Member of the International Union for the
Conservation of Nature and Natural Resources; Advisory Board of Ngorongoro Conservation Area Authority;
Board of Trustees of Kenya National Parks; UNESCO
Board of Natural Resource Research. From 1973 to
1979, he was head of the Division of Natural Resources
in the United Nations Economic Commission for Africa
in Addis-Ababa. In 1979, he was appointed Managing
Director of the newly established Lake Basin Development Authority. He is the author of several scientific
papers.

WEEKLY REVIEW, THE. With the slogan, "the magazine
for the people who matter," this was established by Mr.
Hilary Ng'weno, a Kenyan editor and publisher, in February 1975. It provides a serious analysis of Kenyan,
East African, and world news. Like The Nairobi Times,
it is owned by Stellascope Limited.

WEST GERMANY-KENYA RELATIONS. Since independence,
West Germany has rapidly become the second most important trading partner of Kenya (after Britain), despite the fact that Germany had no previous colonial or
traditional ties with Kenya. Kenya's exports to the Federal Republic of Germany are primarily coffee, tea, processed agricultural products like fruits and vegetables,
cut flowers and other horticultural products. In 1977,
for example, Kenya exported 26,656 tons of coffee to
West Germany valued at a record sum of £70,420,387
sterling. This represented 33.4 percent of the total
volume of all the coffee exported in that year. The
figure for 1978 was 29,146 tons valued at £47,614,630
sterling, which represented 30 percent of the total volume of coffee exported. Kenya has also rapidly become
a leading exporter of carnations to West Germany, where
carnations are the most popular cut flowers.

Next to coffee, tourism is Kenya's most important source of foreign currency. The country has been
receiving a large influx of German tourists. Between
1970 and 1978, the number of German tourists to Kenya has more than doubled, from about 23,000 in 1970
to about 55,000 in 1978. The figure for 1979 was about
60,000 German tourists. Of the 334,000 tourists who
visited Kenya in 1978, 16.6 percent came from the Federal Republic of Germany, thus making the Germans the
largest contingent in Kenyan foreign tourism.

In turn, Kenya is among the leading markets in
Africa for Germany's industrial and capital goods, especially chemicals, machinery, and vehicles.   In the industrial field, a few German firms have established factories and businesses in Kenya, e.g. Achelis, BASF,
Bayer, Gauff, Jos Hansen and Soehne.   German private
investment in Kenya rose from K. Shs. 295 million in
1977 to K. Shs. 304 million in 1978.   Most of this investment has gone into finance companies (e.g. ICDC,
Kenya Industrial Estate, Development Finance Company
of Kenya), the food and drink industry, the hotel industry, textiles and chemicals.   Kenya is also one of the
leading recipients of German aid.   From 1963 to 1979,
Kenya received loans of DM. 468.6 million (capital aid)
and an additional amount of DM. 155 million grants
(technical aid) within bilateral relations.   In addition,
there were donations from private organizations of more
than DM. 100 million.   Apprenticeship and advanced
training of skilled labor and management have been promoted by granting 1,000 scholarships during that period.
President Moi's one-week state visit to the Federal Republic of Germany in February 1980 strengthened these
political and economic ties.   German leaders agreed to
increase their economic assistance to Kenya to DM. 180
million for the years 1980-83.

"WHITE HIGHLANDS."   This term refers to the Kenya Highlands which, through the Kenya Ordinance in Council
1938-39, had exclusively been reserved for white settlement.   It covered an area of approximately three million hectares consisting of about 4,000 farms.   Throughout the colonial period, it was easily the most agricul-
turally developed region of Kenya.   In 1960, the British
Government passed an Order in Council terminating the
exclusive legislation that had forbidden non-Europeans
from owning land or farming in the Kenya Highlands.
From 1961, all races could own land and farm in that
region.

WICKS, SIR JAMES.   Born in Middlesex, England.   Educat-
ed at Royal Grammar School, Guilford Surrey; King's
College, London, where he obtained an LL.B. degree;
Oxford University, where he obtained an M.A. and a
B. Litt.   Barrister-at-Law of Gray's Inn.   Appointed
Puisne Judge in Kenya in 1958.   Appointed Chief Jus-
tice of Kenya on July 14, 1971, following the resigna-
tion of Chief Justice Kitili Mwendwa on July 7, 1971.

Following the break-up of the East African Community
and the setting up of the Kenya Court of Appeal on October 26, 1977, Sir James became Chairman of the Court.

WILLIS, THE RIGHT REV. JOHN JAMIESON. For over
thirty years Willis was an influential missionary in Uganda and Kenya. He was born in 1872. Arrived in East
Africa as a C.M.S. missionary towards the end of 1900,
having served an apprenticeship at Great Yarmouth. Assigned to Ankole, where he witnessed the signing of the
Ankole Agreement on January 25, 1901. In the following year, he was posted to Entebbe in Buganda where
he served the European Community as their first resident Chaplain. In 1905, he was posted to the Nyanza
Province of Kenya and in 1909 he was appointed Archdeacon of Nyanza with his center at Maseno where he
truly laid the foundation of the Anglican Church. He
went back to Uganda in 1920 where he was to succeed
Bishop Tucker as Bishop of Uganda. Consecrated in
England on January 5, being the 50th C.M.S. missionary to be raised to the episcopate. He built the present
Namirembe Cathedral which was consecrated in 1919 to
replace the one burned down in 1910. He played a leading role at the Kikuyu Conference in 1913 which aimed
at bringing unity and harmony among the non-Roman
missions working in East Africa. Retired from East
Africa in 1934 and became Assistant Bishop of Leices-
ter until 1949. He could speak well at least three African languages: Luganda, Dholuo, and Luyia. He
wrote one book, An African Church in Building, which
was published in 1925. He was awarded a C.B.E. and
a D.D. He died at Teignmouth on November 12, 1954,
at the age of 82.

WILSON, FLORENCE KERR. In July 1929, she inaugurated
Wilson Airways Ltd., a commercial air service at Nairobi and Mombasa. She had come out to Kenya with
her husband, Major W.H. Wilson, D.S.O., after the
First World War to start farming at Timau near Nanyuki. Her husband died in 1928. Nairobi's first airfield was a strip of grassland at Dagoretti Corner. Wilson Airways used the Dagoretti airfield for a year, and
then moved to what then became known as "Nairobi
West," but which in 1962 was changed to Wilson Airport, in honor of Florence Wilson. She was a pioneer
of what is today an enormous complex of hangars and
administration buildings, Kenya's home of light and

charter aircraft, the Police Air Wing, the Flying Doctor Service, Search and Rescue Operations and the Aero
Club of East Africa. She was awarded the O.B.E. in
1935. Wilson died on September 29, 1966, at the age
of 88.

WOMEN, PROGRESS OF see MAENDELEO YA WANA-
WAKE; NATIONAL COUNCIL OF WOMEN OF KENYA

WORLD BANK, THE. Established in 1945 and owned by
the governments of 132 countries. It consists of three
institutions: the International Bank For Reconstruction
and Development (IBRD), the International Development
Association (IDA) and the International Finance Corporation (IFC). The Bank lends money only for productive purposes aimed at stimulating economic growth in
the developing countries. The IDA was established in
1960 and it concentrates its aid on the very poor countries. The IFC was established in 1956 to assist the
economic development of developing countries by promoting growth in the private sector of their economies
and helping to mobilize domestic and foreign capital for
this purpose. The world bank is involved in about 48
ongoing projects in Kenya and is therefore contributing
significantly to the economic development of the country.
The projects include road construction and maintenance,
airports, tea factories, education, housing, hydroelectric development, water supply, agriculture, telecom-
munication, wildlife, and tourism.

- Y -

YAAKU (or MOGOGODO). The Yaaku live about 50 kilometers north of Mt. Kenya, near Doldol. They inhabit
the Mukogodo Forest and their language belongs to the
East Cushitic branch of the Afroasiatic family. Since
about 1930, the Yaaku have gradually acquired goats and
cattle and changed from a hunter-gatherer to a cattle
economy. In the process they have also adopted Masai
social organization and culture, including language.

YOUNG KAVIRONDO ASSOCIATION (YKA). Popularly known
as Piny Owacho, the YKA was launched on December
23, 1921, at Lundha in Gem location, Central Nyanza,
at a public rally attended by over 5,000 people from
Central and North Nyanza. The Association was formed

to protest against the following grievances: the recently introduced registration system (the <u>Kipande</u> system) for all Africans; the insecurity of land-tenure in Nyanza; the raising of hut and poll tax from 10 to 16 shillings which had been done in 1920; the one-third cut in African wages effected by European employers in 1921; the labor camps established in the rural areas to coerce Africans to go to work for Europeans at reduced wages; and the change of status of the country from the East African Protectorate to Kenya Colony, which was considered by many African leaders at this time as the root of all the ills that had befallen them in 1920 and 1921.

The Association demanded the appointment of paramount chiefs who would do the work of District and Provincial Commissioners. It also demanded the establishment of government secondary schools in addition to mission primary schools. It also demanded that Africans should have more control over their own development. The leaders of the Association were all "Mission boys"--C.M.S. adherents. Jonathan Okwiri from Uyoma, the President of the Association, was a teacher at Maseno until 1928 when he was appointed Headmaster of the CMS school at Kisumu; the Secretary was Benjamin Owuor Gumba from Seme, also a teacher at Maseno; and the Treasurer was Simeon Nyende from Gem, who was at that time an evangelist and who was later ordained priest. By the middle of 1922, the Association's pressure on the Government was beginning to bear fruit. The policy of building permanent camps in the Reserve was abandoned and the hut and poll tax was reduced from 16 to 12 shillings. The people had also discovered their strength in unity. Early in 1923, Archdeacon Owen managed to convince both the Government as well as the Luo and Luhya leaders that YKA should be transformed into a welfare organization, with Owen himself as its President.

BIBLIOGRAPHY

Introduction

There is such an abundance of official publications, books, articles, theses, journals and magazines dealing with Kenya that it would require a whole book to provide a comprehensive bibliography on the country. The list which follows is, therefore, a select bibliography, although I have endeavored to make it as representative as possible. The section on science is the shortest largely because scientific publications usually do not deal simply with national problems. The books and articles in this bibliography have been organized under the following subject headings:

GENERAL WORKS

(Travel and Description, General Information, Guides and Annual Reports, Statistical Abstracts, Bibliographies)

Amin, M., and Moll, P. Kenya's World-Beating Athletes-- A Photographic History. Nairobi: East African Publishing House, 1972.

Arkell-Hardwick, A. An Ivory Trader in North Kenya. London: Longmans, Green & Co. 1903.

Bhushan, Kul. Kenya 79: Uhuru 15. Sixth issue in an annual guide series started in 1974. Nairobi: Newspread International, 1979.

Botton, Kenneth. The Lion and the Lily--A Guide to Kenya. London: Geoffrey Bles, 1962.

Boyes, J. The Company of Adventurers. London: East Africa Ltd. 1928.

Brockway, Fenner. African Journeys. London: Victor Gollancz, 1955.

Bulpett, C. W. L. (ed.). John Boyes--King of the Wakikuyu. London: Methuen, 1911.

Churchill, W. S. My African Journey. London: Hodder and Stoughton, 1908.

Clough, Marshall S., and Jackson Jr., Kennell A. A Bibliography on "Mau Mau"--Two Parts. Palo Alto, Calif.: Stanford University, 1975.

Cox, Richard. Kenyatta's Country. London: Hutchinson, 1965.

Cranworth, Lord. A Colony in the Making or Sport and Profit in British East Africa. London: Macmillan, 1912.

_____. Kenya Chronicles. London: Macmillan, 1939.

Doro, Marion E. A Bibliographic Essay on Kenya Colony: Political Themes and Research Sources. Current Bibliography on African Affairs, Serial No. 2, Vol. 5, Washington: 1972.

Du Pré, Carole E. The Luo of Kenya: An Annotated Bibliography. Washington D.C.: Institute for Cross-Cultural Research, 1968.

Farson, Negley. Behind God's Back. London: Victor Gollancz, 1940.

_____. Last Chance in Africa. London: Victor Gollancz, 1951.

Foran, W. R. A Cuckoo in Kenya: The Reminiscences of

a Pioneer Police Officer in British East Africa.   London: Hutchinson, 1936.

Gicero, Mugo. Land of Sunshine: Scenes of Life in Kenya Before "Mau Mau." London: Lawrence & Wishart, 1958.

Gregory, Robert G.; Maxon, R. M.; and Spencer, L. P. A Guide to the Kenya National Archives. Syracuse, N. Y.: Syracuse University, 1968.

Hakes, Jay E. A Study Guide for Kenya. Boston University: African Studies Center, 1969.

Hennings, R. O. African Morning. London: Chatto and Windus, 1951.

Hindlip, Lord. British East Africa: Past, Present and Future. London: T. F. Unwin, 1905.

Hobley, C. W. Kenya: From Chartered Company to Crown Colony. London: Witherby, 1929.

Hooper, H. D. Africa in the Making. London: n. p., 1974.

Hotchkiss, W. R. Then and Now in Kenya Colony: Forty Adventurous Years in East Africa. London and New York: Fleming H. Revell, 1937.

Huxley, Elspeth. A New Earth: An Experiment in Colonialism. London: Chatto and Windus, 1960.

_____. The Sorcerer's Apprentice. London: Chatto and Windus, 1948.

Huxley, J. S. African View. London: Chatto and Windus, 1931.

Jackson, F. Early Days in East Africa. London: Edward Arnold, 1930.

Jacobs, Alan H. "Bibliography of the Maasai," in African Studies Bulletin, VIII, 3, December, 1965, pp. 40-60.

Jewell, John H. A. Mombasa. The Friendly Town. Nairobi: East African Publishing House, 1976.

Kenya Government. Blue Books, 1904-1946.

_____. Kenya: An Official Handbook. Nairobi: East African Publishing House, 1973.

_____. Kenya--1963-1973. Nairobi. Ministry of Finance and Economic Planning, 1975.

_____. Statistical Abstract. Published annually since 1961.

_____. Statistical Digest. Published quarterly since 1963.

_____. Ministry of Information and Broadcasting. Kenya Today, a monthly publication since 1954.

Leakey, L. S. B. White African. London: Hodder and Stoughton, 1937.

Lipscomb, J. F. We Built a Country. London: Faber and Faber, 1955.

_____. White Africans. London: Faber and Faber, 1956.

MacDonald, J. R. L. Soldiering and Surveying in British East Africa, 1891-1894. London: E. Arnold, 1897.

Meinertzhagen, Colonel R. Kenya Diary: 1902-1906. London: Oliver and Boyd, 1957.

Mitchell, Philip E. African Afterthoughts. London: Hutchinson, 1954.

Mollison, S. Kenya's Coast: An Illustrated Guide. Nairobi: East African Publishing House, 1971.

New, Charles. Life, Wanderings and Labours in Eastern Africa, with an Account of the First Successful Ascent of the Equatorial Snow Mountain, Kilima Njaro; Remarks Upon East African Slavery. 2nd Edition. London: Hodder and Stoughton, 1874 (First Edition, 1873).

Patterson, J. H. The Man-Eaters of Tsavo and Other East African Adventures. London: Macmillan, 1934. (First Edition, 1904).

Perham, Margery. East African Journey. Kenya and Tanganyika 1929-30. London: Faber and Faber, 1976.

Pickering, Else. When the Windows Were Opened: Life
    on a Kenya Farm. London: Geoffrey Bles, 1957.

Portal, Sir Gerald. The British Mission to Uganda in 1893.
    London: Arnold, 1894.

Preston, R. O. The Genesis of Kenya Colony. Nairobi:
    Colonial Printing Works, 1947.

_____. Oriental Nairobi. Nairobi: Colonial Printing
    Works, 1938.

Roberts, John S. A Land Full of People: Life in Kenya
    Today. New York: Praeger, 1967.

Rodwell, Edward. Coast Causerie, 1. Nairobi: Heine-
    mann, 1972.

_____. Coast Causerie, 2. Nairobi: Heinemann, 1973.

Ruben, Hilary. African Harvest. London: Harvill Press,
    1972.

Seaton, Henry. Lion in the Morning. London: John Mur-
    ray, n. d.

Survey of Kenya. National Atlas of Kenya. Nairobi: 1970.

Thairu, R. W. "Women of Kenya: A Bibliographical Guide,"
    Maktaba. Nairobi: 2, 2 (1975), pp. 8-16.

Thomson, Joseph. Through Masailand. London: Low,
    Marston, Searl and Rivington, 1885.

U.S. Library of Congress. Kenya: Subject Guide to Of-
    ficial Publications. Compiled by John Bruce Howell.
    Washington, D.C. 1978.

Von Hohnel, L. The Discovery of Lakes Rudolf and Stefane,
    2 volumes. London: 1894.

Webster, John B. A Bibliography on Kenya. Syracuse,
    N.Y.: Syracuse University, Program of Eastern Af-
    rican Studies, 1967.

CULTURE

(Fine Arts, Literature, Linguistics)

Abdallah, A. Nassir. Al-Inkishafi: The Soul's Awakening. Editor and translator, William Hichens. 2nd edition. Nairobi: Oxford University Press, n.d. (1st edition, 1939).

Abdulaziz, M. H. Muyaka: Nineteenth Century Swahili Popular Poetry. Nairobi: Kenya Literature Bureau, 1979.

Allen, J. D. V. Al-Inkinshafi: Catechism of a Soul. Nairobi: East African Literature Bureau, 1977.

Angira, Jared. Juices. Nairobi: East African Publishing House, 1972.

_____. Soft Corals. Nairobi: East African Publishing House, 1974.

_____. Silent Voices. London: Heinemann, 1979.

_____. Cascades. London: Longmans, 1980.

Appleby, L. L. A First Luyia Grammar, with Exercises. Revised Edition. Nairobi: 1961 (First published 1947).

Asalache, K. A Calabash of Life. London: Longmans, Green & Co., 1967.

Barra, G. 1000 Kikuyu Proverbs. London: Macmillan, 1960.

Benuzzi, Felice. No Picnic on Mount Kenya. London: Longmans, Green & Co., 1960.

Blixen, Karen. Out of Africa. London: Penguin Books, 1954. First published 1937.

Brennan, Thomas J. Handicrafts in Kenya. Nairobi: 1958.

Chahilu, B. The Herdsman's Daughter. Nairobi: East African Publishing House, 1974.

Cuthberg, Valerie. The Great Siege of Fort Jesus--An

Historical Novel. Nairobi: East African Publishing
House, 1970.

Gatheru, Mugo. Child of Two Worlds. New York: Vintage
Books, 1965.

Gecaga, B. M., and W. H. Kirkaldy-Willis. English-Kikuyu,
Kikuyu-English Vocabulary. Dar es Salaam: Eagle
Press, 1953.

Gecau, Rose. Kikuyu Folktales. Nairobi: East African
Literature Bureau, 1970.

Gorman, T. P.; with Mutura, F. N.; Julius, M.; Wangai,
G. K.; Kanaiya, Z. N. B.; and Ogot, Grace. A Glossary in English, Kiswahili, Kikuyu and Dholuo. London: Cassell & Co., 1972.

Harman, H. Tales Told Near a Crocodile--A Collection of
Stories from Nyanza. London: Hutchinson, 1962.

_____. Black Samson. London: Hutchinson, 1965.

Harries, Lyndon (ed.). Swahili Prose Texts: A Selection
from the Material Collected by Carl Velten from 1893-
1898. London: Oxford University Press, 1965.

Hilders, J. H., and J. C. D. Lawrence. An Introduction
to the Ateso Language. Kampala: Eagle Press, 1956.

_____. An English-Ateso and Ateso-English Vocabulary.
Kampala: Eagle Press, 1958.

Huxley, Elspeth. Red Strangers. London: Chatto & Windus,
1939.

_____. The Flame Trees of Thika: Memories of an Af-
rican Childhood. New York: W. Morrow, 1959.

Imbuga, F. D. The Married Bachelor. Nairobi: East African Publishing House, 1975.

_____. Betrayal in the City. Nairobi: East African
Publishing House, 1977.

_____. The Fourth Trial. Nairobi: Kenya Literature
Bureau, n.d.

Inter-Territorial Language Committee on the East African
    Dependencies. A Standard Swahili-English Dictionary.
    London: Oxford University Press, 1939.

Kavyu, P. N. An Introduction to Kamba Music. Nairobi:
    East African Literature Bureau, 1977.

Kibera, L. Voices in the Dark. Nairobi: East African
    Publishing House, 1970.

_____, and Samuel Kahiga. Potent Ash. Nairobi: East
    African Publishing House, 1968.

Knappert, Jan (trans. and ed.). Traditional Swahili Poetry.
    Leiden: Brill, 1967.

_____. A Choice of Flowers: Swahili Songs of Love
    and Passion (Chaguo La Maua). London: Heinemann,
    1972.

_____. Myths and Legends of the Swahili. London:
    Heinemann, 1970.

Krapf, Ludwig. A Dictionary of the Suahili Language, 2nd
    ed. London: Gregg Press, 1964 (1st edition, 1882).

Kulet, H. R. Ole. Is It Possible? Nairobi: Longman Ken-
    ya, 1971.

_____. To Become a Man. Nairobi: Longman Kenya,
    1976.

Leakey, L. S. B. The First Lessons in Kikuyu. Nairobi:
    Kenya Literature Bureau, 2nd Edition, 1979.

Liyong, Taban lo. Eating Chiefs: Luo Culture from Lolwe
    to Malkal, selected, interpreted and translated. Lon-
    don: Heinemann, 1970.

Macgoye, Marjori Oludhe. Murder in Majengo. Nairobi:
    Oxford University Press, 1972.

Maillu, David G. After 4.30. Nairobi: Comb Books, 1974.

_____. The Kommon Man. Nairobi: Comb Books, 1975.

Mangua, Charles. Son of Woman. Nairobi: East African
    Publishing House, 1971.

_____. A Tail in the Mouth. Nairobi: East African Publishing House, 1972.

Mbiti, John S. English-Kamba Vocabulary. Nairobi: Eagle Press, 1959.

_____. Poems of Nature and Faith. Nairobi: East African Publishing House, 1969.

Mwangi, Meja. Kill Me Quick. London: Heinemann, 1973.

_____. A Carcase for Hounds. London: Heinemann, 1974.

_____. Taste of Death. Nairobi: East African Publishing House, 1975.

_____. Going Down River Road. London: Heinemann, 1976.

_____. The Cockroach Dance. London: Longmans, 1980.

_____. The Bushtrackers. London: Longmans, 1980.

Nassir, Ahmad bin Jume Bhalo. Poems from Kenya: Gnomic Verses in Swahili. Translated and edited by Lyndon Harris. Madison and London: The University of Wisconsin, 1966.

Ngungi, wa Thiongo. Weep Not Child. London: Heinemann, 1964.

_____. The River Between. London: Heinemann, 1965.

_____. The Black Hermit. London: Heinemann, 1968.

_____. A Grain of Wheat. London: Heinemann, 1968.

_____. Homecoming. London: Heinemann, 1972.

_____. The Trial of Dedan Kimathi (with Micere Mugo) London: Heinemann, 1975.

_____. Petals of Blood. London: Heinemann, 1968.

Njau, Rebeka. Ripples in the Pool. Nairobi: Transafrican Publishers, 1975.

Njururi, Ngumbu. Tales from Mount Kenya. Nairobi:
    Transafrican Publishers, 1975 (originally published in
    1966).

Odaga, Asenath B. Tinda: A Collection of Luo Folktales.
    Nairobi: Uzima Press, 1980.

Ogot, Grace A. The Promised Land. Nairobi: East Af-
    rican Publishing House, 1966.

_____. Land Without Thunder. Nairobi: East African
    Publishing House, 1968.

_____. The Other Woman. Nairobi: Transafrican Pub-
    lishers, 1976.

_____. Short Stories from Kenya. Stockholm: Brevs-
    kolan, 1976.

_____. The Graduate. Nairobi: Uzima Press, 1980.

_____. The Island of Tears. Nairobi: Uzima Press,
    1980.

Okola, L. (ed.). Drum Beat. Nairobi: East African Pub-
    lishing House, 1967.

Onyango-Abuje, J. C. Fire and Vengeance. Nairobi: East
    African Publishing House, 1975.

Onyango-Ogutu, B., and A. A. Roscoe. Keep My Words:
    Luo Oral Literature. Nairobi: East African Publish-
    ing House, 1974.

Ruark, Robert. Something of Value--A Story of Kenya, at
    Peace and at War. London: Landsborough Publications
    Ltd., 1958 (First published in 1955).

_____. Uhuru. Greenwich, Conn.: A Crescent Reprint,
    1963. (First published in 1962).

Ruheni, M. What a Life! Nairobi: Longmans Kenya Ltd.,
    1972.

_____. What a Husband! Nairobi: Longmans Kenya Ltd.,
    1974.

Stafford, R. L.   An Elementary Luo Grammar with Vocab-
ularies.   Nairobi: Oxford University Press, 1967.

Toweett, Taaitta.   English-Swahili-Kalenjin Dictionary.   Nairobi: Kenya Literature Bureau, 1979.

_____.   A Study of Kalenjin Linguistics.   Nairobi: Kenya
Literature Bureau, 1979.

Tucker, A. N., and J. Tompo Ole Mpaayei.   A Maasai
Grammar with Vocabulary.   London: Longmans, Green
and Co., 1955.

Wanjala, C.   Faces at Crossroads.   Nairobi: East African
Literature Bureau, 1978.

_____.   The Season of Harvest.   Nairobi: East African
Literature Bureau, 1978.

Whiteley, W. H. (ed.).   A Practical Introduction to Gusii.
Nairobi: East African Literature Bureau, 1956.

_____.   Language in Kenya.   Nairobi: Oxford University
Press, For the Survey of Language Use and Language
Teaching in Eastern Africa and the Institute of African
Studies, University of Nairobi, 1974.

SCIENCE

(Geography, Geology, Medicine,
Natural Science and Technology)

Battiscome, Edward.   Trees and Shrubs of Kenya Colony.
Nairobi: 1936.

Bishop, W. W. (ed.).   Geological Background to Fossil Man:
Recent Research in the Gregory Rift Valley, East Africa.
Edinburgh: Scottish Academic Press for the Geological
Society of London, 1978.

Bogdan, A. V.   A List of Kenya Grasses.   Nairobi: 1951.

Castelino, John B., and Canute, P. M. Khamala (eds.).
Energy Resources in East Africa.   Nairobi: Kenya Na-

tional Academy for Advancement of Arts and Sciences, 1979.

_____. The Role of Water Resources in Development. Nairobi: Kenya National Academy for Advancement of Arts and Sciences, 1979.

Chipeta, G. "A Study of Windpower Availability in Kenya." M.Sc. thesis, University of Nairobi, 1976.

Cole, S. M. An Outline of the Geology of Kenya. London: Pitman, 1950.

Dale, Ivan R., and P.J. Greenway. Kenya Trees and Flowering Shrubs. London: 1961.

Fordham, Paul, and Peter Kinyanjui. The Geography of Kenya. Nairobi: East African Literature Bureau, 1967.

Gregory, J. W. The Great Rift Valley. London: John Murray, 1896.

_____. The Rift Valley and the Geology of East Africa. London: Seeley Service, 1921.

Hartwig, G. W. "Health Policies and National Development in Kenya." Ph.D. thesis. Kentucky University, 1975.

Hove, A. R. T., and Ongweny, G. S. O. "An Outline of Kenya's Groundwater Quality." Journal of East African Research and Development, 4 (1) pp. 67-94, 1973.

Jex-Blake, Lady Muriel. Some Wild Flowers of Kenya. London: 1938.

Kokwaro, J. O. Luo-English Botanical Dictionary of Plant Names and Uses. Nairobi: East African Publishing House, 1972.

_____. Medicinal Plants of East Africa. Nairobi: East African Literature Bureau, 1976.

Morgan, W. T. W. (ed.). Nairobi: City and Region. Nairobi: Oxford University Press, 1967.

Ogendo, R. B. Industrial Geography of Kenya: With Special Emphasis on Agricultural Processing and Fabricating Industries.   Nairobi: East African Publishing House, 1972.

Ojany, F. F.   "The Physique of Kenya: A Contribution in Landscape Analysis," Annals of the Association of American Geographers, Vol. 56, 1966, pp. 183-196.

_____.   "Drainage Evolution in Kenya" in Studies in East African Geography and Development, edited by S. H. Ominde.   London: Heinemann, 1971, pp. 137-145.

_____, and R. B. Ogendo.   Kenya: A Study in Physical and Human Geography.   Nairobi: Longman Kenya Ltd., 1973.

Ojiambo, J. A.   The Trees of Kenya.   Nairobi: Kenya Literature Bureau, 1978.

Ominde, S. H. (ed.).   "The Semi-arid and Arid Lands of Kenya," in East African Geography and Development.   London: Heinemann, 1971, pp. 146-161.

Ouma J. B.   "Evolution of Meander Traits in the Basin of Lake Victoria."   In Studies in East African Geography and Development, Ed. by S. H. Ominde.   London: Heinemann, 1971, pp. 29-40.

Robson, Peter.   Mountains of Kenya.   Nairobi: East African Publishing House.   Published for the Mountain Club of Kenya, 1969.

Soja, E. W.   The Geography of Modernisation in Kenya-- A Spatial Analysis.   Syracuse: 1968.

Someren, V. D. van.   A Bird Watcher in Kenya.   Edinburgh, n. d.

Vogel, L. C., et al. (eds.).   Health and Disease in Kenya. Nairobi: East African Literature Bureau, 1974.

Walmsley, Ronald W.   Nairobi: The Geography of a New City.   Kampala: The Eagle Press, 1957.

Woodheath, T.   Studies of Potential Evaporation in Kenya. Nairobi: Water Development Department, 1968.

SOCIAL SCIENCE

(Anthropology, Demography and Population, Education,
Religion, Sociology, Race Relations)

Abreu, C. J. E. "Self-help in Education: The Contribution of African and Asian Voluntary Organizations to
the Development of Education in Kenya, 1900-73."
M. Ed. thesis, University of Nairobi, 1974.

Anderson, John. The Struggle for the School: The interaction of Missionary, Colonial Government and Nationalist enterprise in the Development of Formal Education in Kenya. London: Longmans, 1970.

Askwith, Tom G. Adult Education in Kenya. Nairobi: The
Eagle Press, 1961.

Bernardi, Bernardo. The Mugwe: A Failing Prophet. London: Oxford University Press, 1959.

Berntsen, J. L. "Maasai and lloikop: Ritual Experts and
Their Followers." M. A. thesis, University of Wisconsin, 1973.

Blacker, J. G. G. "Population Growth and Urbanisation in
Kenya." in L. N. Blomberg and G. Abrams, United
Nations Mission to Kenya on Housing, 1964. United Na-
tions, 1964.

Bondestam, Lars. Population Growth in Kenya. Uppsala:
Research Report No. 12. Scandinavian Institute of African Studies, 1972.

Brantley, Cynthia. "Gerontocratic Government: Age-sets
in Pre-Colonial Giriama." Africa, 48, No. 43, 1978,
pp. 248-64.

Bujra, Janet Mary. "An Anthropological Study of Political
Action in a Bajuni Village in Kenya." Ph. D. thesis,
University of London, 1968.

Butt, Audrey. The Nilotes of Anglo-Egyptian Sudan and
Uganda. Ethnographic Survey of Africa, East and Cen-
tral Africa, Part IV. London: International African
Institute, 1952.

Cagnolo, Father C. The Akikuyu: Their Customs, Traditions and Folklore. Translated by V. M. Pick. Nyeri: The Mission Printing School, 1933.

Caplan, Ann Patricia. Choice and Constraint in a Swahili
Community, Property, Hierarchy and Cognatic Descent
on the East African Coast. London and New York: Oxford University Press, 1975.

Carey, Walter J. Crisis in Kenya: Christian Common
Sense on Mau Mau and the Colour Bar. London: A. R.
Mowbray, 1953.

Carlebach, Julius. The Jews of Nairobi. Nairobi: The
Nairobi Hebrew Congregation, 1962.

Cowan, L. Gray. The Cost of Learning: The Politics of
Primary Education in Kenya. New York: Teachers
College Press, 1970.

De Blij, Harm J. Mombasa: An African City. Evanston:
Northwestern University Press, 1968.

de Wolf, Jan Jacob. Differentiation and Integration in Western Kenya. A Study of Religious Innovation and Social
Change Among the Bukusu. The Hague: Mouton, 1977.

Dutto, Carl A. Nyeri Townsmen, Kenya. Nairobi: East
African Literature Bureau, 1975.

East Africa High Commission. East African Population
Census, 1948. Nairobi: 1952.

East Africa Protectorate. Census Return 1911. Nairobi: 1911.

Evans-Pritchard, E. E. "Luo Tribes and Clans," in Human Problems in British Central Africa, No. 7, 1949,
pp. 24-40.

_____. "Marriage Customs of the Luo of Kenya," Af-
rica, XX: 2, April, 1950, p. 132.

Fadiman, Jeffrey. Mountain Warriors: The Pre-Colonial
Meru of Mt. Kenya. Athens, Ohio: Ohio University
Centre for International Studies. Africa series No. 27, 1976.

Feddes, Andrew, and Cynthia Salvadori. Turkana: Pastoral
Craftmen. Nairobi: Transafrica, 1977.

Bibliography   234

_____. Peoples and Cultures of Kenya. Nairobi: Trans-
    africa, 1979.

Frank, William. Habari na desturi za Waribe. London:
    Macmillan, 1953.

Fraser, J. Nelson. Education Report. Nairobi: 1909.

Frost, Richard. Race Against Time. London: Rex Col-
    lings, 1979.

Gecaga, Bethuel M. Home Life in Kikuyuland. Nairobi:
    East African Literature Bureau, 1949.

Ghai, Dharam P. (ed.). Portrait of a Minority: Asians
    in East Africa. Nairobi: Oxford University Press,
    1965.

Groot, Francis. "African Lakeside Town. A Study of Ur-
    banisation in Western Kenya with particular reference
    to Religion." Ph.D. thesis, Pontificia Universitas Gre-
    goriana, Rome, 1975.

Gulliver, Pamela, and P. H. Gulliver. The Central Nilo-
    Hamites. Ethnographic Survey of Africa: East and
    Central Africa, Part VII. London: International Af-
    rican Institute, 1953.

Gulliver, P. H. The Family Herds: A Study of Two Pas-
    toral Tribes in East Africa, the Jie and Turkana. Lon-
    don: Routledge and Kegan Paul, 1955.

Hake, Andrew. African Metropolis. Nairobi's Self-help
    City. London: Chatto and Windus for Sussex Univer-
    sity Press, 1977.

Hange, Hans-Egil. Luo Religion and Folklore. Oslo: Uni-
    versitetsforlaget, 1974.

Henin, Roushdi A. Alternative Population Projections for
    Kenya 1969-1989. Nairobi: The Population Studies and
    Research Institute, University of Nairobi, 1979.

Heyer, J.; Ireri, D.; and Moris, J. Rural Development in
    Kenya. Nairobi: East African Publishing House, 1971.

Hobley, C. W. Bantu Beliefs and Magic: With Particular

Reference to the Kikuyu and Kamba Tribes of Kenya
Colony. London: Witherby, 1938. First published
in 1922.

Hollis, A. C. The Masai: Their Language and Folklore.
Oxford: Clarendon Press, 1905.

_____. The Nandi: Their Language and Folklore. Ox-
ford: Clarendon Press, 1909.

Huntingford, G. W. B. Nandi: Work and Culture. London: Colonial office, 1950.

_____. The Nandi of Kenya: Tribal Control in a Pas-
toral Society. London: Routledge and Kegan Paul,
1953.

_____. The Southern Nilo-Hamites. Ethnographic Sur-
vey of Africa: East Central Africa, Part VIII. London: The International African Institute, 1953.

Huxley, Elspeth, and Margery Perham. Race and Politics
in Kenya. Revised edition. London: Faber and Faber, 1955.

Indaru, Peter Albert. Man with the Lion Heart: Biography
of Canon Ezekiel Apindi. Accra: Africa Christian
Press, 1974.

Jackson, Kennell A. "An Ethnographic Study of the Oral
Traditions of the Akamba of Kenya." Ph.D. thesis,
University of California, Los Angeles, 1968.

Jacobs, Alan H. "The Traditional Political Organisation
of the Pastoral Maasai." D. Phil. thesis, Oxford University, 1965.

Jones, Thomas Jesse. Education in East Africa. New
York: Phelps-Stokes Fund, 1925.

Karp, Ivan. Fields of Change Among the Iteso of Kenya.
London: Routledge and Kegan Paul, 1978.

Kenya Government. Report of the Education Commission.
Chairman: J. W. Barth. Nairobi: 1919.

_____. Report on the census of non-natives, 24th
April, 1921. Nairobi: 1921.

_____. Report on the census of non-natives, 21st February, 1926. Nairobi: 1927.

_____. Report on the census of non-natives, 6th March, 1931. Nairobi: 1932.

_____. Report on African Education in Kenya. Chairman: L. J. Beecher, Nairobi: 1949.

_____. Report on the census of non-natives, 25 February, 1948. Nairobi: 1953.

_____. Kenya Population Census, 1962. Nairobi.

_____. Report of the Education Commission, 2 volumes. Chairman: S. H. Ominde, Nairobi: 1964-65.

_____. Kenya Population Census, 1969. Nairobi.

Kenyatta, Jomo. Facing Mount Kenya: The Tribal Life of the Gikuyu. London: Secker and Warburg, 1938.

_____. My People of the Kikuyu and the Life of Chief Wangombe. London: United Society for Christian Literature, 1944.

Kieran, John A. P. "The Holy Ghost Fathers in East Africa, 1863-1914." Ph.D. Thesis, London University, 1966.

King, K. J. Pan-Africanism and Education. A Study of Race Philanthropy and Education in the Southern States of America and East Africa. Oxford: Clarendon Press, 1971.

Kipkorir, Benajmin E. "The Alliance High School and the Origins of the Kenyan African Elite 1926-1962." Ph.D. thesis, University of Cambridge, 1969.

_____, with F. B. Welbourn. The Marakwet of Kenya. Nairobi: East African Literature Bureau, 1973.

Kiteme, K. "The Impact of a European Education Upon Africans in Kenya: 1846-1940." Ed.D. thesis, Yeshiva University, 1970.

Kitson, Frank. Gangs and Counter-Gangs. London: Barrie and Rockliff, 1960.

Kover, M. H. "The Kikuyu Independent Schools Movement:

Interaction of Politics and Education in Kenya, 1923-
1935." Ed.D. thesis, University of California, Los
Angeles, 1970.

Krapf, J. L. Travels, Researches and Missionary Labours,
During an Eighteen Years Residence in Eastern Africa.
London: Trubner, 1860.

Lambert, H. E. Kikuyu Social and Political Institutions.
London: Oxford University Press, 1956.

Larby, Norman. The Kamba. The Peoples of Kenya, No.
8. Nairobi: Highway Press, 1944.

Le Vine, R. A., and Le Vine, B. B. Nyansongo: A Gusii
Community in Kenya. New York: John Wiley, 1966.

McIntosh, B. G. "The Scottish Mission in Kenya, 1891-
1923." Ph.D. thesis, Edinburgh University, 1969.

Macpherson, R. The Presbyterian Church in Kenya. Nairobi: 1970.

Manners, R. A. "The Kipsigis--Change with Alacrity,"
in Markets in Africa: Eight Subsistence Economies in
Transition. Editors Paul Bohannan and George Dalton.
New York: Doubleday, 1965, pp. 214-49.

_____. "The Kipsigis Culture Change in a 'Model' East
African Tribe." in Contemporary Change in Traditional Societies, editor, J. H. Steward, vol. 1. 1967.

Massam, J. A. The Cliff Dwellers of Kenya. London:
Frank Cass & Co., 1968 (First published 1927).

Mayer, Philip. The Lineage Principle in Gusii Society,
Memorandum No. 2. London: Oxford University Press,
1949.

_____. "Gusii Bridewealth, Law and Custom," Rhodes
Livingtone Papers, XVIII. London: Oxford University
Press, 1950.

_____. Two Studies in Applied Anthropology in Kenya.
London: Colonial Office, 1951.

_____. "Gusii Initiation Ceremonies," Journal of the

Royal Anthropological Institute, London, 83, 1953, pp. 9-39.

Mayor, A. W. (ed.). _Thuond Luo_ (Luo Heroes). Nairobi: The Kenya Highway Press, 1938.

Mbithi, Philip M. _Rural Sociology and Rural Development: Its Application in Kenya_. Nairobi: East African Literature Bureau, 1974.

_____, and Rasmussen, R. _Self-Reliance in Kenya. The Case of Harambee_. Uppsala: Scandinavian Institute of African Studies, 1977.

Mboya, Paul. _Luo Kitgi gi Timbegi_ (The Luo: their character and customs). Nairobi: East African Standard, 1938.

Merker, M. _Die Masai: Ethnographische Monographie einer ostafrikanischen Semiten-Volkes_. Berlin: 1910.

Middleton, John. _The Kikuyu and Kamba of Kenya_. Ethnographic Survey of Africa: East Central Africa, Part V. London: The International African Institute, 1953.

Morgan, W. T. W., and N. Manfred Shaffer. _The Population of Kenya, Density and Distribution: A Geographical Introduction to the Kenya Population Census, 1962_. Nairobi: Oxford University Press, 1966.

Muga, E. _African Response to Western Christian Religion_. Nairobi: East African Literature Bureau, 1975.

Muraya, P. N. "Kenya African Teachers' College, Githunguri, 1939-1952." B.A. dissertation, University of Nairobi, 1972.

Murray, J. M. "The Kikuyu Female Circumcision Controversy." Ph.D. thesis, University of California, Los Angeles, 1974.

Mutua, Rosalind W. _Development of Education in Kenya, 1846-1963_. Nairobi: East African Literature Bureau, 1975.

Ndeti, Kivuto. _Elements of Akamba Life_. Nairobi: East African Publishing House, 1972.

Ngala, Ronald G. Nchi na desturi za Wagiriama. Nairobi:
   East African Literature Bureau, 1949.

Ocholla-Ayayo, A. B. C. Traditional Ideology and Ethics
   Among the Southern Luo. Uppsala: Scandinavian Institute of African Studies, 1976.

Okullu, Henry. Church and Politics in East Africa. Nairobi: Uzima Press, 1975.

_____. Church and Marriage in East Africa. Nairobi:
   Uzima Press, 1976.

Oloo, Celina N., and Virginia Cone. Kenya Women Look
   Ahead. Nairobi: 1965.

Ominde, Simeon H. The Luo Girl from Infancy to Marriage.
   London: Macmillan, 1952.

_____. Land and Population Movements in Kenya. Lon-
   don: Heinemann, 1968.

_____. The Population of Kenya, Uganda and Tanzania.
   London: Heinemann, 1975.

Orchadson, Jan Q. The Kipsigis. Abridged. East African Literature Bureau, 1961.

Osogo, J. N. B. "The History of Kabaa-Mangu High School
   and the Contribution of the Holy Ghost Fathers upon Education in Keyna." M.A. thesis, University of East Africa (Nairobi), 1970.

Otiende, J. D. Habari Za Abaluyia. Nairobi: East African Literature Bureau, 1949.

Pala, Achola O. "La femme africaine dans la société
   prècoloniale au Kenya" in La femme africaine dans
   la société précoloniale, Achola O. Pala et Madina Ly.
   Paris: UNESCO, 1979, pp. 11-137.

Parkin, David J. Palms, Wine and Witnesses. Public
   Spirit and Private Gain in an African Farming Community. San Francisco: Chandler Publishing Co.,
   1972.

Penwill, D. J. Kamba Customary Law: Notes Taken in

the Machakos District of Kenya Colony. London: Macmillan, 1951.

Peristiany, J. G. The Social Institutions of the Kipsigis.
London: Routledge, 1939.

Philp, H. R. A. A New Day in Kenya. London: World
Dominion Press, 1936.

Prins, A. H. J. The Coastal Tribes of the North-Eastern
Bantu (Pokomo, Nyika and Teita). Ethnographic Sur-
vey of Africa: East Central Africa, Part III. London:
The International African Institute, 1952.

_____. East African Age-Class Systems. Djakarta:
J. B. Wolters, 1953.

_____. The Swahili-Speaking Peoples of Zanzibar and
the East African Coast (Arabs, Shirazi and Swahili).
Ethnographical Survey of Africa, Part XII. London:
The International Africa Institute, 1961.

Raju, B. M. Education in Kenya. London: Heinemann,
1974.

Routledge, W. S., and Katherine Routledge. With a Prehistoric People: The Akikuyu of British East Africa.
London: Edward Arnold, 1910.

Saberwal, Satish. The Traditional Political System of the
Embu of Central Kenya. Nairobi: East African Publishing House, for Makerere Institute of Social Research, 1970.

Sangree, Walter H. "The Bantu Tiriki of Western Kenya,"
in Peoples of Africa. James L. Gibbs, Jr. ed. New
York: Holt, Rinehart and Winston, 1965, pp. 41-80.

_____. Age, Prayer and Politics in Tiriki, Kenya.
London: Oxford University Press, 1966.

Sankan, S. S. Ole. The Maasai. Nairobi: East African
Literature Bureau, 1971.

Schneider, Harold K. "Pokot Resistance to Change," in
Continuity and Change in African Cultures. William
R. Bascom and Melville J. Herskovits, eds. Chicago:
University of Chicago Press, 1959, pp. 144-67.

Scott, H. E. (Mrs.). A Saint in Kenya: A Life of Marion Scott Stevenson. London: 1932.

Shah Senhlata, R. "A History of Asian Education in Kenya, 1886-1963." M. A. thesis, University of East Africa (Nairobi), 1968.

Sheffield, J. R. (ed.). Education, Employment and Rural Development, A Report of the Kericho Conference, 1966. Nairobi: East African Publishing House, 1967.

_____. Education in Kenya. New York: Teachers College Press, 1973.

Sifuna, Daniel N. Vocational Education in Schools: A Historical Survey of Kenya and Tanzania. Nairobi: East African Literature Bureau, 1976.

Silberman, Leo. "The Social Survey of the Old Town of Mombasa." Journal of African Administration, January 2, 1950, pp. 14-21.

Smith, J. S. The History of the Alliance High School, 1927-1965. Nairobi: Heinemann, 1973.

Smith, M. I. "The East African Airlifts of 1959, 1960 and 1961," Ph.D. thesis, University of Syracuse, 1966.

Southall, Aidan. Lineage Formation Among the Luo. London: Oxford University Press, for International African Institute, Memo. No. 26, 1952.

Spencer, Paul. The Samburu: A Study in Gerontocracy in a Nomadic Tribe. University of California Press, 1965.

Tanner, R. E. S. "Cousin Marriage in the Afro-Arab Community of Mombasa, Kenya," Africa, 34, No. 2. April, 1964, pp. 127-38.

Wagner, Gunter. "The Political Organization of the Bantu of Kavirondo," in African Political Systems, M. Fortes and E. E. Evans-Pritchard (eds.). London: Oxford University Press, 1940, pp. 197-236.

_____. The Bantu of North Kavirondo. London: Oxford University Press, Volume I, 1949; Volume II, 1956.

_____. "The Abaluyia of Kavirondo," African Worlds,

D. Forde (ed.). London: Oxford University Press, 1965, pp. 27-54.

Wanyoike, E. N. An African Pastor: The Life and Work of the Rev. Wanyoike Kamawe, 1888-1970. Nairobi: East African Publishing House, 1974.

Weeks, S. Divergence in Educational Development: The Case in Kenya and Uganda. New York: Teachers College Press, 1967.

Welbourn, F. B., and Ogot, B. A. A Place to Feel at Home. London: Oxford University Press, 1966.

Whisson, M. G. "The Place of the School in the Present Day Luo Society." Ph.D. thesis, Cambridge University, 1963.

_____. Change and Challenge: A Study of the Social and Economic Changes Among the Kenya Luo. Nairobi: Christian Council of Kenya, 1964.

Wilson, Gordon. "Mombasa--A Modern Colonial Municipality," in Social Change in Modern Africa, Aidan Southall (ed.). London: Oxford University Press, 1961, pp. 98-112.

Wipper, Audrey. "Equal Rights for Women in Kenya." Journal of Modern African Studies, 9, No. 3. September, 1971, pp. 429-42.

_____. Rural Rebels: A Study of Two Protest Movements in Kenya. Nairobi: Oxford University Press, 1977.

Wiseman, E. M. Kikuyu Martyrs. London: Highway Press, 1958.

Wright, Marcia. "Women in Peril: A Commentary upon the Life Stories of Captives in Nineteenth Century East Central Africa." African Social Research, 20, December 1975, pp. 800-19.

Zarwan, John. "Social Evolution of the Jains in Kenya." Hadith 6, History and Social Change in East Africa, 1976, pp. 134-44.

HISTORY

(Prehistoric, Archaeology, Pre-Colonial,
Colonial and Post-Colonial)

Abuso, P. A. "A Traditional History of the Abakuria, c.
1400-1914." M.A. thesis, University of Nairobi, 1975.

Adebola, A. S. "A History of Western Education Among
the Kikuyu, 1898-1952." Ph.D. thesis, University of
Ibadan, 1978.

Allen, James de Vere. Lamu. Nairobi: Kenya Museum
Society, 1972.

_____ . "Swahili Culture Reconsidered: Some Historical
Implications of the Material Culture of the Northern
Kenya Coast in the Eighteenth and Nineteenth Centur-
ies." Azania, 9, 1974, pp. 105-37.

Alpers, Edward A. The East African Slave Trade. Historical Association of Tanzania Paper No. 3. Nairobi:
East African Publishing House, 1967.

_____ . Ivory and Slaves in East Central Africa - Changing Patterns of International Trade to the Late Nineteenth Century. Berkeley and Los Angeles: University
of California Press, 1975.

Atieno-Odhiambo, E. S. "The Colonial Government, the
Settlers and the Trust Principle in Kenya to 1939."
Transafrican Journal of History, II, 2, (1972), pp.
94-113.

_____ . "The Rise and Decline of the Kenya Peasant,
1888-1922," East African Journal, IX, 5, May, 1972,
pp. 11-15.

_____ . "History of the Kenya Executive Council, 1907-
1939." Ph.D. thesis, University of Nairobi, 1973.

_____ . The Paradox of Collaboration and Other Essays.
Nairobi: East African Literature Bureau, 1974.

Ayot, H. O. Historical Texts of the Lake Region of East
Africa. Nairobi: Kenya Literature Bureau, 1979.

_____. A History of the Luo-Abasuba. Nairobi: Kenya Literature Bureau, 1979.

Barker, Eric E. A Short History of Nyanza. Nairobi: East African Literature Bureau, 1958.

Beachey, R. W. Documents: Slave Trade of Eastern Africa. London: Rex Collings, 1971.

_____. The Slave Trade of Eastern Africa. London: Rex Collings, 1976.

Bennett, George. Kenya: A Political History. The Colonial Period. London: Oxford University Press, 1963.

Bennett, Norman R. "The Church Missionary Society in Mombasa, 1873-1894," Boston University Papers in African History, Vol. I. Editor, J. Butler. Boston: Boston University Press, 1964, pp. 159-95.

Berg, F. S. "The Swahili Community of Mombasa, 1500-1900," Journal of African History, 9 No. 1, 1968, pp. 35-56.

_____. "Mombasa Under the Busaidi Sultanate: The City and Its Hinterland in the 19th Century." Ph.D. thesis, University of Wisconsin, 1971.

_____. "The Coast from the Portuguese Invasion to the Rise of the Zanzibar Sultanate." In Zamani: A Survey of East African History, ed. B. A. Ogot, 2nd edition, pp. 115-34. Nairobi: East African Publishing House/Longman, 1973 (1st edition 1968).

_____, and B. J. Walter. "Mosques, Population and Urban Development in Mombasa," Hadith I, 1968, pp. 47-100. Nairobi: East African Publishing House.

Boswel, P. G. H. "Human Remains from Kanam and Kanjera, Kenya Colony," Nature, 135, 371, 1935.

Boxer, Charles R., and de Azevedo, Carlos. Fort Jesus and the Portuguese in Mombasa, 1593-1729. London: Hollis & Carter, 1960.

Brantley, Cynthia. The Giriama and British Colonialism in Kenya: A Study in Resiliency and Rebellion, 1800-1920, forthcoming.

Brett, E. A. Colonialism and Underdevelopment in East
    Africa: The Politics of Economic Change 1919-1939.
    London: Heinemann, 1973.

Brooks, C. A. "The Conquest of the Gusii, 1900-1914."
    M. A. thesis, University of Nairobi, 1970.

Buijtenhuijs, Robert. Le Mouvement 'Mau Mau' Une révolte
    paysanne et anti-coloniale en Afrique noire. Paris:
    Mouton, 1971.

_____. "Mau Mau": Twenty Years After. The Myth
    and the Survivors. The Hague: Mouton, 1973.

Carman, John A. A Medical History of Kenya: A Personal
    Memoir. London: Rex Collings, 1976.

Carothers, John C. The Psychology of Mau Mau. Nairobi:
    Government Printer, 1954.

Cashmore, T. H. R. "Studies in District Administration
    in the East Africa Protectorate, 1895-1918." Ph. D.
    thesis, University of Cambridge, 1965.

Chittick, Neville, H. "Discoveries in the Lamu Archipelago,"
    Azania, 11, pp. 37-68, 1967.

_____. "The Coast Before the Arrival of the Portu-
    guese," in Zamani: A Survey of East African History,
    editor, B. A. Ogot, pp. 98-114. Nairobi: East Afri-
    can Publishing House/Longmans, 1973.

_____, and Rotberg, Robert I. (ed.). East Africa and
    the Orient. Cultural Syntheses in Pre-Colonial Times.
    New York: Africana Publishing Company, 1975.

Clayton, A. "Labour in the East Africa Protectorate 1895-
    1918." Ph. D. thesis, St. Andrews University, 1971.

_____. Counter-Insurgency in Kenya. Nairobi: Trans-
    african Publishers, 1976.

Clark, W. E. Le Gros, and Leakey, L. S. B. "The Mio-
    cene Hominoidea of East Africa," in Fossil Mammals
    of East Africa, No. 1. London: British Museum (Na-
    tural History), 1951.

Cole, S. M.   The Prehistory of East Africa.   London:
     Weidenfeld and Nicolson, 1963.

Cooper, Fredrick.   Plantation Slavery on the East Coast
     of Africa.   New Haven and London: Yale University
     Press, 1977.

Coppen, Y.; Howell, F. C.; Isaac, G. Ll; and Leakey,
     R. E. F. (eds.).   Earlier Man and Environments in
     the Lake Rudolf Basin.   Chicago: University of Chi-
     cago Press, 1976.

Corfield, F. D.   The Origins and Growth of Mau Mau--A
     Historical Survey.   Nairobi: Government of Kenya,
     (Cmn. 1030) 1960.

Coupland, R.   East Africa and Its Invaders: From the
     Earliest Times to the Death of Seyyid Said in 1856.
     Oxford: Clarendon Press, 1938.

_____.   The Exploitation of East Africa 1856-1890:   The
     Slave Trade and the Scramble.   London: Faber and
     Faber, 1939.

De Blij, Harm J.   Mombasa.   n. p. :   n. d.

De Kiewiet, Marie.   "History of the Imperial British East
     Africa Company, 1876 to 1895," Ph. D. thesis, Univer-
     sity of London, 1955.

Dilley, M. R.   British Policy in Kenya Colony.   New York:
     Thomas Nelson & Sons, 1937.

Ehret, C.   Southern Nilotic History: Linguistic Approaches
     to the Study of the Past.   Evanston Ill. :   Northwestern
     University Press, 1971.

_____.   Ethiopians and East Africans: The Problems of
     Contacts.   Nairobi: East African Publishing House,
     1972.

Eliot, Sir Charles.   The East African Protectorate.   Lon-
     don: Edward Arnold, 1905.

Foran, W. R.   The Kenya Police: 1887-1960.   London:
     R. Hale, 1962.

Freeman-Grenville, G. S. P. Documents of the East African Coast. London: Rex Collings, 1975.

Furedi, F. "The African Crowd in Nairobi: Popular Movements and Elite Politics," Journal of African History,
vol. XIV, No. 2. (1973) pp. 275-290.

_____. "The Kikuyu Squatters in the Rift Valley, 1918-
1929," in Hadith 5: Economic and Social History of
East Africa, edited by B. A. Ogot. Nairobi: East African Literature Bureau, 1975, pp. 177-194.

Galbraith, John S. Mackinnon and East Africa 1878-1895.
Cambridge Commonwealth Series. London: Cambridge
University Press, 1972.

Garlake, P. S. The Early Islamic Architecture of the East
African Coast. London: Oxford University Press.
Memoir No. 1 of the British Institute in Eastern Af-
rica, 1966.

Ghaidan, Usam. Lamu: A Study of the Swahili Town. Nairobi: East African Literature Bureau, 1975.

Gold, Alice E. "Economic History of the Nandi 1840-1914."
Ph.D. thesis. University of California, Los Angeles,
1980.

Goldsmith, F. H. John Ainsworth: Pioneer Kenya Administrator, 1864-1946. London: Macmillan, 1955.

Gramly, R. M. "Meat-feasting Sites and Cattle Brands:
Patterns of Rockshelter Utilization in East Africa."
Azania, 10, (1975), pp. 107-21.

_____. "Pastoralists and Hunters: Recent Prehistory
in Southern Kenya and Northern Tanzania." Ph.D.
thesis, Harvard University, 1975.

Gray, John Miller. The British in Mombasa 1824-26--
Being the History of Captain Owen's Protectorate. Ken-
ya Historical Society, Transaction, Volume I. London:
Macmillan, 1957.

Greaves, L. B. Carey Francis of Kenya. London: Rex
Collings, 1969.

Gregory, J. W. The Foundation of British East Africa, London: H. Marshall, 1901.

Gregory, Robert G. Sidney Webb and East Africa: Labour's Experiment with the Doctrine of Native Paramountcy. University of California Press, 1962.

_____. India and East Africa: A History of Race Relations Within the British Empire 1890-1939. London: Oxford University Press, 1971.

Grigg, E. M. W. (Later Lord Altrincham). Kenya's Opportunity: Memories, Hopes and Ideas. London: Faber and Faber, 1955.

Harlow, V.; Chilver, E. M.; and Smith, A. (eds.). History of East Africa, Volume II. Oxford: Clarendon Press, 1965.

Harries, Lyndon P. Islam in East Africa. London: Parrett and Neves, 1954.

Harris, Jack W. K., and Ingrid Herbich. "Aspects of early Pleistocene Hominid Behaviour East of Lake Turkana, Kenya," in Geological Background to Fossil Man, edited by W. W. Bishop. Edinburgh: Scottish Academic Press, 1978, pp. 542-544.

Harris, Joseph E. Abolition and Repatriation in Kenya. Nairobi: East African Literature Bureau. Historical Association of Kenya, Pamphlet No. 2, 1977.

_____. Recollections of James Juma Mbotela. Nairobi: East African Publishing House, 1977.

Hay, Margaret Jean. "Economic Change in Luoland: Kowe 1890-1945." Ph.D. thesis, University of Wisconsin, 1972.

Henderson, Ian, with Philip Goodhart. The Hunt for Kimathi. London: Hamish Hamilton, 1958.

Hill, M. F. The Dual Policy in Kenya. Nakuru: Kenya Weekly News, 1944.

_____. Permanent Way: The Story of the Kenya and Uganda Railway. Nairobi: East African Railways and Harbours, 1950.

Hinawy, Mbarak Ali. Al-Akida and Fort Jesus, Mombasa:
    The Life History of Mohammed bin Abdallah bin Mbarak
    Bakhashweini, with Songs and Poems of His Time. Lon-
    don: Macmillan, 1950.

Hobley, C. W. Kenya from Chartered Company to Crown
    Colony: Thirty Years of Exploration and Administra-
    tion in British East Africa. London: H. F. and G.
    Witherby, 1929.

Huxley, Elspeth. White Man's Country: Lord Delamere
    and the Making of Kenya. 2 volumes. London: Chat-
    to and Windus, 1935.

_____. Settlers of Kenya. Nairobi: Highway Press,
    1948.

_____. No Easy Way: A History of the Kenya Farmers
    Association and the Unga Limited. Nairobi: East Af-
    rican Standard, n. d.

Janmohamed, Karim K. "African Labourers in Mombasa,
    c. 1895-1940." Hadith 5, Economic and Social His-
    tory of East Africa, 1976, pp. 154-76.

_____. "Ethnicity in an Urban Setting: A Case Study
    of Mombasa." Hadith 6, History and Social Change in
    East Africa, 1976, pp. 186-206.

_____. "A History of Mombasa, c. 1895-1939: Some
    Aspects of Economic and Social Life in an East Afri-
    can Port Town During Colonial Rule." Ph. D. thesis,
    Northwestern University, 1978.

Johnston, H. H. The Uganda Protectorate, 2 volumes,
    New York: Dodd, Mead, 1904.

Kent, P. E. "The Country Around the Kavirondo Gulf of
    Victoria Nyanza," Geological Journal, volume C, 1942.

_____. The Miocene Beds of the Kavirondo Kenya."
    Quarterly Journal of Geological Society, vol. C, 1944.

Kenya Historical Review--Journal of the Historical Associa-
    tion of Kenya.

Kenya Past and Present--Journal of the Museum Society of
    Kenya.

King, K. J. "The Maasai and the Protest Phenomenon, 1900-1960." Journal of African History, volume XII, 1971.

Kipkorir, B. E. "Mau Mau and the Politics of the Transfer of Power in Kenya, 1957-1960," Kenya Historical Review--Special Issue on Mau Mau, vol. 5, No. 2., 1977, pp. 313-328.

_____. People of the Rift Valley. London: Evans Brothers, 1978.

Kirkman, J. S. The Arab City of Gedi. London: Oxford University Press, 1954.

_____. Man and Monuments on the East African Coast. London: University of London Press, 1964.

_____. Fort Jesus: A Portuguese Fortress on the East African Coast. Memoir No. 4 of the British Institute in Eastern Africa. Oxford: Clarendon Press, 1974.

Lamphear, John. "The Kamba and the Northern Mrima Coast," in Pre-colonial Africa Trade, edited by Richard Gray and David Birmingham, pp. 75-101. London: Oxford University Press, 1970.

Leakey, L. S. B. The Stone Age Cultures of Kenya Colony. Cambridge: Cambridge University Press, 1931.

_____. Adam's Ancestor: The Evolution of Man and His Culture. London: Harper Torchbook, 1960.

_____. By the Evidence: Memoirs 1932-1951. New York and London: Harcourt Brace Jovanovich, 1974.

Leakey, M. D. "Report on the Excavations at Hyrax Hill, Nakuru, Kenya Colony, 1937-1938." Transaction of the Royal Society of South Africa. XXX, IV, pp. 271-409, 1945.

_____; Owen, W. E.; and Leakey, L. S. B. Dimple-based Pottery from Central Kavirondo, Kenya. Nairobi: Coryndon Museum, Nairobi, 1948.

Leakey, Meave G., and R. E. F. Leakey (eds.). Koobi Fora Research in Geology, Palaeontology and Human Origins. Volume I. Oxford: Clarendon Press, 1978.

Lewis, I. M. "Somali Conquest of the Horn of Africa."
Journal of African History, volume IV, No. 2, 1960.

Lonsdale, J. M. "A Political History of Nyanza 1888-
1945." Ph.D. thesis, Cambridge University, 1964.

_____. "The Politics of Conquest: The British in West-
ern Kenya 1894-1908." Historical Journal, XX, (iv)
1977, pp. 841-70.

_____. "When Did the Gusii (or Any Other Group) Be-
come a Tribe?" Kenya Historical Review, vol. V,
(i) (1977), pp. 123-33.

_____. "Copying with the Contradictions: The Develop-
ment of the Colonial State in Kenya 1895-1914," Journal of African History, 20 (1979), pp. 487-505.

McDermott, P. L. British East Africa, or IBEA: A History of the Formation and Work of the Imperial British East Africa Company. London: Chapman and Hall, 1893.

McIntosh, B. G. Ngano. Nairobi Historical Studies No.
1. Nairobi: East African Publishing House, 1969.

McKay, William Francis. "A Precolonial History of the
Southern Kenya Coast." Ph.D. thesis, Boston University, 1975.

Majdalany, Fred. State of Emergency: The Full Story of
Mau Mau. Boston: Houghton Mifflin, 1963.

Mangat, J. S. A History of the Asians in East Africa c.
1886-1945. Oxford: Clarendon Press, 1966.

Martin, Esmond B. "Notes on Some Members of the
Learned Class of Zanzibar and East Africa in the
Nineteenth Century." International Journal of Afri-
can Historical Studies, 4, No. 3, 1971, pp. 525-45.

_____. The History of Malindi: A Geographical Analy-
sis of an East African Coastal Town from the Portuguese Period to the Present. Nairobi: East African
Literature Bureau, 1973.

_____. "Arab Migrations to East Africa in Medieval
Times." International Journal of African Historical
Studies, 7, No. 3, 1974, pp. 367-90.

Matson, A. T. Nandi Resistance to British Rule 1890-1906. Nairobi: East African Publishing House, 1972.

Mbotela, James. The Freeing of the Slaves. London: Evans Brothers, 1956.

Middleton, John. "Kenya: Administration and Changes in African Life 1912-1945." In History of East Africa, Vol. 2, ed. Vincent Harlow, E. M. Chilver and Alison Smith, pp. 333-92. Oxford: Clarendon Press, 1965.

Miller, Charles. The Lunatic Express. New York: Macmillan, 1971.

Moyse-Bartlett, Lt. Col. H. The King's African Rifles: A Study in the Military History of East and Central Africa, 1890-1945. Aldershot: Gale and Palden, 1956.

Mungeam, G. H. British Rule in Kenya 1895-1912: The Establishment of Administration in the East Africa Protectorate. Oxford: Clarendon Press, 1966.

_____ (ed.). Kenya: Select Historical Documents 1884-1923. Nairobi Historical Studies No. 3. Nairobi: East African Publishing House, 1979.

Munro, J. Forbes. Colonial Rule and the Kamba: Social Change in the Kenya Highlands 1889-1939. Oxford: Clarendon Press, 1975.

Muriuki, G. "Chronology of the Kikuyu," Hadith, 3, 1971.

_____. A History of the Kikuyu 1500-1900. Nairobi: Oxford University Press, 1974.

_____. People Round Mt. Kenya. London: Evans Brothers, 1978.

Mutoro, Henry W. "A Contribution to the Study of Cultural and Economic Dynamics of the Historical Settlements of East Africa Coast with Particular Reference to the Ruins at Takwa, North Kenya Coast." M.A. thesis, University of Nairobi, 1979.

Mwaniki, Henry S. K. The Living History of the Embu and Mbeere to 1906. Nairobi: East African Literature Bureau, 1973.

_____. Embu Historical Texts. Nairobi: East African
Literature Bureau, 1974.

Mwanzi, Henry A. "Social Change Among the Kipsigis" in
Hadith 6, History and Social Change in East Africa,
edited by Bethwell A. Ogot. Nairobi: East African
Literature Bureau, 1976, pp. 31-43.

_____. A History of the Kipsigis. Nairobi: East Af-
rican Literature Bureau, 1977.

Myrick, B.; Easterbrook, D. L.; and Roelker, J. R. Three
Aspects of Crisis in Colonial Kenya. Syracuse, N.Y.:
Syracuse University Press, 1975.

Nelson, C. "Comparative Analysis of Thirteen Later Stone
Age Sites in East Africa." Ph.D. thesis, University
of California, Berkeley, 1973.

Nicholls, C. S. The Swahili Coast: Politics, Diplomacy
and Trade on the East African Littoral, 1798-1856.
London: George Allen and Unwin, 1971.

Oakley, K. P. "The Kanam Jaw," Nature, 185, pp. 945-
946.

_____. "Bone Harpoon from Gamble's Cave, Kenya."
The Antiquaries Journal, Vol. 41, No. 182. London,
1961, pp. 86-87.

Ochieng', William R. An Outline History of Nyanza Up
to 1914. Nairobi: East African Literature Bureau,
1974.

_____. A Pre-Colonial History of the Gusii of Western
Kenya from c. A.D. 1500 to 1914. Nairobi: East
African Literature Bureau, 1974.

_____. Eastern Kenya and Its Invaders. Nairobi: East
African Literature Bureau, 1975.

_____. The First Word: Essays on Kenya History.
Nairobi: East African Literature Bureau, 1975.

_____. A History of the Kadimo Chiefdom of Yimbo in
Western Kenya. Nairobi: East African Literature
Bureau, 1975.

_____. An Outline History of the Rift Valley of Kenya up to 1900 A.D. Nairobi: East African Literature Bureau, 1975.

_____. The Second Word: More Essays on Kenya History. Nairobi: East African Literature Bureau, 1977.

_____. People Round the Lake. London: Evans Brothers, 1979.

Ogot, Bethwell A. "British Administration in the Central Nyanza District of Kenya 1900-1960," Journal of African History, IV: 2, (1963), pp. 249-74.

_____. A History of the Southern Luo, Vol. I. Nairobi: East African Publishing House, 1967.

_____ (ed.). Zamani: A Survey of East African History. New Edition, Nairobi: East African Publishing House/Longmans, 1974 (1st Edition 1968).

_____ (ed.). Politics and Nationalism in Colonial Kenya. Nairobi: Historical Association of Kenya, Hadith 4, East African Publishing House, 1972.

_____ (ed.). Kenya Before 1900. Nairobi: East African Publishing House, 1976.

_____. "History, Anthropology and Social Change--the Kenya Case," in Hadith 6, History and Social Change in East Africa, 1976, pp. 1-13.

Oliver, Roland and Gervase Mathew (eds.). History of East Africa volume I. Oxford: Clarendon Press, 1963.

Onyango-Abuje, J. C. "History of Archaeological Research in East Africa from 1890-1970," in Kenya Historical Review, vol. 2, No. 2. pp. 251-262, 1974.

_____. "L. S. B. Leakey: The Man and His Contribution to the Understanding of the Evolution of Man in Africa," Journal of Eastern Africa Research and Development, Vol. 5, No. 2, pp. 121-136, Nairobi, 1975.

_____. "Reflections on Culture Change and Distribution During the Neolithic Period in East Africa," in Hadith VI, History and Social Change in East Africa.

Nairobi: East African Literature Bureau, 1977, pp. 14-30.

_____. "A Contribution to the Study of the Neolithic in East Africa with Particular Reference to Nakuru-Naivasha Basins." Ph.D. thesis, University of California, Berkeley, 1977.

_____. "Crescent Island: A Preliminary Report on Excavations at an East African Neolithic Site," Azania, Volume XII, 1977, pp. 147-159.

_____. "From the End of the Acheulean to the Age of Agriculture in Eastern Africa," in A Survey of the Prehistory of Eastern Africa, edited by Thomas H. Wilson. Nairobi: 1977, pp. 80-100.

_____. "Temporal and Spatial Distribution of Neolithic Cultures in East Africa," Proceedings of the VIII Panafrican Congress on Prehistory and Quaternary Studies, Nairobi, 1977. Edited by R. E. Leakey and Bethwell A. Ogot, Nairobi: 1980, pp. 288-292.

_____, and Simiyu Wandibba. "Palaeoenvironment and Its Influence on Man's Activities in East Africa During the Latter Part of Upper Pleistocene and Holocene." In Hadith 7, Ecology and History in East Africa, Nairobi: Kenya Literature Bureau, 1979, pp. 24-40.

Osogo, J. A History of the Baluyia. Nairobi: Oxford University Press, 1966.

_____. Nabongo Mumia. Nairobi: East African Literature Bureau, 1967.

Perham, Margery. Lugard: Thirty Years of Adventure 1858-1898. London: Collins, 1956.

Phillipson, Laurel and David. East Africa's Prehistoric Past. Nairobi: Longmans, for the British Institute in Eastern Africa, 1978.

Posnansky, M. "The Excavations at Lanet, Kenya, 1957," Azania, Vol. II, pp. 89-114, 1967.

_____. Prelude to East African History. London: Oxford University Press, 1966.

Pouwels, Randall L. "Tenth Century Settlement of the East

African Coast: The Case for Qarmation/Ismaili Connections." Azania, 9, 1974, pp. 65-74.

_____ . "Islam and Islamic Leadership in East African
Coastal Communities 1700-1914," Ph.D. thesis, University of California, Los Angeles, 1979.

Prins, A. H. J. Sailing from Lamu: A Study of Maritime
Culture in Islamic East Africa. Assen: Van Gorcom,
1965.

Ranger, T. O. Dance and Society in Eastern Africa 1890-
1970: The Beni Ngoma. Berkeley and Los Angeles:
University of California Press, 1975.

Richards, C. G. Archdeacon Owen of Kavirondo. Nairobi:
East African Standard, n.d.

Richards, Elizabeth. Fifty Years in Nyanza 1906-1956.
The History of the C.M.S. and the Anglican Church in
Nyanza Province, Kenya. Maseno, 1956.

Robbins, L. H. "Archaeology in the Turkana District,
Kenya." Science 170, pp. 359-366, 1972.

Rosberg, C. G., and Nottingham, J. The Myth of "Mau
Mau." New York: Praeger, 1966.

Said-Ruete, R. Said bin Sultan 1791-1856--Ruler of Oman
and Zanzibar. His Place in the History of Arabia and
East Africa. London: Ousley, 1929.

Salim, A. I. "The Movement for 'Mwambao' or Coast
Autonomy in Kenya, 1956-63." Hadith 2, 1970, pp.
212-28.

_____ . "Sir Ali bin Salim," in Kenya Historical Biog-
raphies, eds. A. I. Salim and Kenneth King. Nairobi,
Historical Studies No. 2. Nairobi: University of Nairobi, 1971, pp. 112-41.

_____ . "Early Arab-Swahili Political Protest in Colonial
Kenya." Hadith 4, Politics and Nationalism in Colonial
Kenya, 1972, pp. 71-84.

_____ . The Swahili-Speaking Peoples of the Kenya Coast
1895-1965. Nairobi: East African Publishing House,
1973.

_____. "'Native or Non-Native?' The Problem of Identity and the Social Stratification of the Arab-Swahili of Kenya." Hadith 6, History and Social Change in East Africa, 1976, pp. 65-85.

_____. People of the Coast. London: Evans Brothers, 1978.

Salvadori, Max. La Colonisation Européene au Kenya. Paris: Larose Editeurs, 1938.

Savage, D. C., and Munro, J. F. "Carrier Corps Recruitment in the British East Africa Protectorate 1914-18." Journal of African History, 7, 1966.

Shimanyula, James Bandi. Elija Masinde and the Dini Ya Musambwa. Nairobi: Transafrica, 1978.

Siirianen, A. "The Iron Age Site at Gatung'ang'a, Central Kenya." Azania, I. pp. 219-239, 1971.

Smith, A. B. "History of the East African Posts and Telecommunications Administration 1837-1967." Ph.D. thesis, University of East Africa (Nairobi), 1968.

Smith, Alison. "The Southern Interior 1840-84," in History of East Africa, vol. I. Editors, Roland Oliver and Gervase Mathew, pp. 253-96. Oxford: Clarendon Press, 1963.

Sopper, R. E. "Kwale: An Early Iron Age Site in Southern-Eastern Kenya." Azania II, pp. 1-17.

Spear, Thomas T. The Kenya Complex--A History of the Mijikenda People of the Kenya Coast to 1900. Nairobi: Kenya Literature Bureau, 1979.

Stanner, W. E. H. "The Kitui Kamba." Ph.D. thesis, University of London, 1939.

Stichter, Sharon. "Women and the Labour Force in Kenya 1895-1964." Rural Africana, No. 29, 1975-76, pp. 45-67.

_____. "The Formation of a Working Class in Kenya," in The Development of an African Working Class: Studies in Class Formation and Action. Eds. Richard Sandbrook and Robin Cohen. London: Longmans, 1975.

Strandes, Justus. The Portuguese Period in East Africa. Translated by Jean F. Wallwork. Nairobi: East African Literature Bureau, 1961. (First published 1899).

Strayer, Robert W. The Making of Mission Communities in East Africa: Anglicans and Africans in Colonial Kenya: 1875-1935. London: Heinemann, 1978.

Strobel, Margaret. Muslim Women in Mombasa 1890-1975. New Haven and London: Yale University Press, 1979.

_____. "Slave and Free in Mombasa," Kenya Historical Review, 6, Nos. 1-2, 1978.

Sutton, J. E. G. The East African Coast: An Historic and Archaeological Review. Historical Association of Tanzania Paper No. 1. Nairobi: East African Publishing House, 1966.

_____. "The Interior of East Africa," in African Iron Age, edited by P. L. Shinnie. London: Oxford University Press, 1971. pp. 143-182.

_____. The Archaeology of the Western Highlands of Kenya. Memoir No. 3. of the British Institute in Eastern Africa. Nairobi: British Institute in Eastern Africa, 1973.

Tamarkin, M. "Social and Political Change in a Twentieth Century African Urban Community in Kenya." Ph.D. thesis, London University, 1973.

Temu, A. J. "The Role of the Bombay Africans (Liberated Africans) on the Mombasa Coast, 1874-1904." In Hadith 3, 1971, pp. 53-81.

_____. British Protestant Missions. London: Longmans, 1972.

Thuku, Harry. An Autobiography. Nairobi: Oxford University Press, 1970.

Tignor, Robert L. The Colonial Transformation of Kenya: The Kamba, Kikuyu and Maasai from 1900 to 1939. New Jersey: Princeton University Press, 1976.

Trimingham, J. Spencer. Islam in East Africa. Oxford: Clarendon Press, 1964.

Turton, E. R. "The Pastoral Tribes of Northern Kenya 1800-1916." Ph.D. thesis. London University, 1970.

Veny's Ladislav. A History of the Mau Mau Movement in Kenya. Prague: Charles University, 1970.

Waller, R. D. "The Lords of East Africa: The Maasai in the Mid-Nineteenth Century, c. 1840-1885." Ph.D. thesis, University of Cambridge, 1979.

Walter, Bobby Joe. "The Territorial Expansion and Organization of the Nandi: 1850-1905. A Study in Political Geography." Ph.D. thesis, University of Wisconsin, 1968.

Wandibba, S. "An Attribute Analysis of the Ceramics of the Early Pastoralist Period from the Southern Rift Valley, Kenya." M.A. thesis, University of Nairobi, 1977.

Were, Gideon S. A History of the Abaluyia of Western Kenya, c. 1500-1930. Nairobi: East African Publishing House, 1967.

_____. Western Kenya Historical Texts. Nairobi: East African Literature Bureau, 1967.

Wilson, Christopher J. Before the Whiteman in Kenya. London: McCorquodale, 1952.

Wilson, Thomas H. (ed.). A Survey of the Prehistory of Eastern Africa. Nairobi: The VIII Panafrican Congress of Prehistory and Quaternary Studies, 1977.

_____. "Takwa: An Ancient Swahili Settlement of the Lamu Archipelago." In Kenya Past and Present, 10, 1978, pp. 7-17.

Wolff, Richard D. The Economics of Colonialism, British and Kenya 1870-1930. New Haven and London: Yale University Press, 1974.

Wrigley, C. G. "Kenya: The Patterns of Economic Life

1902-45." In History of East Africa, vol. 2. Editors
V. Harlow, E. H. Chilver & Alison Smith, pp. 209-
64. Oxford: Clarendon Press, 1965.

Ylvisaker, Marguerite. "The Political and Economic Relationship of the Lamu Archipelago to the Adjacent Kenya Coast in the 19th Century." Ph.D. thesis. Boston
University, 1975.

Zwanenberg, R. M. A. van. The Agricultural History of
Kenya. Nairobi: Historical Association of Kenya Paper No. 1. East African Publishing House, 1972.

_____. Colonial Capitalism and Labour in Kenya 1919-
1939. Nairobi: East African Literature Bureau, 1975.

POLITICS

(Constitutional, Government, Law, Politics,
Political Parties and Foreign Affairs)

Aaronovitch, S. and K. Crisis in Kenya. London: Lawrence and Wishart, 1947.

Abuor, C. Ojuando. White Highlands No More. A Modern Political History of Kenya. Volume I. Nairobi:
Pan African Researches, 1971.

Amin, Mohamed. Tom Mboya--A Photographic Tribute.
Nairobi: East African Publishing House, 1969.

Andrews, C. F. The Indian Question in Kenya. Nairobi:
The Swift Press, 1921.

Arnold, Guy. Kenyatta and the Politics of Kenya. Nairobi: Transafrican Publishers, 1975.

Askwith, Tom. The Story of Kenya's Progress. Nairobi:
Eagle Press, 1953.

Barnett, Donald L. Mau Mau from Within: The Autobiography of Karari Njama. Analysis of Kenya's Peasant
Revolt. London: MacGibbon and Kee, 1966.

_____ (ed.). The Hardcore by Karigo Muchai. Richmond, B.C.: L.M.S. Press, 1973.

_____ (ed.). Man in the Middle by Ngugi Kabiro. Richmond, B. C.: L. M. S. Press, 1973.

_____ (ed.). The Urban Guerilla by Mathu, Mohammed.
Richmond, B. C.: L. M. S. Press, 1974.

Bennett, George. "The Development of Political Organization in Kenya," Political Studies, vol. 2, June, 1957,
pp. 113-30.

_____. "Early Procedural Developments in the Kenya
Legislative Council." Parliamentary Affairs, X: 3, 4,
1957, Part I pp. 296-307; Part II pp. 469-79.

_____. "Kenyatta and the Kikuyu." International Af-
fairs, XXXVI: 4 October, 1961, pp. 477-82.

_____. "Imperial Paternalism: The Representation of
African Interests in the Kenya Legislative Council,"
in Essays in Imperial Government, edited by Kenneth
Robinson and F. Madden. Oxford: Basil Blackwell,
1963.

_____, and Carl G. Rosberg. The Kenyatta Election
1960-61. London: Oxford University Press, 1961.

Berman, B. J. "Administration and Politics in Colonial
Kenya." Ph. D. thesis, Yale University, 1974.

Bewes, T. F. C. Kikuyu Conflict. London: Highway
Press, 1953.

Bienen, Henry. Kenya: The Politics of Participation and
Control. Princeton: Princeton University Press, 1974.

Blundell, Sir Michael. So Rough a Wind. London: Weid-
enfeld & Nicolson, 1964.

Brown, J. L., and Muir, J. D. "The Functioning of the
Kenya Industrial Court." Journal of Modern African
Studies, Volume 14, No. 4, December, 1976, pp. 703-
04.

Buell, Raymond L. The Native Problem in Africa. 2 volumes. New York: Macmillan, 1928.

Campbell, Sir Colin. Report by Sir Colin Campbell on the

Administration of the City Council of Nairobi.   Nairobi:
1957.

Capon, Rev. M. G.   Towards Unity in Kenya.   Nairobi:
Christian Council of Kenya, 1962.

Carey-Jones, N. S.   The Anatomy of Uhuru: An Essay on
Kenya's Independence.   Manchester: Manchester University Press, 1966.

Chege, J. W.   Copyright Law and Publishing in Kenya.   Nairobi: Kenya Literature Bureau, 1978.

Cloete, Stuart.   Storm over Africa: A Study of the Mau
Mau Rebellion, Its Causes, Effects and Implications
in Africa South of the Sahara.   Cape Town: Culem-
borg Publishers, 1956.

Cotran, Eugene.   Report on Customary Criminal Offenses
in Kenya.   Nairobi: Government of Kenya: 1963.

Cox, Richard.   Pan Africanism in Practice.   PARMESCA
1958-1964.   London: Oxford University Press, 1964.

Dealing, J. R.   "Politics in Wanga, c. 1650-1914."   Ph.D.
thesis, Northwestern University, 1974.

Delf, George.   Jomo Kenyatta: Towards Truth About the
"Light of Kenya."   New York: Doubleday, 1961.

Elphinstone, Howard.   Africans and the Law.   Nairobi:
Eagle Press, 1951.

Engholm, O. F.   "African Elections in Kenya, March
1957," in Five Elections in Africa, edited by W. J. M.
Mackenzie and Kenneth E. Robinson.   Oxford: Clarendon Press, 1960, pp. 391-461.

Errington, Kathleen.   A Digest of the East African and Kenya Law Reports, 1897-1952.   Nairobi: 1953.   Government Printer.

Evans, Peter.   Law and Disorder.   London: Secker and
Warburg, 1956.

Fuller, C. and Chambers R.   "Training for Administration
of Development in Kenya."   Journal of Administration
Overseas, Vol. 4, No. 2, 1965.

Gertzel, "Provincial Administration in Kenya." Journal of
Commonwealth Political Studies, Vol. 4, No. 3, 1966.

_____. The Politics of Independent Kenya. London:
Heinemann, 1970.

_____; Goldschmidt, M.; and Rothchild, D. Govern-
ment and Politics in Kenya. Nairobi: East African
Publishing House, 1969.

Ghai, Y. P., and J. P. W. B. McAuslan. Public Law
and Political Change in Kenya: A Study of the Legal
Framework of Government from Colonial Times to the
Present. Nairobi: Oxford University Press, 1970.

Gicheru, H. B. Ndoria. Parliamentary Practice in Kenya. Nairobi: Transafrica Publishers, 1976.

Gikoyo, Gucu G. We Fought for Freedom. Nairobi: East
African Publishing House, 1979.

Godfrey, M. E., and Mutiso, G. S. M. Politics, Economics and Technical Training--A Kenyan Case Study.
Nairobi: Kenya Literature Bureau, 1979.

Great Britain. Report of the Commission on the Civil Services of the East African Territories and the East Africa High Commission, 1953-54. 2 Volumes. Chairman: David J. Lidbury. London: 1954.

Hannigan, A. St. J. J. What Is Local Government? A
Study of Local Government in Kenya and England. Kampala: East African Literature Bureau, 1958.

Hill, M. F. Kenya. The Land of Endeavour. Nairobi:
East African Standard, 1953.

Howarth, A. Kenyatta--A Photographic Biography. Nairobi: East African Publishing House, 1967.

Hyden, Goran. "Local Government Reform in Kenya."
East Africa Journal, Vol. 7, No. 4, 1970.

_____; R. Jackson; and John Okumu. Development Ad-
ministration: The Kenyan Experience. Nairobi: Oxford University Press, 1970.

Hyder, Kindy. Life and Politics in Mombasa. Nairobi: East African Publishing House, 1972.

Itote, Waruhiu. "Mau Mau" General. Nairobi: East African Publishing House, 1967.

Jackson, Tudor. The Law of Kenya: An Introduction. Nairobi: East African Literature Bureau, 1970.

Kaggia, Bildad. Roots of Freedom 1921-1963. The Autobiography of Bildad Kaggia. Nairobi: East African Publishing House, 1975.

Kariuki, Josiah Mwangi. Mau Mau Detainee: The Account by a Kenyan African of his Experiences in Detention Camps 1953-1960. London: Oxford University Press, 1963.

Kenya. The Kenya Gazette. 1899+.

_____. Law Reports of Kenya. Annually.

_____. Constitution of Kenya. Nairobi, 1963.

_____. Report of the Local Government Commission of Inquiry, 1966. Chairman: W. S. Hardacre.

_____. Report of the Commission on the Law of Marriage and Divorce, 1968. Chairman: J. F. Spry.

_____. Report of the Commission on the Law of Succession, 1968. Chairman: H. Slade.

_____. Report of the Commission on the Law of Adoption. Nairobi, 1974. Chairman: H. Slade.

_____. Report of the Commission of Inquiry (Public Service Structure and Remuneration Commission). Nairobi: 1971. Chairman: D. N. Ndegwa.

Kenya Institute of Administration. An Introduction to Kenya Law, 2nd Edition. Nairobi: 1975.

Kenyatta, Jomo. Kenya: The Land of Conflict. London: Panaf Service, 1944.

_____. Harambee! The Prime Minister of Kenya Speeches 1963-1964. Nairobi: Oxford University Press, 1964.

_____. Suffering Without Bitterness: The Founding of
the Kenya Nation. Nairobi: East African Publishing
House, 1968.

_____. The Challenge of Uhuru: The Progress of Ken-
ya 1968-1970. Nairobi: East African Publishing House,
1971.

King, Kenneth. "The Kenya Maasai and the Protest Phenomenon, 1900-1960." Journal of African History, XII,
1971, pp. 117-37.

Koinange, Mbiyu. The People of Kenya Speak for Themselves. Detroit: Kenya Publication Fund, 1955.

La Fontaine, Sydney H., and J. H. Mower. Local Government of Kenya, Its Origins and Development. Nairobi: The Eagle Press, 1955.

Lamb, Geoff. Peasant Politics: Conflict and Development
in Murang'a. Devizes: Davison Publishing Ltd., 1974.

Leakey, L. S. B. Kenya: Contrasts and Problems. London: Methuen, 1936.

_____. Mau Mau and the Kikuyu. London: Methuen,
1952.

_____. Defeating Mau Mau. London: Methuen, 1954.

Leys, N. M. Kenya. London: Hogarth Press, 1924.

_____. A Last Chance in Kenya. London: Hogarth
Press, 1931.

_____. Colour Bar in East Africa. New York: Negro
Universities Press, 1941.

McAuslan, P. "Administrative Law in Kenya." East African Law Today, 1966.

Mboya, Paul. Utawala na Maendeleo ya Local Government,
South Nyanza 1926-1957. Nairobi: The Eagle Press,
1959. (The Work and Progress of Local Government
in South Nyanza 1926-1957).

Mboya, Tom. The Kenya Question: An African Answer.
London: Fabian Colonial Bureau, 1956.

_____. Kenya Faces the Future. New York: American Committee on Africa, 1959.

_____. Freedom and After. London: André Deutsch, 1963.

_____. The Challenge of Nationhood. London: Heinemann, 1970.

Mockerie, Parmenas Githendu. An African Speaks for His People. London: Leonard and Virginia Woolf, 1934.

Mohiddin, A. "The Formulation and Manifestation of Two Socialist Ideologies--Kenya and Tanzania." Ph.D. thesis, McGill University, 1973.

Moi, Daniel T. arap. Transition and Continuity in Kenya: Select Speeches, August 1978-October, 1979. Nairobi: East African Publishing House, 1979.

Muga, Erasto. Crime and Delinquency in Kenya. Nairobi: East African Literature Bureau, 1975.

Mulusa, Thomas. Our Government--How the Government of Kenya Works. Nairobi: East African Literature Bureau, 1970.

Muriithi, K., and Ndoria, Peter. War in the Forest. The Autobiography of a Mau Mau Leader. The Personal Story of J. Kiboi Muriithi as told to Peter N. Ndoria. Nairobi: East African Publishing House, 1971.

Murray-Brown, Jeremy. Kenyatta. London: George Allen & Unwin, 1972.

Mutiso, Gideon Cyrus. Kenya: Politics, Policy and Society. Nairobi: East African Literature Bureau, 1975.

Nellis, J. R. The Ethnic Composition of Leading Kenyan Government Positions. Uppsala: Scandinavian Institute for African Studies, Research Report, No. 24, 1974.

Nyangira, N. Relative Modernization and Public Resource Allocation in Kenya. Nairobi: East African Literature Bureau, 1975.

Oculi, Okelo. "Imperialism, Settlers and Capitalism in Kenya." Mawazo, 4, 3(1975), pp. 113-28.

Odinga, Oginga. Not Yet Uhuru. London: Heinemann, 1968.

Okoth-Ogendo, H. W. O. "The Politics of Constitutional Change in Kenya Since Independence, 1963-69." African Affairs, 71, 282, January, 1972, pp. 9-34.

Okumu, J. J. "Kenya: 1900-1930. A Study in Conflict." Ph.D. thesis, University of California, Los Angeles, 1966.

Omosule, M. "Political and Constitutional Aspects of the Origins and Development of Local Government in Kenya 1895-1963." Ph.D. thesis, Syracuse University, 1974.

Pankhurst, Richard K. P. Kenya: The History of Two Nations. London: Independent Publishing 1955.

Parker, Mary. Political and Social Aspects of the Development of Municipal Government in Kenya with Special Reference to Nairobi. London: Colonial Office, 1949.

_____. How Kenya Is Governed. Nairobi: Eagle Press, 1957.

Penwill, D. J. Kamba Customary Law. London: Macmillan, 1952.

Perham, Margery. The Colonial Reckoning. New York: Alfred Knopf, 1962.

Phillips, Arthur. "The African Court System in Kenya." Journal of African Administration, IV: 4, October, 1952, pp. 135-38.

Pio Gama Pinto: Independent Kenya's First Martyr. Nairobi: Pan African Press Ltd. , 1966.

Rake, Alan. Tom Mboya: Young Man of New Africa. New York: Doubleday, 1962.

Rawcliffe, D. H. The Struggle for Kenya. London: Victor Gollancz, 1954.

Roelker, J. R. "The Contribution of Eliud Wambu Mathu to Political Independence." Ph.D. thesis, Syracuse University, 1975.

Ross, Marc Howard. Grass Roots in an African City: Political Behaviour in Nairobi. Cambridge, Massachusetts
and London: The MIT Press, 1975.

Ross, W. McGregor. Kenya from Within: A Short Political History. London: Allen & Unwin, 1927.

Rothchild, Donald S. Racial Bargaining in Independent Kenya: A Study of Minorities and Decolonization. London:
Oxford University Press, 1976.

Rouyer, A. R. "Political Recruitment of M. Ps. and Political Change." Journal of Developing Areas, 9,
4(1975) pp. 539-62.

Sandford, George R. An Administrative and Political History of the Masai Reserve. London: Colonial Office,
1919.

Sevareid, Peter. An Introduction to Administrative Law in
Kenya. Cases and Materials. Nairobi: Kenya Institute of Administration, 1969.

Slater, Montagu. The Trial of Jomo Kenyatta. London:
Secker and Warburg, 1955.

Snell, Geoffrey S. Nandi Customary Law. London: Macmillan, 1954.

Sockett, Albert E. The Law of the British East Africa
Protectorate. 2 Volumes, Nairobi: Government Printer. 1917/18.

Spurling, A. C. Digest and Guide to the Criminal Law of
Kenya. Nairobi: Government Printer, 1954.

Stoneham, C. T. Mau Mau. London: Museum Press,
1953.

_____. Out of Barbarism. London: Museum Press,
1955.

Stren, Richard. "Factional Politics and Central Control
in Mombasa, 1960-69." Canadian Journal of African
Studies 4, No. 1, 1970, pp. 33-56.

Wamweya, J. Freedom Fighter. Nairobi: East African
Publishing House, 1971.

Waruhiu, S. N. Affiliation Law in Kenya. Kampala: Eagle Press, 1962.

Wasserman, Gary. "The Independence Bargain: Kenya Europeans and the Land Issue, 1960-1962." Journal of Commonwealth Political Studies, XI, 2, (July 1973), pp. 99-120.

_____. "Continuity and Counter-Insurgency: The Role of Land Reform in Decolonizing Kenya, 1962-1970." Canadian Journal of African Studies, VII, I (1973), pp. 133-48.

_____. Politics of Decolonization: Kenya Europeans and the Land Issue 1960-1965. Cambridge: Cambridge University Press, 1976.

Weisbord, Robert G. African Zion: The Attempt to Establish a Jewish Colony in the East Africa Protectorate, 1903-1905. Philadelphia: The Jewish Publication Society of America, 1968.

Werlin, Herbert H. Governing an African City: A Study of Nairobi. New York: Africana Publishing Company, 1974.

Wills, Colin. Who Killed Kenya? London: Dennis Dobson, 1953.

Wilson, Christopher J. Kenya's Warning: The Challenge to White Supremacy in Our British Colony. Nairobi: English Press, 1954.

Wilson, Gordon M. Luo Customary Law and Marriage Laws. Nairobi: Government Printer, 1961.

Wood, Susan. Kenya: The Tensions of Progress. London: Oxford University Press, 1960.

ECONOMICS

(Agriculture, Commerce, Industry, Development, Labor, Communication, Finance)

Amsden, Alice. Foreign Firms and African Labour in Kenya, 1945-1970. London: 1971.

Bigsten, A.   Regional Inequality and Development: A Case
    Study of Kenya.   Nationalekonomiska Institutionen, Gö-
    teborgs Universitet, 1978.

Brown, L. H.   "Agricultural Change in Kenya 1945-60,"
    in Food Research Institute Studies in Agricultural Econ-
    omics, Trade and Development, VIII, 1 (1968), pp. 33-
    90.

Bujra, Janet Mary.   "Women 'Entrepreneurs' of Early
    Nairobi," Canadian Journal of African Studies, 9, No.
    2, 1975, pp. 213-34.

Carey-Jones, N. S.   "The Decolonization of the White High-
    lands of Kenya."   Geographical Journal, 131, 2 (June,
    1965), pp. 186-201.

Christian Council of Kenya.   Who Controls Industry in Ken-
    ya?   Nairobi: East African Publishing House, 1968.

Clayton, A., and Savage, Donald C.   Government and La-
    bour in Kenya 1895-1963.   London: Frank Cass, 1974.

Cone, L. W., and Lipscomb, J. F. (eds.).   The History
    of Kenya Agriculture.   London: 1972.

Crawford, E., and Thorbecke, E.   Employment, Income
    Distribution and Basic Needs in Kenya.   Report of an
    ILO Consulting Mission, Cornell University, 1978.

Datoo, B. A.   Port Development in East Africa: Spatial
    Patterns from the Ninth to the Sixteenth Centuries.
    Nairobi: East African Literature Bureau, 1975.

East Africa Protectorate.   Report of the Labour Commis-
    sion, 1912-13.   Nairobi: 1914.

East African Royal Commission 1953-55 Report.   Cmd.
    9475.   London: British Government, 1955.

Etherington, D. M.   "Land Resettlement in Kenya: Policy
    and Practice?"   East African Economics Review, X,
    1 (June, 1963), pp. 22-35.

_____ .   Smallholder Tea Production in Kenya: An Econ-
    ometric Study.   Nairobi: East African Literature Bu-
    reau, 1973.

Fearn, H.   An African Economy: A Study of the Economic
    Development of the Nyanza Province of Kenya 1903-53.
    London: Oxford University Press, 1961.

Forrester, Marion W.   Kenya Today: Social Prerequisites
    for Economic Development.   S-Gravenhage: Mouton,
    1962.

Furedi, Frank.   "The Social Composition of the Mau Mau
    Movements in the White Highlands."   Journal of Pea-
    sant Studies, 1, 4, 1974.

Ghai, Dharam, and Godfrey, M. (eds.).   Essays on Em-
    ployment in Kenya.   Nairobi: East African Literature
    Bureau, 1979.

_____; _____; and Lisk, F.   Planning for Basic
    Needs in Kenya.   Performance, Policies and Prospects.
    Geneva: International Labour Office, 1979.

Godfrey, M., and Langdon, S.   "Partners in Underdevelop-
    ment?   The Transnationalisation Thesis in a Kenyan
    Context."   The Journal of Commonwealth and Compar-
    ative Politics, vol. XIV, No. 1, 1976.

_____, and Mutiso, G. C. M.   "The Political Economy
    of Self-help: Kenya's Harambee Institutes of Technol-
    ogy."   The Canadian Journal of African Studies, Vol.
    8, 1974.

Haberson, John W.   "Land Reforms and Politics in Kenya,
    1954-70."   Journal of Modern African Studies, 9,
    2(1971), pp. 231-51.

_____.   Nation-Building in Kenya: The Role of Land
    Reform.   Evanston Ill.:   Northwestern University Press,
    1973.

Heady, Harold F.   Range Management in East Africa.   Nai-
    robi: Govt. of Kenya, 1960.

Henriksen, Georg.   Economic Growth and Ecological Bal-
    ance: Problems of Development in Turkana.   Univer-
    sity of Bergen, Norway.   n.d.

Heyer, J.   "Agricultural Development and Peasant Farm-
    ing in Kenya."   Ph.D. thesis, University of London,
    1966.

_____; Maitha, J. K.; and Senga, M. M. (eds.). Agri-
cultural Development in Kenya: An Economic Assess-
ment. Nairobi: Oxford University Press, 1976.

Hill, M. E. Cream Country: The Story of Kenya Co-operative Creameries Ltd. Nairobi: 1956.

_____. Planters Progress: The Story of Coffee in Ken-
ya. Nairobi: 1956.

_____. Magadi: The Story of the Magadi Soda Company.
Birmingham: The Kynoch Press, 1964.

Holtham, G., and Hazlewood, A. Aid and Inequality in Kenya: British Development Assistance to Kenya. London: Croom Helm in Association with the Overseas Development Institute, 1976.

Humphrey, N. The Liguru and the Land. Nairobi: 1947.

ILO. Report on Employment, Incomes and Equality: A
Strategy for Increasing Productive Employment in Kenya. Geneva: 1972.

International Bank for Reconstruction and Development. The
Economic Development of Kenya: Chief of Mission Edward H. Leavey. Baltimore: 1963.

_____. Kenya into the Second Decade: Report of a Mis-
sion Sent to Kenya by the World Bank. Baltimore: 1975.

Kenya Government. A Plan to Intensify the Development of African Agriculture in Kenya--commonly known as the Swynnerton Report. Nairobi: 1954.

_____. Report of the Committee on African Wages.
Chairman: F. W. Carpenter. Nairobi: 1954.

_____. Report of the Committee on the Organization of
Agriculture 1960. Chairman: Donald C. MacGillivray.
Nairobi: 1960.

_____. African Land Development in Kenya 1946-1962.
Nairobi: 1962.

_____. Development Plan 1964-70.

_____. High-Level Manpower Requirements and Re-

sources in Kenya, 1964-1970. Prepared under the direction of Calvin F. Davis. Nairobi: 1965.

_____ . Development Plan 1966-70.

_____ . Report of the Mission on Land Consolidation and
Registration. Chairman: J.C.D. Lawrance, Nairobi:
1966.

_____ . Report of the Agricultural Education Commission. Chairman: J. R. Weir. Nairobi: 1967.

_____ . Development Plan 1970-4.

_____ . Development Plan 1974-79.

_____ . Development Plan 1979-83.

King, John R. Stabilization Policy in an African Setting:
Kenya 1963-73. London: Heinemann, 1979.

King, Kenneth. The African Artisan: Education and the
Informal Sector in Kenya. London: Heinemann, 1977.

Lambert, H. E. The Systems of Land Tenure in the Kikuyu Land Unit. Communications, School of African Studies, No. 22. Cape Town, 1950.

Leitner, Kerstin. "The Situation of Agricultural Workers
in Kenya." Review of African Political Economy, No.
6, May-August, 1976, pp. 34-50.

Leys, Colin. Underdevelopment in Kenya: The Political
Economy of Neo-Colonialism 1964-1971. London:
Heinemann, 1975.

_____ . "Development Strategy in Kenya Since 1971,"
in Canadian Journal of African Studies, Volume 13,
No. 1-2, 1979, pp. 297-320.

Liversage, V. An Economic Study of Dairy Farming in
Kenya. Nairobi: Government Printer, 1934.

Logie, J. P. , and W. G. Dyson. Forestry in Kenya: A
Historical Account of the Development of Forest Management in the Colony. Nairobi: Government Printer,
1962.

Lubembe, C. K. The Inside Labour Movement in Kenya. Nairobi: Equatorial Publishers, 1968.

McMaster, P. G., and N. R. Solly. Coffee and Its Economics in Kenya. Nairobi: 1961.

McWilliam, Michael. "Economic Problems During the Transfer of Power in Kenya." The World Today, 18, 1, (January, 1962), pp. 164-75.

_____. "The World Bank and the Transfer of Power in Kenya." Journal of Commonwealth Political Studies, II, 2 (July, 1964), pp. 1965-9.

Maini, Krishan M. Cooperatives and Law, with Emphasis on Kenya. Nairobi: East African Literature Bureau, 1972.

Maitha, J. K. Coffee in the Kenyan Economy: An Econometric Analysis. Nairobi: East Africa Literature Bureau, 1974.

Marris, Peter, and Somerset, A. African Businessmen: A Study of Entrepreneurship and Development in Kenya. London: Routledge and Kegan Paul, 1971.

Mbithi, Philip M. and Carolyn Barnes. The Spontaneous Settlement Problem in Kenya. Nairobi: East African Literature Bureau, 1975.

Mitchell, Sir Philip. The Agrarian Problem in Kenya. Nairobi: Government Printer, 1948.

Mureithi, L. P. "Employment, Technology and Industrialisation in Kenya." Ph.D. thesis, Claremont University, 1974.

Mutalik-Desai, Priya (ed.). Economic and Political Development in Kenya. Bombay: Himalaya Publishing House, 1979.

Nellis, John R. Who Pays Tax in Kenya? Uppsala: Research Report No. 11. Scandinavian Institute of African Studies, 1972.

_____. "Expatriates in the Government of Kenya," Journal of Commonwealth Political Studies, Vol. XI, No. 3. November, 1973, pp. 251-64.

Newiger, Nikolaus. Cooperative Farming in the Former
    Scheduled Areas of Kenya. Nakuru: 1965.

Njonjo, Apollo L. "The Africanization of the White High-
    lands: A Study in Agrarian Class Struggles in Kenya
    1950-1974." Ph.D. thesis, Princeton University, 1977.

Nottide, C. P. R., and J. R. Goldsack. The Million-Acre
    Settlement Scheme 1962-1966. Nairobi: Department of
    Settlement, 1966.

Odingo, R. S. The Kenya Highlands. Nairobi: East Af-
    rican Publishing House, 1971.

Osolu-Nasubo, N. "A Socio-Economic Study of Kenya High-
    lands 1900-70." Ph.D. thesis, Howard University,
    1973.

Rasmusson, R. Kenyan Rural Development and Aid. Upp-
    sala: Scandinavian Institute of African Studies, 1972.

Reed, H. "Cotton Growing in Central Nyanza, Kenya 1901-
    1939." Ph.D. thesis, Michigan State University, 1975.

Ruthenburg, Hans. African Agricultural Production Devel-
    opment Policy in Kenya 1952-1965. Berlin: Springer-
    Verlag, 1966.

Sandbrook, Richard. Proletarians and African Capitalism:
    The Kenyan Case. Cambridge: Cambridge University
    Press, 1975.

Singh, Makhan. History of Kenya's Trade Union Movement
    to 1952. Nairobi: East African Publishing House,
    1969.

_____. History of Trade Unionism in Kenya: 1952-56.
    Edited by B. A. Ogot. Nairobi: Uzima Press, 1980.

Sorrenson, M. P. K. Land Reform in Kikuyu Country.
    Nairobi: Oxford University Press, 1967.

_____. Origins of European Settlement in Kenya. Nai-
    robi: Oxford University Press, 1968.

Spencer, I. R. G. "The Development of Production and
    Trade in the Reserve Areas of Kenya, 1895-1929."
    Ph.D. thesis, Simon Fraser University, 1975.

Swainson, N. "Foreign Corporations and Economic Growth in Kenya." Ph.D. thesis, University of London, 1977.

_____. "The Rise of a National Bourgeoisie in Kenya." Review of African Political Economy, No. 8, 1977.

_____. The Development of Corporate Capitalism in Kenya, 1918-1977. London: forthcoming.

Taylor, D. R. F. "Special Aspects of Kenya's Rural Development Strategy," in B. S. Hoyle (ed.), Spacial Aspects of Development. London: J. Wiley, 1974.

Thomas, P. A. (ed.). Private Enterprise and the East African Company. Nairobi: 1969.

Zwanenberg, R. M. A. van, and Anne King. An Economic History of Kenya and Uganda 1800-1970. London: Macmillan, 1975.

APPENDIX A:
COMMISSIONERS AND GOVERNORS,
1895-1963

Sir Arthur Hardinge, 1895-1900. Responsible for the East
Africa Protectorate as Consul-General, Zanzibar, up to
1896. In that year, he was appointed Commissioner
and Consul-General for East Africa Protectorate.
Sir Charles Eliot, 1900-1904. In August 1902, the office
of the Commissioner for the East Africa Protectorate
was created.
Sir Donald Steward, 1904-5.
Sir James Hayes-Sadler, 1905-9. Commissioner 1905-6,
then Governor. In November, 1906, the East Africa
Protectorate was placed under Governor and Command-
er-in-Chief. The executive and Legislative Councils
were created.
Sir Percy Girouard, 1909-12.
Sir Henry Belfied, 1912-17.
Sir Charles Bowring, Acting Governor, 1917-1919.
Sir Edward Northey, 1919-1922. In June 1920, the Protec-
torate became a Crown Colony, renamed Kenya.
Sir Robert Coryndon, 1922-1925.
Sir Edward Grigg (later Lord Altrincham), 1925-1930.
Sir Joseph Byrne, 1931-1937.
Sir Robert Brooke-Popham, 1937-1939.
Sir Henry Monck-Mason Moore, 1940-1944.
Sir Philip Mitchell, 1944-1952.
Sir Evelyn Baring (later Lord Howick), 1952-1959.
Sir Patrick Renison, 1959-1962.
Rt. Hon. Malcolm J. Macdonald, 1963.

APPENDIX B:
KENYA CABINET, JUNE 1980

The President: Daniel arap Moi

Ministers of State: James Samuel Gichuru
            Godfrey Gitahi Kariuki
            Nicholas Biwott

Vice-President and Minister
 for Finance: Mwai Kibaki

Minister for Home and Constitutional Affairs: Charles Njonjo

Minister for Livestock Development: James C. N. Osogo

Minister for Culture and Social Services: Jeremiah J. Nyaga

Minister for Economic Plan-
 ning and Development: Zacharia T. Onyonka

Minister for Co-operative Development: Robert S. Matano

Minister for Industry: Munywa Waiyaki

Minister for Local Develop-
 ment: Stanley S. Ole Oloitiptip

Minister for Commerce: Eliud Mwamunga

Minister for Works: Paul Ngei

Minister for Foreign Affairs: Robert Ouko

Minister for Health: Arthur K. Magugu

Minister for Urban Develop-
    ment and Housing: Charles W. Rubia

Minister for Higher Educa-
    tion: John Joseph Kamotho

Minister for Energy: John Henry Okwanyo

Minister for Water Develop-
    ment: Moses Mudavadi

Minister for Tourism: Elijah Mwangale

Minister for Agriculture: Gilbert M'Mbijjiwe

Minister for Basic Education: Jonathan arap Ng'eno

Minister for Environment and
    Natural Resources: Andrew Omanga

Minister for Transport and
    Communications: Henry Kosgey

Attorney General: James Karugu

Minister for Information and
    Broadcasting: Peter Oloo-Aringo

Minister for Labour: Titus Mbathi